THE SOUP AND BREAD COOKBOOK

ALSO BY BEATRICE OJAKANGAS

PUBLISHED BY THE UNIVERSITY OF MINNESOTA PRESS

Breakfast with Beatrice

The Great Holiday Baking Book

Great Old-Fashioned American Desserts

Great Old-Fashioned American Recipes

The Great Scandinavian Baking Book

Great Whole Grain Breads

*Homemade: Finnish Rye, Feed Sack Fashion,
and Other Simple Ingredients from My Life in Food*

Pot Pies

Quick Breads

Scandinavian Cooking

Scandinavian Feasts

THE
SOUP
&BREAD
COOKBOOK

Beatrice Ojakangas

UNIVERSITY OF MINNESOTA PRESS
MINNEAPOLIS LONDON

First published in 2013 by Rodale, Inc.
First University of Minnesota Press edition, 2020

Published by the University of Minnesota Press
111 Third Avenue South, Suite 290
Minneapolis, MN 55401-2520
http://www.upress.umn.edu

Printed in the United States of America on acid-free paper

The University of Minnesota is an equal-opportunity educator and employer.

25 24 23 22 21 20   10 9 8 7 6 5 4 3 2 1

Library of Congress Cataloging-in-Publication Data
Ojakangas, Beatrice, 1934– author.
The soup and bread cookbook / Beatrice Ojakangas.
Minneapolis : University of Minnesota Press, 2020.
Identifiers: LCCN 2020020438 | ISBN 9781517910419 (pb)
Subjects: LCSH: Soups. | Bread. | LCGFT: Cookbooks.
Classification: LCC TX757 .O37 2020 | DDC 641.81/3–dc23
LC record available at https://lccn.loc.gov/2020020438

TO MY AMAZING FAMILY

my husband, Dick Ojakangas

my children and their spouses, Cathy and Nicho Hatsopoulos;
    Greg and Tracie Ojakangas; Susanna and Peter Elliott

my grandchildren, Niko, Tomas, and Isabella Friehs;
    Kieran, Celka, and Lian Ojakangas; Frans and Kaisa Elliott

**AND ALSO TO TRUE LOVERS
OF SOUP AND HOMEMADE BREAD**

CONTENTS

WINTER

ACKNOWLEDGMENTS

Nothing comes to fruition without the support of friends and family.

First of all, thanks go to my husband, Richard, who encouraged me every step of the way, and to my circle of friends who kept tabs on my progress and were willing tasters.

Thanks to Erik Anderson and the staff of the University of Minnesota Press for their enthusiasm and energy to bring *The Soup and Bread Cookbook* back to life.

A special thanks goes to the many volunteers who have assisted me in producing the soup and bread suppers at our church during the Lenten season over the years. The kitchen there is such a fun place to be: we continue to broaden the menu every year and take great pleasure in circling the globe, culinarily speaking.

INTRODUCTION

It is impossible to think of any good meal, no matter how plain or elegant, without soup or bread in it.

–M. F. K. FISHER

When I was a young girl, my mother offered up what could be credited as the inspiration for this book. She suggested that I could never go wrong when eating out if I simply ordered soup from the menu. And with that soup, there would always be some kind of bread or cracker worth noting. I've been sampling soup from around the world ever since. My "soup travels," however, are firmly rooted in the rhythm of the seasons in Minnesota, where I live. I take most of my inspiration from what shows up in the farmers' market and in the local organic foods store. Availability and seasonality both drive my choices, but so do holidays and the mood a certain time of year cultivates.

I usually lean toward lighter menus. In spring, for example, I create special soup and bread combinations for Easter and Mother's Day. It's easy to go light when greens such as sorrel, mustard greens, and asparagus begin showing up in the markets. Once summer arrives and the temperature soars (yes, even in Minnesota), I want to chill everything! The warmer months bring a bounty of wonderful fresh farm-stand produce–all of it fair game for cooling soups. Wild mushrooms pop up in the forests surrounding my home come autumn, and glorious piles of colorful root vegetables beckon at the farmers' market. In winter, I rely on vegetables that can be stored or preserved, whether dried, frozen, or canned.

Nowhere is cooking to the rhythm of the seasons (which ultimately becomes tradition) more obvious to me than in northern Europe. For instance, spring and summer in Finland mean that creamy salmon soup served with a chewy dark rye bun is on the menu. In fall, wild mushrooms dominate the soup selection, and a hearty split pea defines the winter season. All over the world, bread in some form–flat, quick, loaf, cracker, biscuit, stick–is also part of a soup tradition. In France, seafood bouillabaisse is invariably paired with crusty bread; a cheese roll is tucked next to a bowl of *ajiaco,* or chicken soup, in Colombia.

Wanderlust is in my blood, and many of the soups and breads in this book trace a path around the globe, inspired by the ministries my church supports in many parts of the world. To bring awareness to these ministries, we host a global mission meal once a year. To represent Petrozavodsk, Russia, we made borscht and black bread. El Salvador inspired a red kidney bean soup with pupusas. Malaysia's menu turned out to be an Asian-style vegetable soup with spring rolls. Most of what is on offer here, however, are just soups we have enjoyed over the years and breads that go well with each one. The duets are not carved in stone—of course, you can switch the bread/soup combinations however you wish.

A recent holiday invitation from two dear Finnish friends sums up the warm feelings I have had all my life for the humble pairing of soup and bread: "A crust of bread, a bowl of soup, a warm sauna, and a bed await you in our home. Come to visit us in this beautiful northland! Joyfully, Antti and Jane." Breaking bread and sipping lovingly made soup would have been enough, but the sauna and the northland are the swirl of sour cream in the soup! My hope is that after preparing some of the recipes here, you'll feel the same way.

BASICS
Stocks, Broths, and Breads

You can do almost anything with soup stock; it's like a strong foundation. When you have the right foundation, everything tastes good.

–MARTIN YAN

They are terms that are often used interchangeably, but a stock and a broth are two different things. Perhaps the confusion lies not only in the similar way the two are used—as a base for soups—but in their makeup. Both are basically flavored water, with meat and/or vegetables, herbs, and spices long-simmered in the liquid. But there actually is a difference between stocks and broths in that technically, stocks are prepared with bones while broths are not. But that distinction is rarely made in recipes. I've developed three basic stock recipes and one broth recipe that are called for throughout this book.

Like many cooks, I occasionally don't have my own homemade broth or stock on hand, and I have no problem using good-quality boxed or canned versions when time is tight. I prefer them to cubes, dried powders, or pastes because their flavors are more intense, they're lower in sodium, and they typically do not contain preservatives and additives.

Prepared stocks and broths are usually packaged in 32-ounce boxes that measure 4 cups, 48-ounce cans that measure 6 cups, or 14.5-ounce cans that measure 1¾ cups. Once opened, they are safe to keep, refrigerated, for about 1 week. If you aren't planning to use prepared stocks and broths within that time, pour the liquid into ice cube trays or resealable plastic bags and freeze for later use.

Basic Chicken Stock

Roasting the chicken bones gives the stock a rich flavor. I like to freeze it in 2-cup portions in resealable plastic bags and stack them up like tiles in the freezer. **MAKES ABOUT 2 QUARTS**

4 POUNDS CHICKEN NECKS
    AND BONES
3 LARGE SPANISH ONIONS, UNPEELED,
    ENDS TRIMMED, QUARTERED
6 RIBS CELERY, CUT INTO 2-INCH PIECES
3 LARGE CARROTS, CUT INTO
    2-INCH PIECES
1 TABLESPOON OLIVE OIL

1½ TEASPOONS SALT
½ TEASPOON GROUND BLACK PEPPER
4 QUARTS COLD WATER
2 BAY LEAVES
¼ CUP BLACK PEPPERCORNS
STEMS FROM 1 SMALL BUNCH FLAT-
    LEAF PARSLEY
6 SPRIGS THYME

1. Preheat the oven to 450°F. Combine the chicken necks and bones, onions, celery, and carrots in a large roasting pan. Toss with the oil and sprinkle with the salt and pepper.

2. Roast until the chicken and vegetables are golden brown, 30 to 40 minutes.

3. Transfer to a large stockpot and add the water, bay leaves, peppercorns, parsley, and thyme. (The stock can also be made in a slow cooker—see "Tips for Making Broth or Stock in a Slow Cooker," page 11—if you wish to leave the stock unattended.)

4. Bring to a boil, reduce the heat to medium, partially cover, and simmer for 4 hours. Using a slotted spoon, skim away and discard any foam that rises to the top.

5. Remove from the heat and strain through a colander lined with a dampened piece of cheesecloth.

Two-for-One Chicken Stock

Making your own chicken stock can serve two purposes. There's the stock, which not only is a versatile base for soups and sauces but also makes a flavorful cooking liquid for rice or for braising poultry or vegetables. And then there's the meat from the bones of the bird, preferably a large organic hen, that can be used for any number of dishes. Dice it and add to pasta or rice, then toss with diced fresh tomato and chopped herbs to make a quick dinner; shred it and mix with mustard, mayo, salt, and pepper to make a sandwich filling; or mix with diced apple, celery, pecans, dried cranberries, and yogurt to make a quick lunch salad. **MAKES ABOUT 4 QUARTS**

1 LARGE (4½- TO 5-POUND) HEN, PREFERABLY FREE-RANGE ORGANIC

1 LARGE ONION, UNPEELED, ENDS TRIMMED, HALVED

2 CARROTS, CUT INTO 2- TO 3-INCH CHUNKS

1 RIB CELERY, CUT INTO 2- TO 3-INCH CHUNKS

1 LARGE LEEK, SPLIT LENGTHWISE AND WELL WASHED

2 TO 3 CLOVES GARLIC

2 SPRIGS PARSLEY

2 SPRIGS THYME

1 TEASPOON BLACK PEPPERCORNS

1½ TEASPOONS SALT

1. Place in a heavy-bottomed 12-quart stockpot. (The stock can also be made in a slow cooker—see "Tips for Making Broth or Stock in a Slow Cooker," page 11—if you wish to leave the stock unattended.)

2. Add the onion, carrots, celery, leek, garlic, parsley, thyme, peppercorns, and salt. Add enough water to cover completely (about 8 quarts). Bring to a boil, uncovered; then reduce the heat to bring the stock to a slow simmer. Be sure to let the stock simmer slowly in order to produce a clear liquid. Using a slotted spoon, skim off any foam that rises to the surface. Simmer, uncovered, for 6 hours, skimming occasionally. Add water as it evaporates to keep the ingredients covered.

CONTINUED ▶

3. Remove the cooked chicken to a bowl and let cool. Remove the meat from the bones, dice, and refrigerate to use as desired.

4. Return any liquid that has drained off the chicken to the stockpot. Strain the stock through a sieve lined with a few layers of dampened cheesecloth or a muslin kitchen towel. Cool the stock quickly by setting it in an ice bath. (I set it in a large bowl of snow in the winter!) Refrigerate or freeze the stock in resealable plastic bags.

Two-for-One Beef Stock

For the most richly flavored stock, start by browning the beef bones in the oven. As the stock simmers, the chuck roast cooks and can then be the basis for a variety of meals. Chill and slice the meat for hot beef sandwiches, or into chunks for casseroles, a French ragout, roast beef salad, or other favorite quick main dishes.

MAKES ABOUT 4 QUARTS

6 POUNDS BEEF SOUP BONES OR
    MEATY BEEF RIBS

1 LARGE ONION, QUARTERED

3 LARGE CARROTS, CUT INTO
    2-INCH PIECES

2 RIBS CELERY, INCLUDING SOME
    LEAVES, CHOPPED

1 PARSNIP, PEELED AND CHOPPED

½ CUP RED WINE OR WATER

4 SPRIGS PARSLEY

2 CLOVES GARLIC

8 BLACK PEPPERCORNS

1 TABLESPOON SALT

2 TEASPOONS DRIED THYME

1 BAY LEAF

3 POUNDS BEEF CHUCK ROAST

1. Preheat the oven to 450°F. Cover a rimmed baking sheet with foil and coat the foil with cooking spray.

2. Spread the beef bones evenly in the prepared pan, and scatter the onion, carrots, celery, and parsnip over the bones. Roast, uncovered and turning once, until the bones are well browned, about 30 minutes.

3. Drain any accumulated fat off the baking sheet and place the bones and vegetables in an 8- to 10-quart stockpot. (The stock can also be made in a slow cooker—see "Tips for Making Broth or Stock in a Slow Cooker," page 11—if you wish to leave the stock unattended.) Pour the wine or water into the baking sheet and gently scrape up the browned bits using a silicone spatula or wooden spoon. Pour the liquid and the bits into the stockpot.

4. Add the parsley, garlic, peppercorns, salt, thyme, bay leaf, and the roast. Add water to cover.

CONTINUED ▶

5. Bring the liquid to a gentle boil. Reduce the heat, cover, and simmer until the stock is intensely flavored, about 5 hours. Remove the chuck roast and set aside for another use. Line a colander or sieve with a triple layer of dampened cheesecloth. Pour the stock through to strain out the solids. Cool the stock quickly by setting it in an ice bath. (I set it in a large bowl of snow in the winter.)

6. Refrigerate or freeze the stock in resealable plastic bags.

Cooling Stock Safely

Homemade stock is always my first choice, and making it requires little more than assembling several ingredients in a big pot filled with water—and waiting. But there are some safety considerations when it comes to cooling the finished stock. Bringing the temperature down quickly is key, since stock offers up an excellent opportunity for bacteria to grow if left out to cool over a long period of time. The facts are these: When the stock's temperature is between 45°F and 145°F, it's in the "danger zone," but only if it's allowed to stay in that zone for a substantial period of time. Bacteria divide every 20 minutes, and if the stock is left, say, on the counter for just 2 hours, it can be unsafe to eat. To cool quickly, place the bowl or pot, uncovered, into an ice-water bath (ideally this is a sink full of ice water); then stir the stock often. Once it's cooled to lukewarm, the stock can be refrigerated, tightly covered, for up to 5 days or poured into ice cube trays or resealable plastic bags and frozen up to 12 months.

Tips for Making Broth or Stock in a Slow Cooker

- First of all, you need to have a very large (8- to 10-quart) slow cooker.
- Don't fill the pot more than two-thirds full. Liquid in a slow cooker doesn't evaporate as quickly as in a stockpot, and if the slow cooker is too full, the liquid will splatter all over the place. It is helpful to weight down the lid. Some cookers come with a band that stretches across the top of the lid.
- After filling the pot, set the cooker on high until the liquid is simmering. That usually will take 2 hours. After that, you can set the cooker to low.

How to Freeze Stocks and Broths

I prefer to freeze homemade stocks and broths in quart-size heavy-duty, resealable freezer bags, measuring 2 cups into each bag. I stack them up in a high-rimmed cake pan just in case anything leaks out. Other options are rigid plastic containers that can be reused. Leave a little space to allow for expansion. For smaller portions, I pour the stock into ice cube trays. Once frozen, transfer them to resealable plastic bags and use them cube by cube. Frozen stocks and broths will keep up to a year—if you don't use them sooner!

Basic Vegetable Broth

A rich vegetable broth is a great thing to have on hand, especially if you need to cook for a vegetarian or somebody who shuns animal products. I like the color that comes from the onions and potatoes that are not peeled. Of course, they need to be scrubbed free of any grime before adding to the pot. Some cooks say they make vegetable stock out of any vegetables they have on hand. Some save potato peelings for broth. This is definitely a recipe for the frugal cook! **MAKES ABOUT 2 QUARTS**

4 RIBS CELERY, CUT INTO
    2-INCH LENGTHS

3 LARGE CARROTS, CUT INTO
    2-INCH LENGTHS

1 LARGE SWEET ONION, UNPEELED,
    QUARTERED

1 LARGE BOILING POTATO, CUT INTO
    1-INCH SLICES

½ POUND FRESH MUSHROOMS,
    COARSELY CHOPPED, OR ¼ CUP
    DRIED MUSHROOMS

1 LARGE LEEK, HALVED LENGTHWISE,
    CUT INTO 4-INCH LENGTHS,
    AND WELL WASHED

8 LARGE CLOVES GARLIC, UNPEELED,
    SMASHED

1½ TEASPOONS SALT

1½ TEASPOONS SWEET PAPRIKA

2 BAY LEAVES

1 TEASPOON BLACK PEPPERCORNS

4 QUARTS WATER

1. Combine the celery, carrots, onion, potato, mushrooms, leek, garlic, salt, paprika, bay leaves, and peppercorns in an 8-quart stockpot and add the water. Bring to a boil. (The broth can also be made in a slow cooker—see "Tips for Making Broth or Stock in a Slow Cooker," page 11—if you wish to leave the broth unattended.)

2. Reduce the heat and simmer, uncovered, until the liquid is reduced by half, about 1 hour 30 minutes.

3. Line a colander with a double thickness of cheesecloth or a dampened muslin kitchen towel, and pour the stock through. Press lightly with a spoon or spatula. Discard or compost the vegetables.

A Glossary of Bread-Baking Basics

Good bread is the most fundamentally satisfying of all foods; and good bread with fresh butter, the greatest of feasts.

—JAMES BEARD

BAKING SODA AND BAKING POWDER

What's the difference between baking powder and baking soda? It's a question many beginning bakers ask. The answer is in their makeup. Baking powder is a combination of an acid and an alkaline, and when it is subjected to moisture and heat, it makes bubbles in the dough that cause the dough to rise while baking. Baking soda is simply a base. When there is baking soda in a recipe, there usually is also an acid ingredient like vinegar, buttermilk, lemon, cream of tartar, or fruit. Soda will react with the acid ingredient to create bubbles in the dough that make the bread rise.

EGGS

Eggs add rich flavor and a golden color to bread and produce a finer crumb. They are often an important ingredient in many specialty holiday breads. Yeast breads containing eggs in the dough brown quickly during baking.

FATS

Fats like oil, butter, and shortening add tenderness and flavor to bread. Breads made with fats are also moister. Low-fat products contain water and are not recommended for baking either quick breads or yeast breads.

FLOUR

For yeast breads, unbleached bread flour makes the best loaf because it is higher in protein content than all-purpose flour. When water is added to flour, two proteins (glutenin and gliadin) combine to form gluten. Gluten forms a network of proteins that stretch through the dough like a web, trapping air bubbles that form as the yeast ferments. This creates the characteristic airholes of perfect bread.

All-purpose flour will work in most bread recipes, but you may need to use slightly more flour as there is less gluten in the flour to absorb liquid. Cake flour does not contain enough protein to make yeast bread. Cake flour, however, is often used, especially in the South, to make tender biscuits and quick breads.

Whole grain flours add color, texture, and flavor to breads. These flour types don't have enough gluten to make a successful loaf on their own, so bread flour or pure gluten (called vital gluten) is almost always added to provide structure. Half bread flour and half whole grain flour is a proportion that usually works well.

HERBS, SPICES, AND SEEDS

Many ethnic and holiday breads depend on herbs, spices, and seeds for their characteristic flavors. They also enhance texture and appearance.

LIQUIDS

The type of liquid you use will change a bread's characteristics. Water will make a loaf that has more wheat flavor and a crisper crust. Milk and cream-based breads produce a richer bread with a finer texture. They also promote quicker browning in breads because of the additional sugar and butterfat added to the dough.

SALT

Salt is essential to almost every bread recipe. It helps control yeast development and prevents the bread from overproofing. In most breads, salt also adds flavor and brings out the flavors of other ingredients. A standard loaf will require ½ teaspoon salt per cup of flour, although some recipes might call for a little less. One exception to this rule is the Crusty Tuscan Bread (page 128). It naturally develops a very light and airy texture and has a rather bland flavor. In Tuscany, this bread balances meals that are highly spiced or highly salted.

SUGAR

Sugar is the fuel that feeds yeast and promotes fermentation, producing the carbon dioxide that makes the bread rise. Some bread recipes don't use sugar, but depend on starch in the flour to provide food for the yeast. Excess amounts of sugar will result in overly heavy, dense breads that brown too quickly before the center of the bread is done.

TOPPINGS

Toppings can change the crust of a loaf. Egg glaze (or egg wash) is used to attach other ingredients like nuts or seeds to the top of the loaf. For a chewy, crisp crust, spray the dough with water while it's baking. Brushing the baked loaf with butter will soften the crust.

YEAST

Yeast breads are, of course, leavened breads. The simplest are made with just water, flour, and yeast. My mom, like other home bakers in her day, used compressed cake yeast: there was no such thing as dry yeast back then.

Today, I use active dry yeast almost exclusively. Not only is compressed cake yeast hard to find, but it has a shelf life of just two weeks. Active dry yeast, on the other hand, is readily available and will keep for several months stored in a cool dry place or in the freezer.

Active dry yeast comes in ¼-ounce packages. One package measures from 2¼ to 2¾ teaspoons yeast, depending on the brand—usually a little less than 1 tablespoon. In this book, therefore, I have specified "1 package (¼ ounce) or 1 scant tablespoon active dry yeast." (Use the tablespoon measure if you buy yeast in bulk.) If you are not sure if your yeast is active, dissolve it in warm water and add a pinch of sugar. If it bubbles up within 5 minutes, it is good. If not, toss the mixture and start with a fresh packet. If you bake a lot of bread, it is more economical to buy yeast in bulk from a whole foods coop or a wholesale store. When dissolving the yeast in liquid before adding it to the bread mixture, the liquid should be between 105°F and 115°F. If the dry yeast is combined with flour and other dry ingredients first, then the temperature of the liquid added to the bread mixture should be higher: 120°F to 130°F. Use a thermometer to check.

There is much discussion around the difference between active dry yeast and instant dry yeast. The truth is, there is very little difference. Some maintain that instant dry yeast is stronger than active dry yeast and that you need to use less of it. Whatever the case, the trick is to watch the dough, especially after it is shaped into a loaf. When it has almost doubled in bulk, it is ready to bake. The rising of yeast dough depends more on the temperature of the environment (your kitchen) than on time or the type of yeast used. If the loaf is overproofed (meaning it has risen and then deflated during the rise), it likely will flatten while baking because the bubbles that formed when the bread was rising could not hold up. When it is slightly underproofed, there tends to be more "oven spring" while baking. "Oven spring" describes the increase in the volume of a dough during the first 10 to 12 minutes of baking, due to increased rate of expansion of gases.

QUICK BREADS

Quick breads are leavened with baking powder or baking soda (like muffins) or steam (like popovers).

BREAD-BAKING TECHNIQUES

Begin by reading the recipe carefully. Make sure you have all of the ingredients assembled. Start with a simple bread loaf recipe, like the Fresh Baguette, especially when learning to make yeast breads.

Fresh Baguette

My favorite method of getting a crisp crust on baguettes might seem a bit over the top—and more than you want to attempt. I keep a pan of river rocks in the bottom of my oven so that they heat up as the oven itself does. I also keep a baking stone on the center rack of the oven. It takes at least an hour for the oven to heat both the rocks and the stone. Then, I slide the risen loaves onto the stone and pitch about a cup of water onto the rocks, which creates the steam necessary to achieve a crusty loaf.

The following recipe offers an alternative method for baking a very acceptable baguette, not quite so crusty but still excellent. **MAKES 2**

1 PACKAGE (¼ OUNCE) OR 1 SCANT
    TABLESPOON ACTIVE DRY YEAST
1¾ CUPS WARM WATER (105°F TO 115°F)

4 CUPS UNBLEACHED BREAD FLOUR,
    PLUS ADDITIONAL IF NEEDED
2 TEASPOONS SALT

1. In a large bowl, sprinkle the yeast over the warm water and let stand until the yeast looks foamy, about 5 minutes. With a wooden spoon, stir in 2 cups of the flour until combined. Set aside until the dough begins to rise to make a sponge, 25 minutes. Alternatively, to further develop the flavor, cover and refrigerate the sponge overnight.

2. In a food processor, combine the remaining 2 cups flour and the salt. Pulse 2 or 3 times until mixed. Alternatively, mix the flour and salt in a large bowl or in the bowl of a stand mixer fitted with the paddle attachment.

3. Add the sponge to the flour mixture. In the food processor, process until the dough comes together in a soft ball that completely comes away from the sides of the bowl. Alternatively, add the sponge to the flour mixture in the mixing bowl and mix until a shaggy dough forms. If the dough seems dry, add more water 1 tablespoon at a time. Or, if the dough seems too moist, add more flour, 1 tablespoon at a time. Turn out onto a lightly floured surface, cover with a bowl, and let sit for 15 minutes until the dough comes together. Knead until the dough forms a smooth ball, about 10 minutes.

CONTINUED ▶

4. Place the dough in a lightly greased bowl and turn to coat. Cover with a cloth and let rise in a warm place until doubled in bulk, about 1 hour. (The dough can be refrigerated overnight, if necessary.)

5. Lightly grease two 17 × 14-inch baking sheets. Punch the dough down and divide into 2 equal pieces. Shape each piece into a long, slender loaf about 21 inches long and 3 inches wide.

6. Place the loaves diagonally on the baking sheets and let rise, uncovered, about 30 minutes until almost doubled in bulk. (You can refrigerate the loaves at this point to bake several hours later or the next day. Brush or spray with cool water before refrigerating.)

7. Position an oven rack in the middle of the oven and preheat to 475°F. Using a razor blade, a French *lame*, or a serrated knife, make 4 or 5 diagonal slashes in the risen loaves and spray with cool water. Bake one loaf at a time (refrigerate the second until ready to bake) until golden and the loaf sounds hollow when tapped, 25 to 30 minutes. Transfer to a rack to cool.

VARIATION
. . . .

Ciabatta Loaves

Make the Fresh Baguette dough using only 3 cups flour and reducing the salt to 1½ teaspoons. When ready to shape the dough for baking, lightly flour or line the baking sheets with parchment. Divide the dough into 4 pieces, and form each into a 3 × 7-inch oval. Place 2 loaves on each prepared sheet and dust lightly with flour. Cover and let rise until almost doubled in bulk, about 45 minutes. Position an oven rack in the middle of the oven and preheat to 425°F. Spritz the loaves with water. Bake one sheet at a time, for 25 to 30 minutes, spritzing every 5 to 10 minutes to achieve a crispy crust. **MAKES 4**

A Basic Vegetable Soup

This is a go-to template that calls for whatever you happen to have on hand to make the soup. It is an all-season soup and very forgiving, which is why there are no measures given. Serve with a slice of bread such as the basic home-baked bread in the next recipe, topped with your favorite cheese or savory spread.

BUTTER OR OIL

ONION, CHOPPED

CELERY, FINELY CHOPPED

CARROTS, FINELY CHOPPED

POTATOES, CUT INTO 1-INCH CHUNKS,
    OR COOKED BEANS

TOMATOES, FRESH OR CANNED

ANY OTHER VEGETABLES YOU
    HAVE ON HAND AND LIKE

BOILING WATER OR BROTH

SALT

GROUND BLACK PEPPER

FRESH OR DRIED HERBS

1. In a heavy pot, heat the butter or oil. Add the onion, celery, and carrots and sauté them over medium-low heat until the vegetables become aromatic, 5 to 10 minutes.

2. Add the potatoes or beans, tomatoes, and other vegetables of your choice. Add boiling water or broth to cover all the vegetables. Simmer until the soup comes together, about 30 minutes. Add the seasonings of your choice about halfway through the cooking time.

Basic Home-Baked Bread

This is the easiest loaf you will ever bake. It is also the most basic, which makes it easy to vary the recipe. Switch the liquid from water to milk or juice or broth, and you have a different flavored loaf. Vary the sugar (or leave it out), the shortening (or leave it out), and the mixture of flours, and you can come up with even more flavors. Add seeds, dried fruits, or nuts, and you get even more variety.

This recipe goes back to the basic proportion of approximately three parts flour to one part liquid, plus yeast and salt. The sugar adds flavor, and the butter or shortening imparts flavor and tenderness.

You do not need to use up all the flour called for in this recipe, or you may need more flour than called for. The amounts vary depending on many factors, including weather, which is why I only give the approximate amount needed. It is always better to use less, rather than more, flour; dough that has too much flour worked into it may not rise well—so be a flour miser. **MAKES ONE 9¼ × 5¼-INCH LOAF**

1 PACKAGE (¼ OUNCE) OR 1 SCANT
    TABLESPOON ACTIVE DRY YEAST
1 CUP WARM WATER (105°F TO 115°F)
1 TABLESPOON SUGAR
1 TEASPOON SALT

1 TABLESPOON SOFT BUTTER OR OIL
3 CUPS (MORE OR LESS) UNBLEACHED
    BREAD FLOUR OR ALL-
    PURPOSE FLOUR

1. In a large bowl, sprinkle the yeast over the warm water. Add the sugar, salt, and butter or oil. Mix and let stand until the yeast begins to foam, about 5 minutes.

2. Add the flour, a little at a time, beating well from the beginning to keep the dough smooth.

3. Turn the dough out onto a floured board and knead, adding small spoonfuls of flour as needed, until the dough is soft and smooth—not sticky—to the touch.

4. Put the dough in a lightly greased or oiled bowl, turning to coat. Cover and let rise in a warm place until doubled in bulk, about 1 hour.

5. Punch down the dough. Turn out onto a floured board and knead to release the air bubbles.

6. Preheat the oven to 375°F. Butter a 9¼ × 5¼-inch loaf pan.

7. Form the dough into a loaf and set in the pan. Cover and let rise until the loaf is about ½ inch above the edge of the pan, about 30 minutes. Bake until golden brown and a wooden skewer inserted into the loaf comes out clean, 35 to 45 minutes. Turn out onto a rack to cool.

VARIATIONS

Whole Wheat Bread

Replace ½ cup of the bread flour with whole wheat flour.

Rye Bread

Replace ½ cup of the bread flour with medium or dark rye flour. If desired, you may replace the sugar with dark molasses.

Fruit and Nut Bread or Cheese Bread

After the first rise, knead ½ to 1 cup dried cranberries, raisins, or other chopped dried fruits, chopped nuts, or diced cheddar or Swiss cheese into the dough until evenly distributed. Then form and bake as directed.

SPRING

Spring officially begins on March 21, although that date is notorious for a late-season snowstorm here in Minnesota!

No matter, it signals a fresh beginning, a time to trade in heavy winter coats, snow boots, and bulky mittens for lighter clothing and to transition away from thick, stick-to-the-ribs soups and stews toward soups featuring the ingredients that define the season: asparagus, spring peas, nettles, morels, and tender greens.

As if the awakening of the earth isn't enough to celebrate, spring has its share of holidays worth gathering for. May Day, Easter, Memorial Day, and Midsummer Day offer opportunities to share a meal with loved ones—why not make it a casual get-together over soup and bread? I love the Polish tradition of serving borscht on Easter morning. One of the most convivial ways to serve it is buffet style. Offer a boiling pot of broth and with small bowls filled with sliced kielbasa, hard-cooked eggs, cooked beets, diced ham, and grated horseradish. Guests can spoon their choice of ingredients into their own soup bowls and top it off with the boiling broth. Tradition calls for serving it with rye bread that has been blessed on Easter Saturday.

Mother's Day opens up a host of opportunities to bring soup into the mix. No-cook Spicy Mango Melon Soup and Lemon Poppy Seed Muffins (pages 40 and 41) are ideal for a special brunch or lunch that both moms and kids can enjoy. In Minnesota, Mother's Day coincides with one of the state's most anticipated events: the opening of fishing season. Walleye is the prized fish. If there is a fisherman or woman in the family, dinner is likely to be a simple Walleye Chowder (page 78) and a Fresh Baguette (page 17)—or a good-quality purchased one if time is tight!

On the first sunny weekend morning of spring, I make French Spring Vegetable Soup (page 54) with Garlic Toast Rounds (page 55), a nod to a wonderful memory of the version I enjoyed on the French Riviera years ago. I adorn the table with a colorful Provençal tablecloth to set the mood. A big pot of soup, a bowl of pistou, a basket of bread, chilled crisp white wine, and five guests—the ultimate in good eating.

Note: All milk can be whole unless otherwise specified.

New Potato Spring Pea Soup
(WITH) Chive-Dill Batter Bread

NEW POTATO SPRING PEA SOUP
....

Sweet, tender-skinned new potatoes are great simply roasted with garlic and butter, but incomparable in this soup paired with the tender green peas of late spring. **MAKES 4 SERVINGS**

2 TABLESPOONS BUTTER

1½ CUPS DICED NEW POTATOES
    (ABOUT ½ POUND)

½ CUP FINELY DICED SWEET ONION

2 CLOVES GARLIC, MINCED

1 TABLESPOON ALL-PURPOSE FLOUR

1 TABLESPOON GROUND CUMIN

1 TEASPOON GROUND CORIANDER

PINCH OF RED-PEPPER FLAKES

2 CUPS BASIC CHICKEN STOCK (PAGE 6)
    OR LOW-SODIUM STORE-BOUGHT

1 CUP WHOLE OR 2% MILK

2 TEASPOONS SUGAR

1 CUP FRESH OR FROZEN BABY PEAS

1 TABLESPOON LIME JUICE

SALT AND GROUND BLACK PEPPER

SOUR CREAM OR YOGURT

CHOPPED FRESH CILANTRO

1. Melt the butter in a large 3- to 4-quart soup pot over medium heat. Add the potatoes, onion, and garlic. Cook, stirring, for 5 minutes.

2. Stir in the flour, cumin, coriander, and pepper flakes. Continue cooking over medium heat, stirring constantly, until fragrant, about 30 seconds.

3. Whisk in the stock, milk, and sugar and bring to a boil. Cover, reduce the heat to low, and cook until the potatoes are tender, about 15 minutes. Add the peas and cook 5 minutes longer.

4. Stir in the lime juice and salt and black pepper to taste. Serve hot, garnished with sour cream or yogurt and cilantro.

CHIVE-DILL BATTER BREAD

Chives are the first herbs to come up in the garden once the snow has melted, a certain sign of spring. Young chives add mild onion flavor not only to omelets and salads but also to this batter bread. **MAKES 4 TO 8 SERVINGS**

1 PACKAGE (¼ OUNCE) OR 1 SCANT
   TABLESPOON ACTIVE DRY YEAST
¼ CUP WARM WATER (105°F TO 115°F)
2 TABLESPOONS SUGAR
1 TEASPOON SALT
2 TABLESPOONS FINELY CHOPPED
   FRESH CHIVES

1½ TABLESPOONS DRIED DILLWEED
2 TABLESPOONS BUTTER
1 CUP 1% OR FAT-FREE COTTAGE
   CHEESE, LARGE OR SMALL CURD
1 LARGE EGG, LIGHTLY BEATEN
2 CUPS ALL-PURPOSE FLOUR

1. Grease a 1½-quart casserole or soufflé dish generously and set aside. In the bowl of a stand mixer, combine the yeast, warm water, sugar, salt, chives, and dill. Set aside until the yeast begins to foam, about 5 minutes.

2. Add the butter, cottage cheese, egg, and ½ cup of the flour. Beat on low speed until well mixed.

3. Add the remaining 1½ cups flour and beat to make a stiff batter. Cover and let rise for 10 minutes.

4. Transfer the batter to the casserole dish. Cover and let rise in a warm place until almost doubled in bulk, about 45 minutes.

5. Preheat the oven to 350°F. Bake until golden and a wooden skewer inserted into the center of the loaf comes out clean and dry, 35 to 40 minutes. Remove the loaf from the casserole and place on a rack to cool.

Asparagus Soup (WITH) Turkey and Tomato Open-Faced Sandwiches

ASPARAGUS SOUP

There's nothing like asparagus to symbolize spring, which is the only season in which it should be eaten. Cooked quickly and pureed in a soup, it makes an irresistible combination with a simple, open-faced sandwich. **MAKES 4 SERVINGS**

2 CUPS BASIC CHICKEN STOCK (PAGE 6) OR LOW-SODIUM STORE-BOUGHT

1 CUP WATER

1 CUP COARSELY CHOPPED SWEET ONION

1 SMALL YELLOW POTATO, CHOPPED

1 BUNCH ASPARAGUS (ABOUT 1 POUND), CUT INTO QUARTERS

PINCH OF DRIED TARRAGON

SALT AND GROUND BLACK PEPPER

1. In a medium saucepan, combine the chicken stock, water, onion, and potato.

2. Bring to a boil; then reduce the heat and simmer until the potato is tender, about 10 minutes. Add the asparagus and cook 5 minutes longer. Add the tarragon.

3. Remove and reserve 12 asparagus tips to use as garnish. Transfer the remaining soup to a blender and puree until smooth. Season to taste with salt and pepper. Ladle into soup bowls and garnish with the reserved asparagus tips.

TURKEY AND TOMATO OPEN-FACED SANDWICHES

Keep deli-style cooked turkey slices on hand to make these sandwiches.

MAKES 4 SERVINGS

4 THICK SLICES BASIC HOME-BAKED
    BREAD (PAGE 20), WHITE, RYE,
    OR WHOLE WHEAT
4 TABLESPOONS CREAMY GARLIC AND
    HERB CHEESE (SUCH AS BOURSIN), AT
    ROOM TEMPERATURE

8 SLICES DELI-SLICED TURKEY,
    PLAIN OR SMOKED
2 TOMATOES, CUT INTO A TOTAL
    OF 8 SLICES
4 SPRIGS BASIL

1. Preheat the broiler and toast the bread on a baking sheet until lightly browned. Turn over and toast the other side.

2. Spread the toast with the garlic and herb cheese. Top each with 2 slices of the turkey and 2 slices of tomato. Garnish with the basil.

Roasted Red Pepper Soup
WITH Herbed Biscuit Muffins

ROASTED RED PEPPER SOUP

Roasting red peppers intensifies their sweet flavor, but I'm not a fan of the standard roasting method–a messy process of roasting, seeding, and peeling the whole peppers. I concocted my own way of doing it, and it works perfectly, especially for this soup. **MAKES 6 SERVINGS**

6 LARGE RED BELL PEPPERS

1 TABLESPOON OLIVE OIL

4 TABLESPOONS (½ STICK) BUTTER

1 LARGE SWEET ONION, CHOPPED

1 LARGE LEEK (WHITE PART ONLY), WELL WASHED AND CHOPPED

3 SMALL YUKON GOLD POTATOES, PEELED AND CUBED

4 CUPS BASIC CHICKEN STOCK (PAGE 6) OR LOW-SODIUM STORE-BOUGHT

½ TEASPOON SALT

½ TEASPOON GROUND BLACK PEPPER

½ CUP SOUR CREAM

1. Position a rack in the top of the oven and preheat to 475°F. Line a baking sheet with foil.

2. Halve the bell peppers lengthwise, discard the tops, and remove the seeds. Cut the halves in half lengthwise again and toss with the olive oil. Place the peppers, skin side up, on the prepared pan.

3. Roast the peppers until some of the skins are blistered, about 10 minutes. Remove the peppers from the oven and wrap the foil in the pan around them. Let stand for 20 minutes.

4. Meanwhile, melt the butter in a large saucepan over medium-low heat. Add the onion and leek and cook until tender, about 10 minutes. Add the potatoes, stock, salt, and black pepper. Bring to a boil and then simmer, covered, until the potatoes are tender, about 30 minutes.

5. Peel the bell peppers and finely chop. Add them to the potato mixture.

6. Working in batches, puree the mixture in a blender. Return the soup to the pot and heat just until warmed through. Do not boil.

7. Divide the soup among 6 bowls. Spoon the sour cream into a small resealable plastic bag. Snip one corner. Pipe the sour cream into each soup.

HERBED BISCUIT MUFFINS

I use cake flour in place of all-purpose flour in these muffins to give them a tender, biscuit-like consistency. A little sugar brings out the flavor of the herbs. **MAKES 12**

2½ CUPS SIFTED CAKE FLOUR

1 TABLESPOON SUGAR

1 TEASPOON DRIED THYME LEAVES

1 TEASPOON CRUMBLED DRIED
    MARJORAM LEAVES

½ TEASPOON CRUMBLED DRIED
    SAGE LEAVES

2 TEASPOONS BAKING POWDER

½ TEASPOON BAKING SODA

½ TEASPOON SALT

4 TABLESPOONS (½ STICK)
    BUTTER, MELTED

⅔ CUP BUTTERMILK

1. Preheat the oven to 400°F. Lightly grease 12 cups of a muffin tin.

2. In a large bowl, combine the flour, sugar, thyme, marjoram, sage, baking powder, baking soda, and salt. Mix well.

3. Stir in the butter and buttermilk, until the mixture just forms a soft dough, about 20 strokes. Spoon the batter into the muffin cups, dividing evenly.

4. Bake until golden brown and a wooden pick inserted into the center of a muffin comes out clean, 12 to 15 minutes. Serve hot.

Spring Tonic Soup and Croutons
(WITH) Cardamom Almond Scones

SPRING TONIC SOUP AND CROUTONS

Serve this soup for lunch or brunch along with a bowl of big, juicy strawberries and fragrant cardamom-scented scones. **MAKES 4 OR 5 SERVINGS**

1 TABLESPOON OLIVE OIL

3 LEEKS, WHITE AND TENDER GREEN
  PARTS ONLY, WELL WASHED
  AND CUT INTO ½-INCH PIECES

1 RED BELL PEPPER, DICED

2 CLOVES GARLIC, MINCED

2 MEDIUM CARROTS, DICED

1 BUNCH RADISHES, TRIMMED AND
  THINLY SLICED

2 CUPS CHOPPED BABY SPINACH

5 CUPS BASIC VEGETABLE BROTH
  (PAGE 12) OR LOW-SODIUM
  STORE-BOUGHT

1 TABLESPOON FRESH THYME LEAVES

2 TO 4 TABLESPOONS LEMON JUICE

SALT AND GROUND BLACK PEPPER

CRISP CROUTONS

SOUR CREAM

ALFALFA SPROUTS

1. Heat the oil in a large soup pot over medium-low heat. Add the leeks, bell pepper, garlic, and carrots and cook, covered, over low heat, stirring often, until the vegetables are tender, 15 to 20 minutes.

2. Add the radishes, spinach, broth, and thyme. Bring to a boil; reduce to a simmer and cook for 15 minutes. Add the lemon juice and salt and black pepper to taste.

3. To serve, place a few croutons in each soup bowl and ladle the soup over them. Top each bowl with sour cream and sprouts.

CARDAMOM ALMOND SCONES

For the best cardamom flavor, buy it in the pods (and remove the seeds from the pods) or whole cardamom seeds and grind them in a coffee or spice mill. Not only are these scones perfect for springtime, but they make a great offering with coffee for any holiday. Use any extra scones as a base for shortcake. **MAKES 12**

3 CUPS ALL-PURPOSE FLOUR

1 CUP CHOPPED ALMONDS

½ CUP SUGAR

1 TABLESPOON BAKING POWDER

1 TEASPOON FRESHLY GROUND
  CARDAMOM SEEDS

2 STICKS (8 OUNCES) COLD BUTTER,
  CUT INTO SMALL PIECES

3 LARGE EGGS

½ TO ⅔ CUP PLAIN YOGURT (FAT-FREE,
  2%, OR WHOLE MILK) OR BUTTERMILK

1. Preheat the oven to 400°F. Lightly grease a large baking sheet or line with parchment paper.

2. In a large bowl, combine the flour, almonds, ⅓ cup of the sugar, the baking powder, and cardamom. Using a pastry blender, two knives, or a pastry fork, cut in the butter until it is in pea-size pieces.

3. In a small bowl, mix together the eggs and ½ cup of the yogurt or buttermilk. Add it to the dry ingredients and blend quickly, just until the dough comes together, adding a bit more yogurt or buttermilk, if needed.

4. Using a large ice-cream scoop or ½-cup measure, scoop the dough into mounds and place on the prepared baking sheet, about 3 inches apart. Sprinkle the mounds of dough with the remaining sugar and press them down lightly.

5. Bake until lightly browned, 10 to 15 minutes. Transfer the scones to a rack or place directly into a serving basket. Serve warm.

Herb Vegetable Soup
(WITH) Wheat Germ Batter Bread

HERB VEGETABLE SOUP

This cream-based soup is appealing on those early spring evenings when there's still a chill in the air. Couple this with thick slabs of freshly baked Wheat Germ Batter Bread and perhaps a favorite cheese on the side. **MAKES 6 SERVINGS**

1 TABLESPOON BUTTER

1 LARGE ONION, CHOPPED

2 CLOVES GARLIC, MINCED

3 CUPS BASIC CHICKEN STOCK (PAGE 6) OR LOW-SODIUM STORE-BOUGHT

1 CUP PEELED, SEEDED, AND CHOPPED TOMATOES

4 MEDIUM CARROTS, SLICED

4 SMALL RED POTATOES, SCRUBBED AND CUT INTO ½-INCH PIECES

1 CUP HALF-AND-HALF

2 TEASPOONS MINCED FRESH MARJORAM

1 TEASPOON MINCED FRESH THYME, PLUS SPRIGS FOR GARNISH

⅛ TEASPOON GROUND WHITE PEPPER

1. Melt the butter in a 4- to 5-quart saucepan over medium heat. Add the onion and garlic and cook until tender, about 3 minutes.

2. Add the stock, tomatoes, carrots, and potatoes and bring to a boil. Cover, reduce the heat, and simmer until the carrots and potatoes are tender, about 30 minutes. Set aside.

3. Transfer the mixture to a blender and puree until smooth. Return to the pot. Add the half-and-half, marjoram, minced thyme, and white pepper. Bring to a simmer over medium heat. Alternatively, cover and refrigerate until chilled throughout and serve cold. Garnish individual servings with sprigs of thyme.

WHEAT GERM BATTER BREAD

When you're pressed for time, or even when you are not, this flat loaf—which is light and tender—makes an excellent accompaniment for almost any soup.

MAKES 6 SERVINGS

1 PACKAGE (¼ OUNCE) OR 1 SCANT
    TABLESPOON ACTIVE DRY YEAST
¼ CUP WARM WATER (105°F TO 115°F)
3 TABLESPOONS SUGAR
⅛ TEASPOON GROUND GINGER
1¼ CUPS UNBLEACHED
    ALL-PURPOSE FLOUR

1 CUP WHOLE WHEAT FLOUR
¼ CUP WHEAT GERM
½ TEASPOON SALT
1 CUP MILK, SCALDED AND COOLED
2 TO 3 TEASPOONS MELTED BUTTER

1. In a large bowl, sprinkle the yeast over the warm water. Add 1 teaspoon of the sugar and the ginger and stir to mix. Let stand until the yeast begins to foam, about 5 minutes.

2. Stir in the all-purpose and whole wheat flours, wheat germ, remaining sugar, salt, and milk and beat for 50 strokes.

3. Line a baking sheet with parchment paper or grease generously. Turn the dough out onto the prepared pan. Spread out to make an 8-inch round and let rise 30 minutes.

4. Preheat the oven to 400°F. Bake until golden and the center of the loaf springs back when touched, 20 to 30 minutes. Brush with the melted butter. Cut into 6 wedges and serve warm.

Root Vegetable Soup
⬤WITH Caraway Rye Pretzels

ROOT VEGETABLE SOUP

I've been called the queen of root vegetables—and for good reason. I love a simple tomato-based soup like this one, with the vegetables left in chunks and fragrant of cumin. It's a very forgiving and adaptable soup: in the summer, I add fresh veggies as they come into the market and the garden. **MAKES 6 TO 8 SERVINGS**

4 CUPS BASIC CHICKEN STOCK OR TWO-FOR-ONE BEEF STOCK (PAGE 6 OR 9) OR LOW-SODIUM STORE-BOUGHT

3 CUPS TOMATO JUICE, HOME-CANNED OR STORE-BOUGHT

3 THIN-SKINNED BOILING POTATOES, SCRUBBED AND CHOPPED

4 CARROTS, SLICED

2 MEDIUM PARSNIPS, PEELED AND SLICED

1 ONION, CUT INTO EIGHTHS

1 RIB CELERY, THINLY SLICED

1 CLOVE GARLIC, SMASHED

¼ CUP FINELY CHOPPED FRESH PARSLEY

¼ TEASPOON GROUND BLACK PEPPER

¼ TEASPOON GROUND CUMIN

¼ TEASPOON SALT

1 TOMATO, CHOPPED

1. In a large saucepan, combine the broth and tomato juice and bring to a boil over medium heat. Add the potatoes, carrots, parsnips, onion, celery, and garlic. Reduce the heat to medium-low and simmer until the vegetables are tender, about 45 minutes.

2. Season with the parsley, pepper, cumin, and salt. Add the chopped tomatoes, bring to a boil, and serve hot.

CARAWAY RYE PRETZELS

It is thought that the word *pretzel* is derived from the German word *brezel*, which refers to the prayer position in which the hands are crossed at the breast. For me, pretzels are synonymous with the Easter season, when I make these fragrant breads. **MAKES 16**

1 PACKAGE (¼ OUNCE) OR 1 SCANT
    TABLESPOON ACTIVE DRY YEAST

2 CUPS WARM WATER (105°F TO 115°F)

3 CUPS RYE FLOUR

2½ CUPS BREAD FLOUR

2 TEASPOONS SUGAR

½ TEASPOON SALT

1 TABLESPOON PLUS 2 TEASPOONS
    CARAWAY SEEDS

1 EGG WHITE

2 TEASPOONS WATER

1 TEASPOON KOSHER SALT

1. In a large bowl, sprinkle the yeast over the warm water, stir, and let stand until the yeast looks foamy, about 5 minutes. Add the rye flour, 2 cups of the bread flour, the sugar, the table salt, and 1 tablespoon of the caraway seeds and stir until a soft dough forms. Cover and let rest about 15 minutes.

2. Turn the dough out onto a well-floured surface. Knead until smooth and elastic, about 8 minutes. Add enough of the remaining ½ cup bread flour to prevent the dough from sticking to your hands.

3. Place the dough in a large, lightly oiled bowl and turn to coat. Cover and let rise in a warm place until doubled in bulk, about 30 minutes.

4. Preheat the oven to 475°F. Line 2 baking sheets with parchment paper. Punch the dough down and divide into 4 portions. Cut each portion into 4 pieces.

5. Roll each piece into a 15-inch rope. (Cover the remaining dough while working to prevent it from drying out.) Twist each rope into a pretzel shape. Place the pretzels 1½ inches apart on the baking sheets.

6. Whisk the egg white with the water and brush onto the tops of each pretzel. Sprinkle with the kosher salt and the remaining 2 teaspoons caraway seeds. Bake until golden, about 12 minutes. Transfer to a rack to cool.

Sausage and Vegetable Minestra with Rosemary Focaccia

SAUSAGE AND VEGETABLE MINESTRA

Minestra is Italian for a soup in a light broth, with tiny pasta and a few vegetables. *Minestrone*, on the other hand, means a "big soup" made with lots of vegetables. The spinach goes into the pot late in the recipe so it will wilt but not get mushy. **MAKES 6 SERVINGS**

2 TABLESPOONS OLIVE OIL

1 POUND ITALIAN-STYLE SAUSAGE LINKS, CUT INTO 1-INCH PIECES

1 TABLESPOON MINCED GARLIC

2 CUPS DICED ONIONS

½ CUP DRY WHITE WINE

2 CUPS SEEDED AND DICED TOMATOES

4 CUPS BASIC CHICKEN STOCK (PAGE 6) OR LOW-SODIUM STORE-BOUGHT

1 POUND GREEN BEANS, CUT INTO 2-INCH LENGTHS (ABOUT 4 CUPS)

½ CUP ORZO PASTA

3 CUPS CHOPPED FRESH SPINACH

3 TABLESPOONS FINELY CHOPPED FLAT-LEAF PARSLEY

1 TABLESPOON RED WINE VINEGAR

½ CUP FRESHLY GRATED PARMESAN CHEESE, PLUS MORE FOR SERVING

1. Heat the oil in a 4- to 5-quart soup pot over medium-high heat. Add the sausage and cook, stirring, until browned. Add the garlic and onions and cook until the onions are fragrant and wilted, 4 to 5 minutes.

2. Push the vegetables to the side, add the wine, and stir to incorporate the browned bits from the bottom of the pan. Boil until almost evaporated; then add the tomatoes, chicken stock, and green beans.

3. Add the orzo and simmer 10 minutes. Stir in the spinach and cook until it is wilted. Add the parsley and vinegar. Just before serving, stir in the Parmesan cheese. Top individual servings with additional Parmesan cheese.

ROSEMARY FOCACCIA

I remember the first time I had focaccia. I can't tell you how many years ago it was, but I was in a train station in Italy. It was sold by the piece, in 4 × 8-inch rectangles, an inch or so thick with an airy texture and a delicious, salty olive oil topping. Since then, I've made focaccia for large groups and for small ones, with lots of toppings and with a few. Sometimes I top it with grated cheese, but I like it best dressed simply with olive oil, rosemary, and coarse salt. **MAKES 12 SQUARES**

1 PACKAGE (¼ OUNCE) OR 1 SCANT
    TABLESPOON ACTIVE DRY YEAST
1 TEASPOON SUGAR
2 CUPS WARM WATER (105°F TO 115°F)
3½ TO 4 CUPS UNBLEACHED
    BREAD FLOUR

1 TEASPOON SALT
½ CUP OLIVE OIL
3 TABLESPOONS FRESH ROSEMARY,
    COARSELY CHOPPED
½ TEASPOON COARSE KOSHER SALT

1. In a large bowl of a stand mixer, combine the yeast, sugar, and ½ cup of the warm water. Let stand until the yeast is foamy, about 5 minutes.

2. Add the remaining 1½ cups warm water, 1 cup of the flour, the table salt, and ¼ cup of the olive oil. Fit the mixer with the paddle attachment and beat the mixture on medium speed until a very soft, smooth batter forms. Let stand until the batter begins to rise, about 15 minutes.

3. Replace the paddle attachment with the dough hook. With the mixer on medium speed, gradually add in the remaining flour to make a soft, smooth dough. Place the dough on a greased 10 × 15-inch rimmed baking sheet.

4. Let the dough rise until it is puffy, about 1 hour. With your fingers, press down on the dough, pushing it toward the corners of the pan. Cover with plastic wrap and let sit for an additional 20 minutes. Preheat the oven to 450°F. Remove the plastic wrap and dimple the dough all over with your fingertips. Drizzle with the remaining ¼ cup olive oil and sprinkle the rosemary all over. Sprinkle with the kosher salt.

5. Bake until the focaccia is browned all over, 20 to 25 minutes. Remove from the oven and let cool about 10 minutes before cutting into 12 squares.

May Day Celebration Soup
(WITH) Scottish Currant Bannock

MAY DAY CELEBRATION SOUP

Leeks, green onions, and baby spinach comprise this simple soup, a perfect one to serve for a May Day or Beltane celebration around a bonfire. Serve it in mugs and offer the bannock, cut into chunks and piled into a napkin-lined basket.

MAKES 6 SERVINGS

2 TABLESPOONS BUTTER

1½ POUNDS NEW OR FINGERLING POTATOES, SCRUBBED

1 BUNCH GREEN ONIONS (SCALLIONS), CUT UP

1 SMALL LEEK, WHITE AND TENDER GREEN PARTS ONLY, WELL WASHED AND CHOPPED

4 CLOVES GARLIC, CHOPPED

SALT AND GROUND BLACK PEPPER

4½ CUPS BASIC CHICKEN STOCK (PAGE 6) OR LOW-SODIUM STORE-BOUGHT

1 BAG (5 OUNCES) BABY SPINACH, CHOPPED

¾ CUP WHOLE MILK OR LIGHT CREAM

1. Melt the butter in a heavy saucepan over medium-low heat. When it foams, add the potatoes, green onions, leek, and garlic. Toss them in the butter until they are well coated. Sprinkle with salt and pepper and cover. Steam on gentle heat for about 10 minutes.

2. Add the chicken stock and simmer until the vegetables are fork-tender, 10 to 15 minutes. Add the spinach and cook until wilted, about 5 minutes.

3. Puree the soup in the blender, return to the pot, and whisk in the milk or cream. Taste and adjust the seasoning. Serve hot.

SCOTTISH CURRANT BANNOCK

When you bake this buttermilk loaf in a big round, it resembles a giant scone. Sometimes I scoop the dough into balls and bake them to make individual buns. This makes a good breakfast bread too. **MAKES 8 SERVINGS**

2 CUPS ALL-PURPOSE FLOUR	½ TEASPOON SALT
2 TABLESPOONS SUGAR	2 TABLESPOONS BUTTER
1 TEASPOON BAKING POWDER	1 CUP BUTTERMILK
½ TEASPOON BAKING SODA	½ CUP DRIED CURRANTS

1. Preheat the oven to 375°F. Line a baking sheet with parchment paper.

2. In a large bowl, combine the flour, sugar, baking powder, baking soda, and salt. Cut the butter into the flour mixture with a pastry blender. Add the buttermilk and mix until the dough is soft. Mix in the currants until incorporated throughout.

3. Turn the dough out onto a lightly floured surface. Knead for 5 minutes, or until smooth. Form the dough into a 7-inch round. Place on the prepared baking sheet. Using a razor blade, a French *lame,* or a serrated knife, score the bannock from edge to edge to divide it into 4 sections. Score a second cross on top of the first to divide the round into 8 sections. Alternatively, scoop the dough to make 8 buns and place them on the baking sheet.

4. Bake until a wooden skewer inserted into the bread comes out clean and dry, 40 minutes for the loaf, 25 minutes for the buns.

Spicy Mango Melon Soup
WITH Lemon Poppy Seed Muffins

SPICY MANGO MELON SOUP

This makes a beautiful pairing for a Mother's Day brunch. If you can find fresh, diced mango in your supermarket, it eliminates the need to peel and cut away the fruit from a whole mango. Pair this dessert-like soup with a plate of sliced strawberries and peeled oranges. **MAKES 4 SERVINGS**

2 LARGE MANGOES, CHOPPED
   (ABOUT 2 CUPS)
4 CUPS CHOPPED CANTALOUPE
½ CUP WHOLE OR 2% MILK
1 CUP PLAIN WHOLE-MILK OR
   LOW-FAT YOGURT

JUICE OF 1 LIME
1 TEASPOON GRATED FRESH GINGER
PINCH OF CAYENNE PEPPER
CHOPPED FRESH MINT

1. In a food processor or blender, combine the mangoes, cantaloupe, and milk and process until pureed.

2. Add the yogurt, lime juice, ginger, and cayenne. Taste and adjust the seasoning if needed. Cover and chill in the refrigerator.

3. Ladle into soup bowls or mugs, and garnish with fresh mint.

LEMON POPPY SEED MUFFINS

Flecked with poppy seeds, these easy-to-stir-up muffins freeze well in resealable plastic bags. They'll keep up to three months. To reheat, bring them to room temperature, wrap in foil, and warm in a low-temperature oven. **MAKES 12**

2 CUPS ALL-PURPOSE FLOUR

¼ CUP POPPY SEEDS

2 TEASPOONS BAKING POWDER

¼ TEASPOON SALT

8 TABLESPOONS (1 STICK) BUTTER,
   AT ROOM TEMPERATURE

1 CUP SUGAR

2 LARGE EGGS, LIGHTLY BEATEN

1 TABLESPOON FINELY GRATED
   LEMON ZEST

1 CUP MILK

1. Preheat the oven to 400°F. Lightly grease 12 cups of a muffin tin or line with paper liners (coat the liners with cooking spray).

2. In a medium bowl, stir together the flour, poppy seeds, baking powder, and salt.

3. In a large bowl, cream the butter and sugar together until light and fluffy. Add the eggs and lemon zest and mix well. Add the flour mixture and milk to the large bowl and stir with a wooden spoon just until the flour is moistened, about 20 strokes.

4. Divide the batter evenly among the muffin cups. Bake until lightly browned and a wooden skewer inserted into the center of a muffin comes out clean, 15 to 20 minutes. Transfer to a rack to cool. Serve warm.

Fresh Nettle Soup
WITH Three-Grain Almond Hardtack

FRESH NETTLE SOUP
. . . .

I first enjoyed this soup when we lived in Finland for a year. Little did I know that I was eating a soup of ingredients that were growing right in my own flower beds at home. Nettles are rich in vitamins, serotonin (which I know I can definitely use in the spring), and histamines. Wear gloves when you prepare them, as the nettles can sting and cause little rashlike hives on your hands. Once cooked, they lose this property. If you can't find nettles, use fresh kale or spinach instead. Scandinavians tradition-ally garnish this soup with slices of hard-cooked egg. **MAKES 5 OR 6 SERVINGS**

10 CUPS NETTLE LEAVES, STEMS
   REMOVED

1 TABLESPOON OLIVE OIL

6 GREEN ONIONS (SCALLIONS), CHOPPED

2 CUPS WATER

2 TABLESPOONS ALL-PURPOSE FLOUR

2 CUPS BASIC CHICKEN STOCK (PAGE 6)
   OR LOW-SODIUM STORE-BOUGHT

1 TEASPOON SALT

⅛ TEASPOON GROUND GINGER

PINCH OF WHITE PEPPER

½ CUP HEAVY CREAM

2 HARD-COOKED EGGS, CHOPPED OR
   CUT INTO SLICES

2 TABLESPOONS CHOPPED FRESH CHIVES

1. Wash and dry the nettle leaves. Place them in a large soup pot. Drizzle with the oil. Add the green onions and water and place over medium heat. Cook until tender, 10 to 15 minutes. The nettles are safe to touch at this point. Reserving the cooking liquid, drain the nettles and transfer to a food processor or blender.

2. Add about 1 cup of the reserved cooking liquid to the processor or blender and chop the greens finely. Gradually add the flour as you process. Add some more of the cooking liquid to the processor as needed to keep the mixture workable.

3. Return the mixture to the pot along with the remaining cooking liquid and add the chicken stock. Bring to a boil and whisk in the salt, ginger, and white pepper. Stir in the cream.

4. Ladle into soup bowls, garnish with the hard-cooked eggs and chives, and serve hot.

THREE-GRAIN ALMOND HARDTACK

A thin slice of Jarlsberg cheese on a piece of this hardtack is the perfect accompaniment to fresh nettle soup. Traditional hardtack is a cracker-type bread made of just flour, water, and salt. This hardtack is embellished with almonds, sugar, and a variety of grains. It is a tender, rich cracker that keeps up to three months in an airtight container stored in a cool place. A hardtack rolling pin—one with hobnails carved into the roller—is ideal for rolling out the dough. **MAKES ABOUT TWENTY 2 × 4-INCH RECTANGLES**

1½ STICKS (6 OUNCES) BUTTER,
    AT ROOM TEMPERATURE
½ CUP SUGAR
3 CUPS ALL-PURPOSE FLOUR
1 CUP DARK RYE FLOUR
1 CUP ROLLED OATS

1 CUP ALMONDS
1½ TEASPOONS SALT
1 TEASPOON BAKING SODA
1½ CUPS MILK
1 TABLESPOON LEMON JUICE OR
    DISTILLED WHITE VINEGAR

1. Preheat the oven to 350°F. Lightly grease two 17 × 11-inch baking sheets.

2. In a large bowl, cream the butter and sugar with a fork until smooth. Add the all-purpose and rye flours. In a blender, grind the rolled oats until fine and add to the flour mixture. Add the almonds to the blender and grind them until fine but not a paste; add to the flour mixture. Add the salt and baking soda. Mix with a fork until crumbly.

3. Combine the milk and the lemon juice; then add it to the flour mixture and stir until a stiff dough forms.

4. Divide the dough into two equal parts. Working with one part at a time and using a hardtack or standard rolling pin, roll the dough to the edges of a prepared baking sheet. Repeat with the remaining piece of dough and baking sheet. Pierce all over with a fork.

5. Using a serrated knife, score the dough into 2 × 4-inch rectangles. Bake until lightly browned and crisp, about 25 minutes. Let cool completely; then remove and store in an airtight container. The hardtack will keep up to three weeks in a cool place or in the freezer for several months.

Asparagus Sipping Soup
with Sesame Sunflower Breadsticks

ASPARAGUS SIPPING SOUP

Most abundant from April to June, asparagus is one of spring's most flavorful and nutritious vegetables. Not only is it low in calories, but it is a good source of folate and potassium. This soup is a thin one, ideal served in shot glasses or small punch cups and offered as guests walk in the door. Arrange the breadsticks in a basket to go along with it. **MAKES 8 SERVINGS**

4 TABLESPOONS (½ STICK) BUTTER

1 YELLOW ONION, DICED

3 CLOVES GARLIC, MINCED

¼ CUP DRY VERMOUTH OR DRY
  WHITE WINE

1½ POUNDS ASPARAGUS, CUT INTO
  1-INCH PIECES

3 CUPS BASIC CHICKEN STOCK (PAGE 6)
  OR LOW-SODIUM STORE-BOUGHT,
  PLUS ADDITIONAL AS NEEDED

¾ CUP HEAVY (WHIPPING) CREAM

SALT AND GROUND BLACK PEPPER

1. Melt the butter in a heavy soup pot over medium heat. Add the onion and garlic and cook, stirring occasionally, until tender and translucent, 3 to 4 minutes.

2. Add the vermouth or wine and cook until most of the liquid has evaporated. Add the asparagus and stock. Bring the soup to a simmer. Reduce the heat to medium-low, cover, and cook until the asparagus is tender, about 20 minutes.

3. Transfer the soup to a blender and process until smooth. Stir in the cream and additional stock, if needed. Season to taste with salt and pepper.

4. Return the soup to the pot and heat through. Spoon into heatproof punch cups or small glasses.

SESAME SUNFLOWER BREADSTICKS

Sesame and sunflower seeds add an extra bit of crunch to these always popular sticks. To make them extra thin and crunchy, run the dough through a pasta machine fitted with the fettuccine blades. **MAKES 24 THICK BREADSTICKS, OR ABOUT 7 DOZEN VERY THIN BREADSTICKS**

1 PACKAGE (¼ OUNCE) OR 1 SCANT TABLESPOON ACTIVE DRY YEAST

1½ CUPS WARM WATER (105°F TO 115°F)

1 TABLESPOON HONEY

¼ CUP CANOLA OR OLIVE OIL

2 CUPS WHOLE WHEAT FLOUR

1 TO 1½ CUPS UNBLEACHED ALL-PURPOSE FLOUR

1½ TEASPOONS SALT

1 EGG WHITE, BEATEN WITH 1 TABLESPOON WATER

¼ CUP SESAME SEEDS

¼ CUP ROASTED UNSALTED SUNFLOWER SEEDS

1. In a large bowl or in the bowl of a stand mixer, sprinkle the yeast over the warm water. Stir in the honey and oil. Let stand until the yeast foams, about 5 minutes.

2. In a medium bowl, combine the whole wheat flour and 1 cup of the all-purpose flour. Stir in the salt.

3. Add the flour mixture to the yeast mixture. Using the paddle attachment, stir until the dough is stiff enough to turn out onto a lightly floured surface. Dust the dough with additional all-purpose flour and knead for 10 minutes, adding flour as necessary to keep it from sticking to your hands and until the dough is no longer sticky.

4. Preheat the oven to 300°F. Lightly grease two baking sheets.

5. On a lightly floured surface, press or roll out the dough to a 14 × 4-inch rectangle. Brush the egg white mixture evenly all over the dough. Sprinkle with the sesame and sunflower seeds. Cut the dough lengthwise into twenty-four ½-inch strips. Twist the strands from one end to the other and place 1 inch apart on the baking sheets. Alternatively, cut the dough into quarters, flatten, and run each through the thickest setting on a pasta machine to make the piece flat. Run the dough through the fettuccine cutter to make thin sticks. Separate the strands and brush with the egg wash. Sprinkle with the sesame and sunflower seeds and arrange on the greased baking sheets.

6. Bake until the breadsticks are crisp, about 30 minutes for thick breadsticks and 15 minutes for thinner ones.

Asian Lemon-Ginger Soup
WITH **Rice Buns**

ASIAN LEMON-GINGER SOUP

The punch of fresh ginger and the spark of lemon make this soup light and refreshing—just like spring is supposed to be. It's a great way to use leftover cooked chicken. **MAKES 4 SERVINGS**

6 CUPS BASIC CHICKEN STOCK (PAGE 6) OR LOW-SODIUM STORE-BOUGHT

3 STALKS LEMONGRASS OR 3 STRIPS LEMON ZEST (ABOUT 4 INCHES LONG AND ½ INCH WIDE)

4 SLICES (¼-INCH-THICK) FRESH GINGER, ABOUT 1 INCH ACROSS

3 OR 4 SMALL CHILE PEPPERS, MINCED (**CAUTION** *USE PLASTIC GLOVES WHEN HANDLING THE CHILE PEPPERS.*)

2 TABLESPOONS SOY SAUCE

8 OUNCES COARSELY CHOPPED MUSHROOMS, SUCH AS SHIITAKE, CREMINI, OR OYSTER

2 CUPS SHREDDED COOKED CHICKEN

2 TEASPOONS MINCED KAFFIR LIME LEAVES OR GRATED LIME ZEST

JUICE OF 1 LIME

¼ CUP FINELY CHOPPED CILANTRO

1. Heat the chicken stock in a 3-quart soup pot over medium heat.

2. Meanwhile, trim away the tough outer layers of the lemongrass stalks. Using the side of a knife, smash them, and then cut two stalks into 2-inch sections. Add to the stock, mince the remaining stalk, and set aside. Alternatively, add the lemon strips to the stock. Add the ginger and 1 tablespoon of the minced chile peppers. Simmer for 15 minutes.

3. Remove the lemongrass and ginger, and add 1 tablespoon of the soy sauce, the mushrooms, chicken, lime leaves or zest, lime juice, and minced lemongrass (if using). Taste and adjust the seasonings. Garnish with the chopped cilantro. Serve piping hot.

RICE BUNS

These are so simple to stir up and result in well-flavored, gluten-free white buns. You can shape the dough into a loaf, if you wish. **MAKES 16**

1½ CUPS WARM WATER (105°F TO 115°F)

1 PACKAGE (¼ OUNCE) OR 1 SCANT TABLESPOON ACTIVE DRY YEAST

2 TABLESPOONS SUGAR

2 LARGE EGGS

1 TEASPOON APPLE CIDER VINEGAR

¼ CUP CANOLA OIL

1½ CUPS WHITE RICE FLOUR

⅔ CUP BROWN RICE FLOUR

1 TABLESPOON XANTHAN GUM

1 TEASPOON SALT

1. Grease a baking sheet and set aside.

2. In a medium bowl, whisk together the warm water, yeast, sugar, eggs, vinegar, and oil. In a large bowl, thoroughly stir together the white and brown rice flours, xanthan gum, and salt.

3. Add the yeast mixture to the flour mixture and, using a hand mixer, beat until the dough thickens and begins to crawl up the beaters, about 3 minutes.

4. Divide the dough into 16 pieces and shape into smooth, round balls using water-moistened hands. Place on the prepared baking sheet.

5. Cover and let rise in a warm place until the buns look puffy, about 1 hour.

6. Preheat the oven to 350°F. Bake the buns until a wooden skewer inserted into the center of a bun comes out clean, 15 to 20 minutes. Remove from the oven and cool on a rack. Store any buns you are not using immediately in an airtight container or in the freezer in resealable plastic bags. They will keep frozen for several months.

VARIATION

Rice Bread

To bake into a loaf, make the dough and turn into a greased 9 × 5-inch loaf pan. Smooth the top of the loaf with water-moistened hands. (It may still bake up bumpy on top!) Cover and let rise in a warm place until the loaf has risen to the rim of the pan, about 1 hour. Bake in a preheated 350°F oven until a wooden skewer inserted into the center of the loaf comes out clean, 40 to 45 minutes. Makes one 9 × 5-inch loaf.

Italian Turkey Meatball Soup
(WITH) Monkey Bread

ITALIAN TURKEY MEATBALL SOUP

This hearty soup is an adaptation of an Italian classic but uses ground turkey instead of ground beef. I prefer to use ground turkey breast because it is leaner than plain "ground turkey," which has the skin in the mix. Ditalini, which translated means "small thimbles," is a pasta shaped like tiny elbow macaroni without the arc.

MAKES 6 TO 8 SERVINGS

2 TABLESPOONS OLIVE OIL

1 SMALL ONION, CHOPPED

2 MEDIUM BOILING POTATOES, PEELED AND DICED

2 MEDIUM CARROTS, DICED

1 RIB CELERY, FINELY CHOPPED

2 CLOVES GARLIC, MINCED

2 CANS (14.5 OUNCES EACH) DICED TOMATOES WITH ITALIAN HERBS

4 CUPS TWO-FOR-ONE BEEF STOCK (PAGE 9) OR LOW-SODIUM STORE-BOUGHT

1 TEASPOON SALT

1 POUND GROUND TURKEY BREAST

2 LARGE EGGS, LIGHTLY BEATEN

½ CUP SOFT BREAD CRUMBS

⅓ CUP PLUS ¼ CUP FINELY GRATED PARMESAN CHEESE, PLUS ADDITIONAL FOR SERVING

½ CUP DITALINI OR OTHER SMALL PASTA SHAPE

3 CUPS BABY SPINACH

2 TABLESPOONS CHOPPED FRESH BASIL

1. Place a heavy 5-quart soup pot over medium heat. After 1 minute, pour in the oil and swirl to cover the bottom of the pot. Add the onion, potatoes, carrots, celery, and garlic and cook, stirring, until the vegetables are soft and fragrant, about 10 minutes.

2. Add the tomatoes (with juice), stock, and ½ teaspoon of the salt and stir to combine. Heat to simmering and cook for 15 minutes.

3. In a medium bowl, combine the turkey, eggs, bread crumbs, ⅓ cup of the Parmesan, and the remaining ½ teaspoon salt and mix until thoroughly combined.

4. Using an ice-cream scoop, shape the mixture into smooth meatballs.

5. Carefully add the meatballs to the simmering soup. Add the remaining ¼ cup Parmesan cheese and simmer until the meatballs are cooked through, about 20 minutes.

6. Add the ditalini and spinach to the hot soup, stir well, and cook for 15 minutes, or until the pasta is cooked through. Stir in the basil and serve the soup in wide bowls, garnished with additional grated Parmesan, if desired.

MONKEY BREAD

There are dozens of variations on this bread, but the basic elements are the same: a yeast bread baked in a tube pan. The dough is rolled into small balls, dipped in butter and herbs, and tucked into the pan. The balls connect as they bake, yet remain distinct enough to tear apart from one another. Pass the loaf whole at the table and let guests pull off a piece of warm, tender bread. **MAKES 12 SERVINGS**

1 PACKAGE (¼ OUNCE) OR 1 SCANT TABLESPOON ACTIVE DRY YEAST

¼ CUP WARM WATER (105°F TO 115°F)

1 CUP MILK, SCALDED AND COOLED TO LUKEWARM

¼ CUP SUGAR

1 TEASPOON SALT

8 TABLESPOONS (1 STICK) BUTTER, MELTED, PLUS ADDITIONAL FOR THE PAN

3 TO 3½ CUPS UNBLEACHED ALL-PURPOSE FLOUR

¼ CUP ITALIAN HERB SEASONING

1. In a large bowl, sprinkle the yeast over the warm water. Stir and set aside until the yeast looks foamy, about 5 minutes.

2. Stir in the milk, sugar, salt, and ¼ cup of the melted butter. Add the flour, ½ cup at a time, beating well after each addition until the dough is stiff, but still a little sticky, and smooth (you may not need all of the flour).

3. Cover and let rise in the bowl until doubled in bulk, about 1 hour.

4. Butter a 9-inch tube pan. Place the herbs on a dinner plate. Pour the remaining ¼ cup melted butter into a shallow bowl. Turn the dough out onto a floured surface and pinch off 2-inch pieces of dough. Shape each piece into a ball. Dip in the melted butter, then in the herbs. Place them in the pan. The pan should be about half full. Cover and let rise until almost doubled in bulk, about 45 minutes.

5. Preheat the oven to 400°F. Bake until golden brown, 25 to 30 minutes. Invert the bread onto a cutting board or serving dish, and serve warm.

Spring Greens Soup and Dill
(WITH) Cracker Bread

SPRING GREENS SOUP AND DILL

Spring greens, sometimes called wild cabbage, are similar to kale in that the central leaves form a very loose head or no head at all. Because it can tolerate cold winters, wild cabbage grows primarily in northern Europe. It's easy to find if you are a forager, or you might find it in farmers' markets in the early spring. It resembles a small head of cabbage yet is more delicate. If you can't find it, substitute young kale or spinach. **MAKES 6 SERVINGS**

¾ CUP CHOPPED GREEN ONIONS (SCALLIONS)

2 TABLESPOONS EXTRA-VIRGIN OLIVE OIL

1 POUND WILD CABBAGE, YOUNG KALE, OR BABY SPINACH

1½ RIBS CELERY, CHOPPED

1 BAKING POTATO, PEELED AND CHOPPED

4 CUPS BASIC CHICKEN STOCK, TWO-FOR-ONE BEEF STOCK, OR BASIC VEGETABLE BROTH (PAGES 6 TO 12) OR LOW-SODIUM STORE-BOUGHT, OR WATER

1 CUP DRY WHITE WINE

¼ CUP CHOPPED FRESH DILL, PLUS ADDITIONAL SPRIGS FOR GARNISH

SALT AND GROUND BLACK PEPPER

1. In a heavy 3-quart saucepan, combine the green onions and oil, stir, cover tightly, and cook over low heat until the onions have softened but not browned, about 10 minutes.

2. Stir in the cabbage, kale, or spinach, the celery, and potato and cook for about a minute. Add the stock or broth, wine, and dill. Simmer, partly covered, until the vegetables are very tender, about 30 minutes.

3. Let the mixture cool briefly; then puree in a blender or a food processor. You may have to do this in two batches. Strain the soup through a sieve into a clean saucepan.

4. To serve, reheat the soup and season to taste with salt and pepper. Ladle into 6 warm soup plates and float a few sprigs of dill into each.

CRACKER BREAD

Cracker bread goes by various names, depending on where it hails from. In the Middle East, it is called lavash, a version that happens to be very expensive to buy here yet costs very little to make. It *is* labor intensive, but the results are so delicious it's worth making at home. **MAKES 32 ROUNDS**

1¼ CUPS WARM WATER (105°F TO 115°F)

¼ CUP WHOLE WHEAT FLOUR

1 PACKAGE (¼ OUNCE) OR 1 SCANT
    TABLESPOON ACTIVE DRY YEAST

1 TEASPOON SALT

2¼ TO 2½ CUPS ALL-PURPOSE FLOUR

1. In the large bowl of a stand mixer fitted with a dough hook, combine the warm water, whole wheat flour, and yeast until moistened. Add the salt and 1 cup of the all-purpose flour. Gradually add enough of the remaining flour to make a soft dough.

2. Knead at medium speed until the dough comes away cleanly from the sides of the bowl, about 10 minutes. Add more flour, if needed, to keep the dough from getting sticky or add more water if the dough is too stiff. Turn the dough out into a lightly greased bowl and turn to coat. Cover and let rise in a warm place until doubled in bulk, about 1 hour.

3. Punch down the dough and divide into quarters, divide each quarter into quarters; then divide each piece in half to make 32 balls about the size of small walnuts. Roll each piece into a ball, and cover with a damp kitchen towel for 30 minutes to rest.

4. Position an oven rack in the middle of the oven and place an ungreased baking sheet on it. Preheat the oven to 450°F.

5. Roll out each ball into a round 6 inches across. The dough should be paper thin, almost translucent. If it is too thick, the breads will bubble up like pita breads and not be crisp and crackerlike. Place as many crackers on the heated baking sheet as you can fit, probably 2 or 3. Bake until lightly browned on the top with small bubbles, about 3 minutes. Adjust the thickness for the remaining batches if the first batch is not crackerlike. Cool the crackers on a rack. Store in an airtight container or in resealable plastic bags. They will keep at room temperature for 1 to 2 weeks, or in the freezer for up to 2 months.

Cold Minted Pea Soup
WITH Quick-and-Easy Breadsticks

COLD MINTED PEA SOUP

When we first moved into our house, I planted some mint. Over the years, it has spread along the walkways, beneath the front steps, and along the foundation of the house. I use sprigs of it to garnish fruit salads and sometimes chilled punches. But it is perhaps best when combined with fresh peas, a wonderful enhancer in this delicious, light main-dish soup, which is perfect for the kind of spring days that feel more like summer. **MAKES 4 SERVINGS**

1½ CUPS FRESH OR THAWED FROZEN
    BABY PEAS

1½ CUPS BASIC CHICKEN STOCK
    (PAGE 6) OR LOW-SODIUM
    STORE-BOUGHT

1 CUP HALF-AND-HALF

1 HEAD ICEBERG LETTUCE, TORN
    INTO PIECES

1 RIB CELERY, CHOPPED

2 TO 3 TABLESPOONS CHOPPED
    FRESH MINT, PLUS ADDITIONAL
    FOR GARNISH

SALT AND GROUND BLACK PEPPER

1. In a food processor or blender, combine the peas, stock, half-and-half, lettuce, celery, and chopped mint. Process until smooth. Season to taste with salt and pepper.

2. Chill thoroughly before serving. Sprinkle a little fresh mint on each bowl.

QUICK-AND-EASY BREADSTICKS

Breadsticks are such fun to make when there are kids involved. Not only do they love rolling the dough out, but they love eating the elongated crackers too.

MAKES ABOUT 5 DOZEN

3 TABLESPOONS CANOLA OIL

2 CUPS UNBLEACHED ALL-
  PURPOSE FLOUR

1 CUP WHOLE WHEAT FLOUR

1 TABLESPOON BAKING POWDER

1 TEASPOON SALT

1 TO 1¼ CUPS MILK

2 TABLESPOONS SESAME SEEDS

1. Preheat the oven to 425°F. Coat a baking sheet with 2 tablespoons of the canola oil.

2. In a large bowl, stir together the all-purpose and whole wheat flours, baking powder, and salt. Add the remaining 1 tablespoon oil and 1 cup of the milk, stirring until a stiff dough forms. Add the remaining ¼ cup milk, if the dough seems too dry to shape.

3. Knead 5 to 6 times in the bowl; then turn it out onto the baking sheet. Pat the dough and roll it out into a 14 × 10-inch rectangle. Sprinkle the sesame seeds all over the dough; then gently pat them into it. Halve the rectangle lengthwise into two 5-inch-wide strips. Cut crosswise into ½-inch-wide strips. Separate the strips slightly.

4. Bake until the breadsticks are crisp, 15 to 20 minutes. Cool the sticks right on the baking sheet; then transfer to an airtight container to store. The breadsticks can be frozen, tightly wrapped or covered, up to 1 month.

French Spring Vegetable Soup
⬤ Garlic Toast Rounds

FRENCH SPRING VEGETABLE SOUP

The vegetables are colorful in this easy and refreshing soup. It keeps well refrigerated and is even better the second day, reheated. If you are lucky enough to have tender, freshly harvested carrots, they only need to be scrubbed, not peeled. **MAKES 6 SERVINGS**

½ CUP DRIED NAVY OR OTHER SMALL
    WHITE BEANS
2 TABLESPOONS OLIVE OIL
1 SMALL YELLOW ONION, CHOPPED
2 SMALL CARROTS, SCRUBBED AND DICED
2 SMALL RIBS CELERY, DICED
2 CUPS PEELED, SEEDED, AND CHOPPED
    TOMATOES
4 CUPS BASIC VEGETABLE BROTH OR
    BASIC CHICKEN STOCK (PAGE 12 OR 6)
    OR LOW-SODIUM STORE-BOUGHT

3 CUPS WATER
1 CUP GREEN BEANS, CUT CROSSWISE
    ON AN ANGLE INTO 1-INCH PIECES
3 CUPS LOOSELY PACKED, COARSELY
    CHOPPED SWISS CHARD LEAVES
SALT AND GROUND BLACK PEPPER
BASIL PESTO (PAGE 121) OR
    STORE-BOUGHT
SHREDDED PARMESAN CHEESE

1. Soak the dried beans in enough water to cover them by 3 inches for at least 3 hours, or overnight. Drain the beans and place them in a medium saucepan with enough water to cover them by 2 inches. Bring to a boil; then reduce the heat and simmer, uncovered, until slightly tender, about 40 minutes. Drain and set aside.

2. Warm the oil in a large soup pot over medium-low heat. Add the onion, carrots, and celery and cook, stirring once in a while, until the vegetables are soft, about 20 minutes. Add the tomatoes, broth or stock, water, and the cooked beans. Continue cooking, uncovered, for 30 minutes. Add the green beans and Swiss chard and cook until the beans are tender, 15 to 20 minutes longer. Season to taste with salt and pepper.

3. Ladle the soup into serving bowls and add pesto, to individual taste, along with a sprinkle of Parmesan cheese.

GARLIC TOAST ROUNDS

Make these toast rounds ahead of time, but be sure to pack them airtight to maintain freshness. Spread with garlic mayonnaise just before serving. The recipe makes one cup of garlic spread. This will be more than is needed for six servings. Store the extra toast rounds for another time, and keep the extra garlic mayonnaise refrigerated. It will keep for up to a week. **MAKES 60 ROUNDS**

1 FRESH BAGUETTE (PAGE 17) OR
   STORE-BOUGHT, THINLY SLICED
1 CUP COARSELY CHOPPED FRESH BASIL
1 CLOVE GARLIC, SMASHED

¼ TEASPOON SALT
⅛ TEASPOON CAYENNE PEPPER
¾ CUP MAYONNAISE

1. Preheat the oven to 350°F. Arrange the bread slices in a single layer on baking sheets. Bake until lightly toasted and crisp on both sides, about 15 minutes.

2. In a food processor, combine the basil, garlic, salt, and cayenne and pulse until finely chopped. Add the mayonnaise and blend until smooth. Chill, covered, for 1 hour to allow flavors to develop.

3. Spread the toast rounds with the garlic mayonnaise before serving.

Chunky Vegetable Soup
with Cheddar Cheese Onion Scones

CHUNKY VEGETABLE SOUP

I like to use chunky vegetables in this soup so that it appears hearty and colorful.

MAKES 8 SERVINGS

1 LARGE SWEET ONION, COARSELY CHOPPED

2 RIBS CELERY, COARSELY CHOPPED

2 MEDIUM CARROTS, COARSELY CHOPPED

¼ CUP OLIVE OIL

1 POUND GREEN CABBAGE, COARSELY CHOPPED

2 TEASPOONS SALT

½ TEASPOON GROUND BLACK PEPPER

2 CUPS COARSELY SHREDDED ROMAINE LETTUCE

3 MEDIUM BOILING POTATOES, SCRUBBED AND CUT INTO ½-INCH DICE

1 CUP GREEN BEANS, CUT INTO 1-INCH PIECES

6 ROMA (PLUM) TOMATOES, COARSELY CHOPPED

4 CUPS BASIC VEGETABLE BROTH OR BASIC CHICKEN STOCK (PAGE 12 OR 6) OR LOW-SODIUM STORE-BOUGHT

1 CUP FRESH OR FROZEN THAWED GREEN PEAS

2 CLOVES GARLIC, MINCED

½ CUP CHOPPED FRESH PARSLEY, PREFERABLY FLAT-LEAF

1. In a large soup pot, cook the onion, celery, and carrots in the oil over medium heat until soft, about 10 minutes.

2. Add the cabbage, salt, and pepper and cook until the cabbage is wilted, stirring occasionally.

3. Add the romaine, potatoes, green beans, tomatoes, and broth or stock and increase the heat to high. Bring to a boil, stirring constantly. Reduce the heat to low, cover, and simmer until the vegetables are tender, 30 minutes to 1 hour. Add the peas and cook 5 minutes longer. Stir in the garlic and parsley. Serve warm.

CHEDDAR CHEESE ONION SCONES

These savory treats are best served the day they are baked. **MAKES 8**

8 TABLESPOONS (1 STICK) COLD BUTTER, SLICED

2 GREEN ONIONS (SCALLIONS), INCLUDING THE GREEN TOPS, THINLY SLICED

2 CUPS ALL-PURPOSE FLOUR

1 TABLESPOON BAKING POWDER

1 TEASPOON SALT

¼ POUND SHARP CHEDDAR CHEESE, FINELY DICED

1 SMALL JALAPEÑO CHILE PEPPER, SEEDED AND DICED (**CAUTION** USE PLASTIC GLOVES WHEN HANDLING THE CHILE PEPPER.)

½ CUP HEAVY (WHIPPING) CREAM

3 LARGE EGGS

1. Preheat the oven to 400°F. Line a baking sheet with parchment paper.

2. Melt ½ tablespoon of the butter in a small skillet over medium heat. Add the green onions and cook, stirring, until soft, about 2 minutes. Set aside to cool.

3. In a large bowl, stir together the flour, baking powder, and salt. Using a pastry blender or fork, cut the remaining butter into the flour mixture until butter bits are the size of peas. Toss in the green onions and cheese and mix until they are coated with flour.

4. Sauté the diced jalapeño in the same skillet until soft, about 2 minutes. Allow to cool; then stir the chile peppers into the flour mixture.

5. In a small bowl, lightly beat together the cream and two of the eggs. Using a wooden spoon, fold this mixture into the flour-butter mixture until it begins to come together to make a stiff dough.

6. Turn the dough out onto a well-floured surface and knead gently just until the dough comes together. On the baking sheet, pat the dough out to a ¾- to 1-inch-thick round and cut into 8 wedges using a straight knife. Leave the wedges in place.

7. Beat the remaining egg and brush the top of the scones with the beaten egg. Bake until golden brown, 20 to 25 minutes. Serve warm.

Spring Chicken Soup
WITH Flowerpot Rolls

SPRING CHICKEN SOUP

This is a combination meant to cure spring fever. Pink lentils are actually salmon colored yet turn golden when cooked. They cook very quickly and tend to lose their shape. Red, yellow, or green lentils can be substituted here; these tend to hold their shape a bit better. **MAKES 4 TO 6 SERVINGS**

1 TABLESPOON BUTTER

1 MEDIUM ONION, CHOPPED

3 MEDIUM CARROTS, FINELY CHOPPED

2 CLOVES GARLIC, MINCED

½ CUP PINK LENTILS, RINSED

4 CUPS BASIC CHICKEN STOCK (PAGE 6) OR LOW-SODIUM STORE-BOUGHT

2 CUPS SHREDDED COOKED CHICKEN

2 TOMATOES, DICED

GRATED ZEST OF 1 LEMON

1 TO 2 TABLESPOONS LEMON JUICE

1. Melt the butter in a 2- to 3-quart soup pot over medium heat. Add the onion, carrots, and garlic. Cook, stirring frequently, until the vegetables just begin to brown, 5 to 8 minutes.

2. Add the lentils and stock. Bring to a boil. Then reduce the heat to low, cover, and simmer until the lentils are tender, about 20 minutes.

3. Add the chicken, tomatoes, lemon zest, and lemon juice and cook until the chicken is heated through. Serve hot.

FLOWERPOT ROLLS

Small clay flowerpots are perfect for baking individual loaves to go with springtime soups. These little rolls are very versatile; choose whatever combination of herbs and seeds suits you. Or, you can choose not to add any extras at all. **MAKES 12**

CANOLA OIL

1 PACKAGE (¼ OUNCE) OR 1 SCANT
    TABLESPOON ACTIVE DRY YEAST

½ TEASPOON SUGAR

1¾ CUPS WARM WATER (105°F TO 115°F)

4 CUPS BREAD FLOUR

1½ TEASPOONS SALT

Optional Additions and Toppings

2 TABLESPOONS MIXED FRESH HERBS

2 TABLESPOONS CHOPPED CHIVES

2 TABLESPOONS SEEDS (CHOOSE 1 OR
    2 TYPES): POPPY SEEDS, SESAME SEEDS,
    PUMPKIN SEEDS, OR SUNFLOWER SEEDS

2 TABLESPOONS CHOPPED WALNUTS

1. First, season twelve 2½-inch flowerpots in the oven. Preheat the oven to 375°F. Wash the pots thoroughly and rub the inside and outside with canola oil. Place right on the oven rack and heat for 25 to 30 minutes. Repeat the oiling and baking three times until the pots appear glazed inside to achieve well-seasoned, nonstick surfaces. Before baking with them, line the bottoms with a round of parchment paper to cover the holes.

2. In a medium bowl, sprinkle the yeast and sugar over the warm water. Let stand until the mixture starts to foam, about 5 minutes.

3. Add 2 cups of the flour to the yeast mixture, stir, and let stand until the mixture begins to rise, about 15 minutes. In a large bowl or food processor, combine the remaining 2 cups of flour and ½ teaspoon of the salt. Add the herbs, chives, seeds, or nuts, if using. Add the yeast mixture to the flour mixture, and process or stir until a soft dough forms. (In dry weather, you may need to add another tablespoon or two of water to create a soft dough; in humid weather, you may need to add flour, a tablespoon at a time, if the dough is too soft.)

CONTINUED ▶

4. Oil the flowerpots (and parchment paper) well, then place on baking sheets for easier handling. Cut the dough into 12 equal pieces and shape into balls. Place one in each flowerpot with the smooth sides up. In a small bowl, stir together ½ cup water and the remaining 1 teaspoon salt and brush over the tops of the rolls. Combine the desired toppings and sprinkle over the buns. Cover the pots with a kitchen towel and let rise until doubled in bulk, about 45 minutes.

5. Preheat the oven to 450°F. Bake until the rolls are browned and sound hollow when tapped, 15 to 20 minutes.

6. Remove the breads from the pots and cool on a rack. Once cooled, return them to the flowerpots for serving.

New Potato and Chive Soup
WITH Onion–Dill Buns

NEW POTATO AND CHIVE SOUP
....

Though they are not really perennials, chives sprout up all over the place in my garden in the spring since they tend to seed themselves. They give a wonderful mild onion flavor to scrambled eggs, creamy soups, and steamed vegetables. Paired with thin-skinned new potatoes, they give this part-creamy, part-chunky soup a gentle bite. **MAKES 4 TO 6 SERVINGS**

3 TABLESPOONS BUTTER

¾ CUP DICED GREEN ONIONS (SCALLIONS)

¾ CUP CHOPPED CELERY

¾ CUP CHOPPED CARROTS

1½ POUNDS NEW POTATOES, RED OR WHITE, DICED

3½ CUPS BASIC CHICKEN STOCK (PAGE 6) OR LOW-SODIUM STORE-BOUGHT

1 TEASPOON FRESH THYME LEAVES, CHOPPED

¼ CUP GRATED PARMESAN CHEESE

¼ CUP CHOPPED FRESH CHIVES

1. Melt the butter in a large saucepan over medium-low heat. Add the green onions, celery, and carrots. Cook over low heat until the vegetables are softened, 7 to 8 minutes. Add the potatoes, stock, and thyme and bring to a boil. Reduce the heat, cover, and simmer until the potatoes are fork-tender, about 30 minutes.

2. Spoon 1 to 2 cups of the soup into a blender and puree. Return to the pot and add the Parmesan. Stir in the chives and serve hot.

CONTINUED ▶

ONION-DILL BUNS
....

This batter bread is easier to stir up than a batch of muffins—there is no kneading and hardly any waiting. All in all, the buns take about 1 hour and 40 minutes from start to serving. **MAKES 12**

1 PACKAGE (¼ OUNCE) OR 1 SCANT
    TABLESPOON ACTIVE DRY YEAST
¼ CUP WARM WATER (105°F TO 115°F)
2 TABLESPOONS SUGAR
1 TEASPOON SALT, PLUS ADDITIONAL
    FOR SPRINKLING
¼ CUP CHOPPED FRESH DILL OR
    2 TABLESPOONS DRIED DILLWEED

2 TABLESPOONS CHOPPED GREEN
    ONIONS (SCALLIONS)
3 TABLESPOONS BUTTER, MELTED
1 CUP COTTAGE CHEESE
1 EGG, LIGHTLY BEATEN
2 CUPS ALL-PURPOSE FLOUR

1. In a large bowl, sprinkle the yeast over the warm water. Add the sugar, salt, dill, green onions, and 2 tablespoons of the butter. Let stand until the mixture starts to foam, about 5 minutes.

2. Stir in the cottage cheese, egg, and ½ cup of the flour. Using an electric mixer, beat on high speed for 2 minutes. Add the remaining 1½ cups flour and beat to make a stiff batter. Cover and let stand for 10 minutes.

3. Grease 12 cups of a muffin tin and spoon the dough into the cups, dividing equally. Cover and let rise in a warm place until doubled in bulk, about 45 minutes.

4. Preheat the oven to 350°F. Bake the buns until golden, 35 to 40 minutes.

5. Remove the warm buns from the muffin cups. Brush the buns with the remaining melted butter and sprinkle with salt. Serve warm or place on a rack to cool.

Ham and Green Bean Soup
(WITH) Southern Biscuits

HAM AND GREEN BEAN SOUP

This is the perfect soup for the day after Easter, when there's lots of ham left over. It couldn't be easier to make—place everything in a pot and add the cream just before serving. **MAKES 6 TO 8 SERVINGS**

8 CUPS WATER

2 POUNDS FULLY COOKED HAM, CHOPPED

4 CUPS GREEN BEANS, CUT INTO ¾-INCH PIECES

3 CUPS CUBED (½-INCH) BOILING POTATOES

2 ONIONS, SLICED

1 CUP LIGHT CREAM OR EVAPORATED MILK

1 TEASPOON SALT

¼ TEASPOON GROUND BLACK PEPPER

1. In a large saucepan or soup pot, combine the water, ham, green beans, potatoes, and onions. Bring to a boil; then reduce the heat to medium-low and simmer until the vegetables are tender, about 45 minutes.

2. Skim off any excess fat. Stir in the cream or evaporated milk, season with the salt and pepper to taste, and serve.

CONTINUED ▶

SOUTHERN BISCUITS

These are wonderful on their own with a bowl of soup, but are also perfect for sandwiching slices of ham. Make a double batch and freeze them (unbaked) in resealable plastic bags. To bake the frozen biscuits, remove them from the bag, place on a baking sheet, and allow an extra ten minutes for baking. **MAKES 12**

2 CUPS ALL-PURPOSE FLOUR

1 TABLESPOON BAKING POWDER

1 TEASPOON SALT

¼ TEASPOON BAKING SODA

8 TABLESPOONS (1 STICK) COLD UNSALTED BUTTER, CUT UP

1 CUP BUTTERMILK

1. Preheat the oven to 400°F. In a large bowl or in a food processor, combine the flour, baking powder, salt, and baking soda.

2. Using a pastry blender or two knives (or the food processor blade), cut the butter into the flour mixture until the mixture resembles feta cheese. Add the buttermilk and mix just until the dry ingredients are moistened. Turn the dough onto a floured surface.

3. Roll or pat the dough to a ¾-inch thickness. Using a 2½-inch round biscuit cutter, cut out the biscuits. Reroll the scraps to get a total of 12 biscuits. Place on an ungreased baking sheet. Bake until golden, about 15 minutes. Serve warm.

Fresh Pea Soup
⬤ with Egg Salad Sandwiches

FRESH PEA SOUP
....

This beautiful pale-green soup is irresistible either hot or chilled. Use fresh peas when they're in season; otherwise, substitute frozen peas. **MAKES 4 SERVINGS**

2 TABLESPOONS BUTTER

2 MEDIUM SHALLOTS, FINELY CHOPPED

2 CUPS BASIC CHICKEN STOCK (PAGE 6) OR LOW-SODIUM STORE-BOUGHT, OR WATER

2 CUPS FRESH GREEN PEAS OR THAWED FROZEN PETITE GREEN PEAS

SALT AND GROUND BLACK PEPPER

1 CUP REDUCED-FAT SOUR CREAM

1. Melt the butter in a small saucepan over medium heat. Add the shallots and cook until soft and translucent, about 3 minutes.

2. Add the stock or water and peas. Increase the heat to medium-high, bring to a boil; then reduce the heat to low, cover, and simmer until the peas are tender, 12 to 18 minutes.

3. Puree in a blender or food processor in batches until the soup is smooth. Whisk in the sour cream and season to taste with salt and pepper before serving.

CONTINUED ▶

EGG SALAD SANDWICHES

These recall my first 4-H demonstration when I was twelve years old. I prepared egg salad sandwiches and eggnog, not a combination I suggest enjoying together! But paired with pea soup, this classic hits all the right notes. **MAKES 4 SERVINGS**

8 SLICES WHOLE WHEAT OR RYE BASIC
    HOME-BAKED BREAD (PAGE 20)
    OR STORE-BOUGHT
2 TO 3 TABLESPOONS BUTTER,
    AT ROOM TEMPERATURE
8 HARD-COOKED EGGS, PEELED
    AND CHOPPED

½ CUP MAYONNAISE
1 TEASPOON DIJON MUSTARD
¼ CUP CHOPPED GREEN ONIONS
    (SCALLIONS)
¼ TEASPOON PAPRIKA
SALT AND GROUND BLACK PEPPER
8 CRISP LETTUCE LEAVES

1. Lay the slices of bread out on a cutting board. Spread with the butter.

2. In a small bowl, combine the eggs, mayonnaise, mustard, and green onions and mix until evenly incorporated. Season with the paprika and salt and pepper to taste.

3. Divide the egg mixture among four slices of bread. Top each with the lettuce leaves. Top with the remaining four slices of bread and press together gently. Cut the sandwiches into quarters on the diagonal to make triangles.

Polish Easter Soup
with Polish Sourdough Rye Bread

POLISH EASTER SOUP

In Polish families, this combination is often served on Easter morning, the bread having been blessed in a religious service the day before. I like to let guests assemble their soup ingredients in individual bowls to keep things casual. Kielbasa sausage is available both cooked (smoked) and fresh. Either type is fine to use.

MAKES 4 TO 6 SERVINGS

6 CUPS WATER

1 POUND POLISH KIELBASA SAUSAGE

1 CUP SLICED MUSHROOMS

1 TABLESPOON PREPARED HORSERADISH, PLAIN OR BEET

SALT AND GROUND BLACK PEPPER

2 CUPS SOUR CREAM

2 TABLESPOONS LEMON JUICE OR VINEGAR

6 HARD-COOKED EGGS, PEELED AND SLICED

1 CUP CUBED COOKED HAM

1 CUP DICED COOKED POTATOES

1 CUP DICED COOKED BEETS (OPTIONAL)

FRESHLY GRATED OR PREPARED HORSERADISH, FOR SERVING

CHOPPED FRESH DILL OR PARSLEY

1. Bring the water to a boil in a large pot. Add the kielbasa and simmer over low heat until the sausage is cooked through, about 1 hour.

2. With tongs, transfer the kielbasa to a cutting board to cool. When cool enough to handle, cut into thin slices, and transfer to a bowl.

3. Meanwhile, add the mushrooms, 1 tablespoon prepared horseradish, and salt and pepper to taste to the broth in the pot. Cover and simmer for about 15 minutes. Let cool.

CONTINUED ▶

4. In a separate bowl, beat the sour cream with about 3 cups of the cooled broth. Return the sour cream mixture to the remaining broth. Add the lemon juice or vinegar. Turn the heat to medium and warm the soup until hot.

5. Arrange the hard-cooked eggs, ham, potatoes, beets, and horseradish in separate bowls. Set out all the bowls, including the bowl with the kielbasa, and have guests fill their serving bowls with their choice of ingredients; then ladle the broth over them. Set out a bowl of fresh dill or parsley for garnishing. If you prepare the ingredients a day ahead, reheat the broth to boiling before serving, and bring the vegetables, ham, and kielbasa to room temperature.

POLISH SOURDOUGH RYE BREAD

Start the sponge two days ahead to give this bread a tangy, sour flavor. The bread can be frozen, tightly wrapped, up to three months. **MAKES THREE 9 × 5-INCH LOAVES**

2 PACKAGES (¼ OUNCE EACH)
  OR 2 SCANT TABLESPOONS
  ACTIVE DRY YEAST
1 TEASPOON SUGAR
3½ CUPS WARM WATER (105°F TO 115°F)
3 CUPS RYE FLOUR

1 CUP WHOLE OR 2% MILK,
  AT ROOM TEMPERATURE
1 TABLESPOON DISTILLED WHITE
  VINEGAR
1 TABLESPOON SALT
5 TO 5½ CUPS BREAD FLOUR
1 TABLESPOON CARAWAY SEEDS

1. In a medium bowl, sprinkle one of the packages of yeast and the sugar over 3 cups of the warm water. Let stand until the yeast begins to foam, about 5 minutes. Stir in the rye flour until smooth, cover, and let stand at room temperature for 48 hours.

2. When the rye mixture bubbles and has a sweet-sour aroma, dissolve the remaining package of yeast in ½ cup warm water. Add the milk and vinegar. Stir in the rye mixture, salt, and 2 cups of the bread flour and beat until the mixture is smooth. Add the remaining flour, ½ cup at a time, stirring well after each addition to make a dough that comes together and holds its shape (you may not need to add all of the flour).

3. Turn the dough out onto a lightly floured surface and knead until smooth and supple, about 8 minutes. Sprinkle the caraway seeds on the dough and knead them in until they are evenly distributed.

4. Place the dough in an oiled bowl and turn to coat. Cover and let rise in a warm place until doubled in bulk, about 1 hour.

5. Punch down the dough and divide into three parts. Lightly grease three 9 × 5-inch loaf pans. Shape each piece of dough into a loaf and place in the pans. Cover and let rise until nearly doubled in bulk, about 1 hour.

6. Preheat the oven to 350°F. Bake until a skewer inserted into the center of a loaf comes out clean and dry, 40 to 45 minutes.

Cream of Spring Mushroom and Asparagus Soup ⬤WITH Wheat Biscuits with Sage Butter

CREAM OF SPRING MUSHROOM AND ASPARAGUS SOUP

Morels, the prized mushrooms that are available fresh for only a few weeks in springtime, are a treat for those lucky enough to live near where they grow wild or where a morel festival happens to take place. For everyone else, there's the internet. Dried morels can be pricey, but their flavor is so intense a little goes a long way.

MAKES 4 SERVINGS

1½ POUNDS ASPARAGUS

2 TABLESPOONS BUTTER OR
    COCONUT OIL

2 TABLESPOONS ALL-PURPOSE FLOUR

3 CUPS BASIC CHICKEN STOCK (PAGE 6)
    OR LOW-SODIUM STORE-BOUGHT

¼ POUND FRESH MORELS, OR 1 OUNCE
    DRIED, RECONSTITUTED (SEE BOX)

¾ CUP HEAVY CREAM

SALT AND GROUND BLACK PEPPER

1. Bring a large pot of water to a boil. Add the asparagus and cook until just tender and bright, about 5 minutes. Drain and rinse under cold water. Cut off the tips and reserve for garnish. Coarsely chop the remaining stalks.

2. Melt the butter or coconut oil in a 3- to 4-quart soup pot over medium heat. Add the flour and cook, stirring, for 1 minute. Whisk in the stock and bring to a boil. Add the chopped asparagus and morels, reduce the heat, cover, and simmer for 30 minutes.

3. Transfer the mixture to a blender and puree until very smooth. Add the cream and blend in. Return the soup to the pot and reheat. Season to taste with salt and pepper. Garnish servings with the reserved asparagus tips. Serve very hot.

Cooking with Dried Morels

To reconstitute dried morels, place in a small bowl and add hot tap water to cover. Let soak for 20 to 30 minutes; then rinse and add directly to the recipe. One ounce dried morels will reconstitute to about 4 ounces (¼ pound) fresh.

WHEAT BISCUITS WITH SAGE BUTTER

Sage is assertive enough to combine with the intense flavor of morels, making these hearty biscuits perfect partners to the soup. **MAKES ABOUT 8**

2 CUPS UNBLEACHED
   ALL-PURPOSE FLOUR
1 CUP WHOLE WHEAT FLOUR
2 TABLESPOONS SUGAR
4 TEASPOONS BAKING POWDER
1 TEASPOON SALT

1½ STICKS (6 OUNCES) COLD BUTTER,
   CUT INTO SMALL PIECES
1 LARGE EGG
¾ TO 1 CUP WATER
SAGE BUTTER (SEE RECIPE)

1. Preheat the oven to 425°F. Line a baking sheet with parchment paper.

2. In a large bowl, stir together the all-purpose flour, whole wheat flour, sugar, baking powder, and salt.

3. Cut in the butter using a pastry blender or two knives until the mixture resembles coarse crumbs. With a fork, mix in the egg and just enough water to make a dough that holds together.

4. Turn the dough out onto a floured surface and knead until smooth, 2 or 3 times. Pat the dough into a 1-inch-thick disc. Using a floured 2½- to 2¾-inch round biscuit cutter, cut out biscuits. Gently pat the scraps together and cut out more biscuits.

5. Arrange the biscuits ½ inch apart on the prepared baking sheet. Bake until lightly browned, 18 to 20 minutes. Transfer to a rack to cool slightly. Serve warm, spread with the butter.

Sage Butter

8 TABLESPOONS (1 STICK) BUTTER
½ CUP CHOPPED FRESH SAGE LEAVES

½ TEASPOON LEMON JUICE
¼ TEASPOON GROUND BLACK PEPPER

In a food processor, combine the butter, sage, lemon juice, and pepper and process until thoroughly blended. **MAKES ABOUT ⅔ CUP**

Springtime Minestrone
⬤ Grilled Turkey Paninis

SPRINGTIME MINESTRONE

Minestrone is Italian vegetable soup, made with whatever vegetables are in season. It typically includes pasta along with beans, onions, celery, carrots, tomatoes, and stock. This version makes use of spring's bounty. **MAKES 4 SERVINGS**

2 TABLESPOONS OLIVE OIL OR
    CANOLA OIL
6 GREEN ONIONS (SCALLIONS),
    THINLY SLICED
2 LARGE CLOVES GARLIC, MINCED
1 POUND FINGERLING POTATOES
    (SEE BOX) OR YUKON GOLD
    POTATOES CUT INTO 1-INCH CHUNKS
8 OUNCES FRESH OR THAWED
    FROZEN ARTICHOKE HEARTS,
    COARSELY CHOPPED
1 CAN (14.5 OUNCES) DICED TOMATOES

4 CUPS BASIC VEGETABLE BROTH OR
    BASIC CHICKEN STOCK (PAGE 12 OR 6)
    OR LOW-SODIUM STORE-BOUGHT
2 CUPS COOKED CHICKPEAS OR
    1 CAN (15 OUNCES) CHICKPEAS,
    RINSED AND DRAINED
1 CUP FRESH OR FROZEN GREEN PEAS
½ POUND ASPARAGUS, CUT INTO
    1-INCH LENGTHS
2 CUPS BABY SPINACH, SLICED INTO
    THIN RIBBONS
BASIL PESTO (PAGE 121)
GRATED PARMESAN OR
    PECORINO CHEESE

1. Heat the oil in a 5-quart soup pot. Add the green onions and garlic. Cook, stirring, until the onions and garlic are fragrant, about 5 minutes. Add the potatoes, artichoke hearts, tomatoes, and broth or stock. Cook over medium heat until the potatoes are fork-tender, 10 to 20 minutes.

2. Add the chickpeas, green peas, asparagus, and spinach. Cook until the vegetables are tender, 2 to 3 minutes. Ladle the soup into bowls. Serve with the pesto and grated cheese for people to add according to personal taste.

Fingerlings

Fingerling potatoes are small, stubby, finger-shaped potatoes usually available in one-pound bags and generally available in three varieties and colors: the Golden Russian Banana, Orange-Hued French, and Purple Peruvian. Any of these add color and variety to this soup.

GRILLED TURKEY PANINIS

If you do not have a panini sandwich press, toast the sandwiches in a skillet over medium heat. **MAKES 4 SERVINGS**

1 AVOCADO

¼ CUP MAYONNAISE (MADE WITH OLIVE OIL)

4 CIABATTA ROLLS, HOMEMADE (SEE VARIATION ON PAGE 18) OR STORE-BOUGHT, SPLIT HORIZONTALLY

1 TABLESPOON OLIVE OIL

4 SLICES PROVOLONE CHEESE

1 CUP WHOLE SPINACH LEAVES

¼ POUND THINLY SLICED ROAST TURKEY BREAST, REGULAR OR SMOKED

2 ROASTED RED PEPPERS, SLICED INTO STRIPS

1. Preheat a panini sandwich press or place a heavy skillet over medium heat.

2. Mash the avocado and mayonnaise together in a bowl until thoroughly combined.

3. Brush the bottom of each roll with oil. Place the bottoms of the rolls on the panini press or skillet.

4. Divide the provolone, spinach, turkey, and red peppers among the sandwich bottoms. Spread the avocado mixture on the cut surface of each top and place the top on the sandwich. Brush the top of the roll with oil.

5. Close the panini press and cook until the rolls are toasted and crisp, with golden brown grill marks, and the cheese has melted, 5 to 8 minutes. If using a skillet, cook over medium heat until browned on the bottom, about 5 minutes; turn over and cook until toasted and browned on the second side, another 5 minutes.

Danish Meatball and Dumpling Soup (WITH) Danish Butter Buns

DANISH MEATBALL AND DUMPLING SOUP

Danes serve this soup on almost every special occasion as part of a traditional menu of sugar-browned potatoes and carrots, roast pork, and sweet and sour red cabbage, with an ice-cream cake for dessert. It is sometimes served as a nightcap signaling the end of a party. Food historian Hugo Jensen said, "Frankly, it's the only way to get rid of people when the party is over." A rich beef broth is the basis of the soup, with tasty little meatballs and little oval-shaped dumplings floating in it. Don't let the long directions intimidate you; the meatballs and dumplings can be made a day ahead, making the day of assembly very quick. **MAKES 8 SERVINGS**

Meatballs

½ POUND GROUND MEAT (PORK, BEEF, OR TURKEY)

½ CUP FINELY CHOPPED ONIONS

1 TEASPOON SALT, PLUS ADDITIONAL FOR THE POACHING LIQUID

¼ TEASPOON GROUND BLACK PEPPER

⅛ TEASPOON GROUND ALLSPICE

3 TABLESPOONS ALL-PURPOSE FLOUR

3 TABLESPOONS MILK

1 EGG WHITE, LIGHTLY BEATEN

Dumplings

8 TABLESPOONS (1 STICK) BUTTER

1 CUP WATER

1 TEASPOON SALT, PLUS ADDITIONAL FOR THE POACHING LIQUID

1 CUP ALL-PURPOSE FLOUR

3 LARGE EGGS

Soup

2 QUARTS TWO-FOR-ONE BEEF STOCK (PAGE 9) OR LOW-SODIUM STORE-BOUGHT

½ CUP COOKED FINELY DICED CARROTS

½ CUP FRESH OR FROZEN BABY PEAS, COOKED

CHOPPED CHERVIL OR PARSLEY

1. **To make the meatballs** In a food processor, combine the meat and onions and process until fine and light. (Danes put the mixture through a food grinder three times until very fine.) Add the salt, pepper, and allspice. In a small bowl, stir together the flour and milk to make a paste; then add it to the meat mixture. Add the egg white and mix well. Let stand for at least 30 minutes before continuing so that the liquids are completely absorbed and the mixture has come together.

2. Bring about 2 inches of water to a boil in a skillet and add 1 teaspoon salt per quart of water. Using a teaspoon, shape the meat mixture into 40 small oval meatballs. Drop 8 to 10 meatballs at a time into the water and boil until cooked through, 4 to 5 minutes. Repeat with the remaining meatball mixture. Using a slotted spoon, transfer the meatballs to a colander and rinse under cold water. Let drip-dry.

3. **To make the dumplings** In a saucepan, combine the butter, water, and salt and bring to a boil. Add the flour all at once, stirring vigorously. When the mixture is smooth, shiny, and thick enough to make a ball that leaves the sides of the pan, remove from the heat and cool for 10 minutes. Beat in the eggs, one at a time until thoroughly mixed.

4. Bring about 2 inches of water to a boil in a skillet and add 1 teaspoon salt per quart of water. Using 2 teaspoons, shape the dough into 40 small, slightly oval-shaped balls. Gently drop half of the balls into the skillet, return the water to a boil, and as soon as it begins to boil, add a small amount of cold water to stop the boiling. Repeat the boiling and cooling three times, at which point, the dumplings will be firm. Repeat with the remaining balls. Using a slotted spoon, transfer the dumplings to a colander to drain.

5. **To assemble the soup** Bring the stock to a boil in a saucepan. Bring the meatballs and dumplings to room temperature. Ladle the broth into 8 heated individual bowls. Add 1 tablespoon each carrots and peas to each bowl. Add 5 meatballs and 5 dumplings to each bowl. Garnish with chervil or parsley and serve immediately.

CONTINUED ▶

DANISH BUTTER BUNS

These buns are as close to a flaky Danish pastry as it gets, with the yeasted rye dough rolled with butter into many thin layers. **MAKES 16**

1 PACKAGE (¼ OUNCE) OR 1 SCANT
    TABLESPOON ACTIVE DRY YEAST
½ CUP WARM WATER (105°F TO 115°F)
½ CUP WARM MILK
1 TABLESPOON SUGAR
½ TEASPOON SALT

2 STICKS (8 OUNCES) COLD BUTTER,
    PLUS 4 TABLESPOONS SOFT BUTTER
2 EGGS
1 CUP LIGHT OR DARK RYE FLOUR
2 CUPS ALL-PURPOSE FLOUR
COARSE SALT
CARAWAY SEEDS

1. In a medium bowl, sprinkle the yeast over the warm water. Stir in the milk, sugar, and salt and let stand until the yeast foams, about 5 minutes. Meanwhile, melt 4 tablespoons (½ stick) of the butter in a small saucepan.

2. Add 1 egg, melted butter, and ½ cup of the rye flour to the yeast mixture and stir.

3. In a large bowl, combine the all-purpose flour and the remaining ½ cup rye flour. Cut 1½ sticks (6 ounces) of cold butter into the flour mixture until the butter is about the size of peas. Pour the yeast mixture over the flour mixture. With a rubber spatula, carefully fold the mixtures together just until the flour is moistened.

4. Cover the bowl and refrigerate for at least 4 hours or up to 2 days. When ready to shape the dough, turn it out onto a lightly floured board and divide the dough into two parts.

5. Shape one part at a time. Cover and refrigerate the remaining dough. Roll the dough out to make a 16-inch square. With a butter knife, spread the surface of the dough with 1 tablespoon of the softened butter. Fold the dough into thirds like a business letter to form a rectangle. Roll the strip to about 24 inches long; then fold the strip in thirds to make an 8-inch square. Roll out to make a 16-inch square again and spread with the remaining 1 tablespoon softened butter. Roll the dough up tightly, jelly roll fashion. With your hands, flatten the roll. Cut it into 8 equal pieces.

6. Place the pieces on a lightly greased baking sheet with the seam side down and the cut edges facing the sides of the baking sheet.

7. Repeat with remaining piece of dough. Let rise, covered, until doubled in bulk, about 2 hours.

8. Preheat the oven to 400°F. In a small cup, beat the remaining egg. Brush the buns with the egg; then sprinkle lightly with coarse salt and caraway seeds. Bake until golden and crispy, 13 to 15 minutes. Transfer the buns to racks to cool.

Walleye Chowder
WITH Parmesan Garlic Bread

WALLEYE CHOWDER

Walleye is the sweetest tasting freshwater fish there is. If you have fishermen or women in the family, and you live in a freshwater lake area, you'll probably have a good supply. Think of this menu if you are going on a fishing trip and staying in a cabin. All of the ingredients are simple to transport, and you can even assemble the garlic bread before leaving home so it is ready to pop into the oven. Use tilapia, a farm-raised fish that has become popular and readily available both fresh and frozen, as an alternative to walleye. This soup has lots of texture from the vegetables. **MAKES 6 TO 8 SERVINGS**

8 SLICES BACON, DICED

1 LARGE SWEET ONION, CHOPPED

1 RIB CELERY, CHOPPED

¼ CUP ALL-PURPOSE FLOUR

8 MEDIUM BOILING POTATOES,
    PEELED AND DICED

4 CUPS BASIC CHICKEN STOCK
    (PAGE 6) OR LOW-SODIUM
    STORE-BOUGHT,OR WATER

½ CUP WHITE WINE

2 CUPS WHOLE OR 2% MILK

1 GREEN BELL PEPPER, CHOPPED

1 RED BELL PEPPER, CHOPPED

2 CUPS FROZEN CORN KERNELS

1 TO 2 TEASPOONS SALT

DASH OF CAYENNE PEPPER

2 POUNDS FRESH OR THAWED FROZEN
    WALLEYE PIKE FILLETS OR TILAPIA,
    CUT INTO 1-INCH CUBES

1. Cook the bacon in a heavy 5-quart soup pot over medium heat until crisp. Drain all but 1 tablespoon of the bacon fat and set the bacon aside on a paper towel–lined plate.

2. Add the onion and celery to the pot and cook, stirring, until the vegetables are softened, 3 to 5 minutes. Sprinkle the flour over the mixture and add the potatoes, stock or water, and wine. Simmer until the potatoes are tender, about 15 minutes.

3. Stir in the milk, bell peppers, and corn. Simmer until the vegetables are crisp-tender, about 3 minutes. Add the salt (to taste), cayenne, and fish. Simmer just until the fish is cooked through, no more than 3 minutes.

4. Ladle the soup into bowls, sprinkle with the bacon, and serve.

PARMESAN GARLIC BREAD

You basically slather slices of baguette (homemade or purchased) with garlic-parmesan butter, wrap the bread in foil, and bake for fifteen minutes or so to assemble this favorite. That's it. **MAKES 6 TO 8 SERVINGS**

2 STICKS (8 OUNCES) BUTTER,
   AT ROOM TEMPERATURE
2 CLOVES GARLIC, MINCED
½ CUP FINELY CHOPPED FRESH PARSLEY
   OR 2 TABLESPOONS DRIED

½ CUP GRATED PARMESAN CHEESE
1 LOAF (ABOUT 1½ POUNDS) FRESH
   BAGUETTE (PAGE 17) OR STORE-
   BOUGHT ITALIAN BREAD, CUT
   INTO 1-INCH-THICK SLICES

1. In a small bowl, mash together the butter, garlic, parsley, and Parmesan until well blended.

2. Preheat the oven to 350°F. Spread both sides of each slice of bread generously with the butter and fit the slices together to reshape the loaf. Wrap in foil and bake for 15 minutes. Serve warm.

Super-Simple Salmon Chowder
WITH Sour Rye Buns

SUPER-SIMPLE SALMON CHOWDER

Fresh salmon is, of course, ideal in this recipe, but often when we've broiled or grilled a salmon fillet, there is some left over, and that's usually when I make this creamy salmon chowder. The important thing here is to not overcook the salmon, so I add it to the pot at the very end. In a pinch you can use canned salmon, which, of course, is already overcooked—but it is handy if you're cooking a last-minute lunch or supper. **MAKES 6 SERVINGS**

2 TABLESPOONS BUTTER

2 MEDIUM YUKON GOLD OR BOILING POTATOES, PEELED AND CUT INTO ½-INCH DICE

1 LARGE SWEET ONION, FINELY CHOPPED

3 GREEN ONIONS (SCALLIONS), INCLUDING THE GREEN TOPS, FINELY SLICED

1 RIB CELERY, FINELY SLICED

2 TABLESPOONS ALL-PURPOSE FLOUR

3 CUPS WATER

1½ TABLESPOONS LEMON JUICE

¾ POUND FRESH SALMON FILLETS, CUT INTO THIN SLICES, OR ABOUT 2 CUPS FLAKED COOKED SALMON

2 CUPS WHOLE MILK OR HALF-AND-HALF

SALT AND WHITE PEPPER

½ CUP CHOPPED FRESH DILL OR 2 TABLESPOONS DRIED DILLWEED

1. Melt the butter in a heavy 4-quart saucepan over medium heat. Add the potatoes, onion, green onions, and celery and cook, stirring often, for 10 to 15 minutes.

2. Stir in the flour. Add the water and lemon juice and simmer, stirring, until lightly thickened.

3. Add the fish and milk or half-and-half to the pot and heat through. Do not boil. Season to taste with salt and white pepper.

4. Ladle into warmed soup plates or bowls, and sprinkle with the fresh dill or dried dillweed.

Rye Sourdough Starter

About two days before you plan to make Sour Rye Buns, mix ½ cup room-temperature milk with ½ cup rye flour. Let stand, uncovered, in a warm place until the mixture begins to bubble and has a pleasantly sour odor, about 48 hours. You may refrigerate the starter at this point or use the entire amount immediately in a bread dough. If you make a bread with it, set aside ½ cup of the bread dough and refrigerate it for subsequent bakings. You can hold the starter for up to a week before using it for another baking. When you plan to start another bread dough, pour about ½ cup warm water over the dough and add ½ cup rye flour. Stir and let stand, covered, for 24 hours before adding to the new bread dough. The starter will become more sour with each baking.

SOUR RYE BUNS

These are serious buns! To achieve the intense sour flavor that makes them so delicious, you need to use rye flour, which imparts a distinctive tang that wheat flour does not. It's vital to begin the starter a couple of days in advance of baking day. And if using a starter seems like too much work, skip it and simply combine the yeast, warm water, and flour in the second paragraph of the directions. The resulting buns will taste more sweet than sour. **MAKES 12**

½ CUP SOURDOUGH STARTER (SEE "RYE SOURDOUGH STARTER")

2½ CUPS WARM WATER (105°F TO 115°F)

1 PACKAGE (¼ OUNCE) OR 1 SCANT TABLESPOON ACTIVE DRY YEAST

3½ CUPS COARSE DARK RYE FLOUR

2 TEASPOONS SALT

2 TO 3 CUPS BREAD FLOUR

1. Prepare the starter, if using, 2 days before you want to bake the bread.

2. Pour the starter and the warm water into a large bowl and add the yeast plus 1 cup of the rye flour. Let stand until the yeast begins to foam, about 5 minutes. Cover and let stand in a warm place until the mixture has a distinct sour aroma, 20 to 40 hours. If you are impatient, let the mixture rise for just 1 to 2 hours.

CONTINUED ▶

3. Stir in the remaining 2½ cups rye flour, the salt, and 1 cup of the bread flour. Beat until the dough is well mixed. Slowly add more bread flour to make a dough that is stiff enough to knead. Let the dough rest for 15 minutes in the bowl.

4. Turn the dough out onto a well-floured surface. Knead (the dough will be sticky!) until well mixed, about 5 minutes. Wash the large bowl, grease it lightly, add the dough, and turn the dough in the bowl—it will be sticky—to coat. Let rise in a warm place until doubled in bulk, 1 to 1½ hours.

5. Lightly grease a baking sheet. Turn the dough out onto a floured board and pat down to about 12 inches in diameter. With a 3-inch cookie cutter, cut out rounds of dough. Place on the baking sheet. Cover and let rise until the buns have puffed up, about 1 hour.

6. Preheat the oven to 375°F.

7. Poke the buns with a fork 4 or 5 times each. Brush with water and bake until the buns are lightly browned, 20 to 25 minutes. Transfer to a rack to cool.

SUMMER

In summertime, "the livin' is easy," as the song goes. With daylight stretching well past dinnertime, cooking is all about putting forth minimal effort for maximum returns. Living is much more pleasant when the "eatin' is good."

We don't often associate homemade soups and breads with summer cooking—maybe because we think it will be just too warm—but that's a pity. In this chapter, I hope to change your mind with these irresistible soups that feature in-season ingredients. One of my favorites, the Spicy Revitalizer (page 90), is an ideal refresher after an afternoon of working or playing in the sun. I like to serve it with crispy homemade breadsticks made with carrots. Chilled fruit soups are perfect for a light lunch or even dessert. Chilled Avocado-Potato Soup (page 104), served with savory crackers, makes a lovely light supper.

We belong to a local farm share that supports local farmers. When our summer farm share yields green beans, young onions, peas, sweet small carrots, and potatoes, I simply cannot resist making my favorite creamy soup with these ingredients. I couple my Summer Vegetable Soup (page 116) with freshly baked rolls made with a simple, stir-together refrigerator yeast dough. It's a perfect meal to enjoy outdoors on a sunny summer evening.

Summer often is filled with the pleasure of out-of-town visitors, usually far-flung friends who find this a perfect time for travel. (Minnesota is an ideal destination, they think, because when we think it's hot outdoors, they feel it is refreshing!) For these occasions, simple soups and breads enjoyed alfresco saves me from fussing with table settings and worrying about fancy decorations. I simply bring the pot of soup out onto the deck with bread or crackers in a basket, stack up bowls and utensils, and let people help themselves and let the conversation flow. Often I add a crisp, refreshing wine, a chunk of favorite cheese, and some fruit to the menu.

Baking bread may seem like another challenge altogether. I like to make my own, of course, but in the summertime, I sometimes break down and buy pita breads and artisan crackers just to have them on hand. Usually I make my own baguettes and slicing breads (see basic recipes on pages 17 and 20), but typically I wait for the season's cooler days when the warmth and aroma of baked bread is welcome. The other way I get around filling the summer kitchen with heat is to have frozen home-baked loaves on hand. I often bake breads and freeze the loaves. Reheating them in a 350°F oven for just 10 minutes won't send the mercury too much higher.

Quick breads are good choices for summertime eating. Blueberry Banana Bread (page 101), which I serve with Chilled Melon Soup (page 100), is a particular favorite, especially for a brunch when guests are likely to sleep in.

Of course, the bread suggestions can be switched around at will. While the pairings here are somewhat arbitrary, I have found they work well together with preparation time and flavor combinations in mind.

Cream of Summer Vegetable Soup **WITH** Whole Wheat Buttermilk Biscuits

CREAM OF SUMMER VEGETABLE SOUP

Fresh garden vegetables are all candidates for inclusion in this smooth soup. If you have herbs like basil, dill, chervil, or even sorrel, by all means include them all! **MAKES 4 SERVINGS**

2 MEDIUM BOILING POTATOES, PEELED AND CHOPPED

1 CUP PEAS, GREEN BEANS, OR BROCCOLI FLORETS

2 GREEN ONIONS (SCALLIONS), CHOPPED

3 CUPS BASIC CHICKEN STOCK (PAGE 6) OR LOW-SODIUM STORE-BOUGHT

1 CUP LIGHT CREAM OR EVAPORATED MILK

⅛ TEASPOON CURRY POWDER

SALT AND GROUND BLACK PEPPER

¼ CUP CHOPPED FRESH HERBS

1. In a medium saucepan, combine the potatoes, peas, green onions, and stock and bring to a boil over high heat. Reduce to a simmer, cover, and cook until the vegetables are tender, 10 to 20 minutes. Let cool.

2. Pour the soup into a blender and puree until smooth. Add the cream and curry powder and blend until thoroughly incorporated. Season to taste with salt and pepper.

3. Return the soup to the saucepan and heat to serving temperature or chill in the refrigerator. Serve sprinkled with the herbs.

WHOLE WHEAT BUTTERMILK BISCUITS

Buttermilk gives these whole grain biscuits a subtle tang. They're just right for serving with a bowl of hot or chilled creamy vegetable soup. **MAKES 12**

1 CUP WHOLE WHEAT FLOUR

¾ CUP ALL-PURPOSE FLOUR

¼ CUP WHEAT GERM

2 TABLESPOONS LIGHT BROWN SUGAR

2 TEASPOONS BAKING POWDER

½ TEASPOON BAKING SODA

¼ TEASPOON SALT

4 TABLESPOONS (½ STICK) COLD
    BUTTER, CUT INTO SMALL PIECES

1 CUP BUTTERMILK

1. Preheat the oven to 400°F. Coat a baking sheet with cooking spray or line with parchment paper.

2. In a large bowl, combine the whole wheat and all-purpose flours, wheat germ, brown sugar, baking powder, baking soda, and salt. With a pastry blender or two knives, cut the butter into the dry ingredients until the mixture resembles coarse crumbs. Add the buttermilk and stir just until a moist dough forms.

3. Turn the dough out onto a generously floured work surface and, with floured hands, knead gently 6 to 8 times just until the dough comes together in a solid mass. Lightly flour the board, and roll out or pat the dough until ½ inch thick. Using a 2½-inch round biscuit cutter dipped in flour, cut out biscuits. Gather the scraps and roll out to make additional biscuits.

4. Place the biscuits about 1 inch apart on the baking sheet. Bake until the biscuits rise to twice their unbaked height and are lightly golden, 8 to 10 minutes. Serve hot.

Fresh Tomato and Cilantro Soup with Toasted Baguette Slices with Tapenade

FRESH TOMATO AND CILANTRO SOUP

When the temperature swirls around 85 or 90 degrees (yes, even in Minnesota), no-cook soups are the order of the day. The herb garden loves the heat, and so do the tomatoes. But me? I sit in a chair with an icy cold rag over my head. Preparing this soup and serving it with a toasted baguette slice spread with tapenade requires little effort. **MAKES 4 SERVINGS**

4 LARGE TOMATOES (ABOUT
    1½ POUNDS), QUARTERED
1 CUP CHILLED TOMATO JUICE
2 TABLESPOONS SHERRY WINE VINEGAR
1½ TEASPOONS SALT
1 TEASPOON CHILI POWDER
    (CHILI SEASONING) OR ANCHO
    CHILE POWDER

8 ICE CUBES
1 LARGE HANDFUL FRESH CILANTRO,
    WASHED AND TOWEL DRIED
    (SAVE A FEW SPRIGS FOR GARNISH)

In a blender, combine the tomatoes, tomato juice, vinegar, salt, chili powder, and ice cubes and process until almost smooth. Add the cilantro and pulse sparingly. If overprocessed, the soup will taste delicious but will have a grayish color. Serve immediately, or cover and refrigerate up to 3 days.

TOASTED BAGUETTE SLICES WITH TAPENADE

Make your own tapenade and store it in the fridge for any time the mood strikes you. It will keep, tightly covered and refrigerated, up to one week. **MAKES 12 SERVINGS**

1 CUP PITTED KALAMATA OLIVES

3 CLOVES GARLIC, PEELED

2 TABLESPOONS CAPERS

3 TABLESPOONS CHOPPED
    FRESH PARSLEY

2 TABLESPOONS LEMON JUICE

2 TABLESPOONS OLIVE OIL

SALT AND GROUND BLACK PEPPER

1 FRESH BAGUETTE (PAGE 17) OR
    GOOD-QUALITY STORE-BOUGHT,
    CUT INTO ½-INCH SLICES
    AND TOASTED

In a blender or food processor, combine the olives, garlic, capers, parsley, lemon juice, and oil and pulse to mince. Season to taste with salt and pepper. Taste and adjust the lemon juice. Spread on baguette slices and serve.

Spicy Revitalizer
WITH Carrot Breadsticks

SPICY REVITALIZER
....

I enjoyed a version of this refreshing soup at a California spa. It was served as a between-meal snack and was especially tasty after workout sessions.

MAKES 4 SERVINGS

4 CUPS TOMATO JUICE

⅛ TO ½ TEASPOON CAYENNE PEPPER

1 CARROT, CUT INTO 4 STICKS

4 RIBS CELERY, 4 INCHES LONG,
   INCLUDING THE LEAVES

Heat the tomato juice in a saucepan over medium heat until steaming. Whisk in the cayenne pepper. Place a carrot stick and a celery stick into each of 4 mugs. Pour the soup into the mugs and serve hot.

CARROT BREADSTICKS

These crunchy sticks disappear as soon as I pull them from the oven! If you are lucky enough to have some left over, store them in an airtight container or resealable plastic bag. They will keep in the freezer up to one month. **MAKES 64**

1 CUP ALL-PURPOSE FLOUR

2 TABLESPOONS GRATED
   PARMESAN CHEESE

2 TABLESPOONS BUTTER OR
   VEGETABLE OIL

½ TEASPOON GROUND CUMIN

½ TEASPOON BAKING POWDER

½ TEASPOON SALT

½ CUP FINELY SHREDDED CARROTS

1 TO 2 TABLESPOONS WATER

1. Preheat the oven to 400°F. Line a baking sheet with parchment paper.

2. In a food processor, combine the flour, Parmesan, butter, cumin, baking powder, and salt. Process just until the dough comes together. Add the carrots and pulse just until the carrots are evenly incorporated into the dough, about 10 on/off pulses. Add the water, 1 tablespoon at a time, and pulse just until the dough comes together in a ball.

3. Roll the dough out on the baking sheet to about an 8-inch square, about ½ inch thick. Using a knife or a pizza cutter, cut the dough into sticks, 2 inches long by ½ inch wide.

4. Bake until crisp, 15 to 17 minutes. Let cool on the pan.

Avgolemono Soup ⬤ Pita Bread

AVGOLEMONO SOUP

The consistency of this traditional Greek soup can vary from near-stew to near-broth, but whatever the texture, it all starts with good-quality chicken stock. It's best made with the homemade version, which yields cooked chicken that can be added to the soup. Rice, orzo, or tapioca are cooked in the stock before the lemon and eggs are added. **MAKES 6 TO 8 SERVINGS**

6 CUPS RICHLY FLAVORED CHICKEN
    STOCK, PREFERABLY TWO-FOR-ONE
    CHICKEN STOCK (PAGE 7)
½ CUP SHORT-GRAIN RICE

2 LARGE EGGS
JUICE OF 2 LEMONS (6 TABLESPOONS)
SALT AND GROUND BLACK PEPPER
2 CUPS SHREDDED COOKED CHICKEN

1. Bring the stock to a boil in a soup pot over high heat. Add the rice, reduce to a simmer, and cook until the rice is tender, about 20 minutes.

2. Beat the eggs in a medium bowl until light yellow. Add the lemon juice and beat until incorporated. Slowly add a ladleful of the hot stock to the eggs. Repeat with 2 more ladlesful of hot stock. Pour the egg-stock mixture back into the soup pot. Season with salt, pepper, and more lemon juice to taste. Add the chicken and cook until heated through. Serve with more pepper.

PITA BREAD

Pita bread is common in Middle Eastern cultures and can be found in the cuisines of several countries, including Greece. These small, round breads puff during baking to form pockets. They can hold a variety of fillings, from traditional falafel or meat fillings and yogurt to tuna, egg salad, or the ingredients in your favorite taco.

MAKES 8

1 PACKAGE (¼ OUNCE) OR 1 SCANT TABLESPOON ACTIVE DRY YEAST
1 CUP WARM WATER (105°F TO 115°F)
1 TEASPOON SUGAR

1 TEASPOON SALT
1 TEASPOON VEGETABLE OR CANOLA OIL
2¾ TO 3 CUPS ALL-PURPOSE FLOUR

1. In a bowl, sprinkle the yeast over the warm water. Stir in the sugar and let stand until the yeast begins to foam, about 5 minutes.

2. Add the salt, oil, and 1 cup of the flour and beat with a wooden spoon until the batter is smooth. Slowly add enough of the remaining flour until the dough is stiff. Let stand 15 minutes. Sprinkle a work surface with flour, turn the dough out onto it, and knead until the dough is smooth and springy, about 10 minutes. Place in a lightly greased bowl and turn over to grease the top.

3. Let the dough rise, covered, until doubled in bulk, about 1 hour. Turn out onto a lightly oiled countertop or board and divide into 8 equal parts. Shape each part into a ball. With a rolling pin, roll each ball into a round 6 inches in diameter and place on an ungreased baking sheet. Cover loosely with plastic wrap and let rise in a warm place until almost doubled in bulk, about 45 minutes.

4. Preheat the oven to 500°F. Bake until lightly browned and puffy, 5 to 7 minutes.

5. Remove from the baking sheet, stack one on top of the other, and cover with waxed paper to cool.

Summer Day Herb-Scented Soup ⬤ Whole Grain Oatmeal Bread

SUMMER DAY HERB-SCENTED SOUP

Spiked with tarragon vinegar and flavored with fresh tarragon and honey, this cooling vegetable soup is an ideal refresher on a hot day. **MAKES 6 SERVINGS**

2 CUPS CHOPPED TOMATOES

1½ CUPS CHOPPED SWEET ONIONS

1½ CUPS PEELED, SEEDED, AND CHOPPED CUCUMBER

1 CUP CHOPPED GREEN OR YELLOW BELL PEPPER

2 CLOVES GARLIC, MINCED

¼ CUP FINELY CHOPPED FRESH PARSLEY

1 TEASPOON CHOPPED FRESH BASIL

1 TEASPOON CHOPPED FRESH OREGANO OR ¼ TEASPOON DRIED

1 TEASPOON CHOPPED FRESH TARRAGON OR ½ TEASPOON DRIED

¼ TEASPOON GROUND CUMIN

4 CUPS REGULAR OR SPICY MIXED-VEGETABLE JUICE, CHILLED

2 TABLESPOONS LEMON JUICE

2 TABLESPOONS LIME JUICE

2 TABLESPOONS TARRAGON VINEGAR

1 TABLESPOON OLIVE OIL

1 TEASPOON HONEY

1. In a large bowl, combine the tomatoes, onions, cucumber, bell pepper, garlic, parsley, basil, oregano, tarragon, cumin, vegetable juice, lemon juice, lime juice, vinegar, oil, and honey. Transfer 4 cups of the vegetable mixture to a blender or food processor and process until smooth. Return the pureed vegetable mixture to the bowl, stirring to combine.

2. Cover and refrigerate. Ladle into chilled mugs or soup cups to serve.

WHOLE GRAIN OATMEAL BREAD

A thick wedge of this homespun oatmeal bread is the perfect accompaniment to any chilled soup. **MAKES 6 SERVINGS**

1 PACKAGE (¼ OUNCE) OR 1 SCANT
    TABLESPOON ACTIVE DRY YEAST
1 CUP WARM WATER (105°F TO 115°F)
1 TABLESPOON BUTTER,
    AT ROOM TEMPERATURE
1 TEASPOON SUGAR

1 TEASPOON SALT
½ CUP WHOLE WHEAT FLOUR
1 CUP UNBLEACHED BREAD FLOUR
¾ CUP ROLLED OATS
1 LARGE EGG WHITE BEATEN WITH
    2 TABLESPOONS WATER

1. In a large bowl, sprinkle the yeast over the warm water. Stir in the butter, sugar, and salt. Stir in the whole wheat flour, bread flour, and ½ cup of the oats. Beat 50 strokes.

2. Line a baking sheet with parchment paper or generously grease it. On the baking sheet, sprinkle 2 tablespoons of the remaining oats in a 9-inch circle. Turn the dough out onto the oats and spread the dough to cover the circle. Cover and let rise for 30 minutes.

3. Preheat the oven to 400°F. Brush the loaf with the egg white mixture and sprinkle with the remaining 2 tablespoons oats. Bake until golden, 20 to 25 minutes. Slide the bread onto a board. Cut into 6 wedges to serve while still warm.

Lemon, Corn, and Shrimp Soup
⬤ Asian-Style Flatbread

LEMON, CORN, AND SHRIMP SOUP

This delicious soup and flatbread combination makes a quick and light summer meal. Both the broth and flatbread take only about twenty minutes to prepare. Make this soup when corn on the cob shows up at the farm stand or in the farmers' market. **MAKES 8 SERVINGS**

2 QUARTS BASIC CHICKEN STOCK (PAGE 6) OR LOW-SODIUM STORE-BOUGHT

½ CUP SAKE

3 TABLESPOONS JAPANESE-STYLE SOY SAUCE OR TAMARI

1 TABLESPOON SUGAR

1 INCH PEELED FRESH GINGER, CUT INTO ¼-INCH SLICES (1-INCH DIAMETER)

1 CUP FRESH OR THAWED FROZEN CORN KERNELS

16 LARGE SHRIMP, PEELED AND DEVEINED

2 TABLESPOONS LEMON JUICE

DASH OF TABASCO SAUCE (OPTIONAL)

8 GREEN ONIONS (SCALLIONS) INCLUDING THE GREEN TOPS, THINLY SLICED

1. In a 5-quart soup pot, combine the stock, sake, soy sauce, sugar, and ginger and bring to boil. Reduce to a simmer and cook 5 minutes. Add the corn, shrimp, and lemon juice and cook until the shrimp turn pink, about 30 seconds. Add the Tabasco, if using.

2. Ladle the soup into bowls and garnish with the green onions. Serve hot.

Corn Off the Cob

To cut fresh corn kernels away from the cob, hold the ear in a slanted position over a bowl and, using a sharp knife, cut down to slice off the kernels. Depending on the size of the ear of corn, you may need two to get 1 cup kernels.

ASIAN-STYLE FLATBREAD

Fragrant sesame oil infuses these savory breads, making them the perfect accompaniment to a soy-seasoned soup. Even though there is yeast in the mixture, the rising period is short and the dough is a snap to stir up. **MAKES 8 SERVINGS**

1 PACKAGE (¼ OUNCE) OR 1 SCANT TABLESPOON ACTIVE DRY YEAST

1 CUP WARM WATER (105°F TO 115°F)

2 CUPS ALL-PURPOSE FLOUR

½ TEASPOON SALT

1 TABLESPOON TOASTED SESAME OIL, PLUS ADDITIONAL FOR COOKING

½ CUP FINELY CHOPPED GREEN ONIONS (SCALLIONS), INCLUDING THE GREEN TOPS

1. In a bowl, sprinkle the yeast over the warm water. Stir in 1 cup of the flour and the salt. Beat with a spoon or small hand mixer until the mixture is very smooth. Stir in the oil, the green onions, and enough of the remaining flour to make a smooth, slightly stiff dough.

2. Divide the dough into 8 portions. Cover with plastic and let rest for 30 minutes. Form the dough into balls. On a lightly floured board, roll out the balls into 8-inch rounds using a rolling pin.

3. Set a nonstick skillet over medium-high heat. Brush the skillet with some sesame oil and heat until hot but not smoking. Cook the discs, one at a time, until golden, about 2 minutes per side. Transfer to a plate and cover with waxed paper or foil to keep warm. Serve warm.

Chilled Carrot and Orange Soup
WITH Old-Fashioned Cream Scones

CHILLED CARROT AND ORANGE SOUP

This gorgeous soup could not be more refreshing, not to mention being full of vitamin A. Use fresh-from-the-garden carrots and juice squeezed straight from oranges for best results. **MAKES 6 SERVINGS**

3 TABLESPOONS BUTTER

1 MEDIUM ONION, FINELY CHOPPED

4 CUPS CARROT SLICES (⅛ INCH THICK)

4 CUPS BASIC VEGETABLE BROTH
(PAGE 12) OR LOW-SODIUM
STORE-BOUGHT, OR WATER

2 TEASPOONS GRATED ORANGE ZEST

¼ TEASPOON GROUND BLACK PEPPER

⅛ TEASPOON SALT

LARGE PINCH OF GROUND CLOVES

1 CUP ORANGE JUICE

2 TEASPOONS LEMON JUICE

FRESH MINT LEAVES

1. Melt the butter in a heavy saucepan over medium heat. Add the onion and cook, stirring, until golden but not browned, about 3 minutes. Add the carrots, broth, orange zest, pepper, salt, and cloves. Simmer, covered, until the carrots are tender, about 15 minutes.

2. Puree the soup in batches in a blender until silky smooth. Transfer to a bowl and stir in the orange and lemon juices. Refrigerate, covered, until chilled, about 2 hours.

3. Serve garnished with mint leaves.

OLD-FASHIONED CREAM SCONES

I sometimes use scones as a base for a dessert shortcake by splitting them horizontally, filling them with fresh berries, and adding a topping of whipped cream. But here, I serve them glazed with a thin layer of cream to accompany a chilled summer soup. The scones can be frozen, stored in resealable freezer bags, up to two months. **MAKES 8**

2 CUPS ALL-PURPOSE FLOUR

2 TABLESPOONS, PLUS
   2 TEASPOONS SUGAR

1 TABLESPOON BAKING POWDER

½ TEASPOON SALT

8 TABLESPOONS (1 STICK) COLD
   BUTTER, CUT INTO SMALL PIECES

2 LARGE EGGS

⅓ CUP HEAVY (WHIPPING) CREAM,
   PLUS ADDITIONAL IF NEEDED

1. Preheat the oven to 400°F. In a food processor, combine the flour, 2 tablespoons of the sugar, the baking powder, and salt and pulse just until mixed, 1 or 2 seconds. Add the butter and pulse until the mixture resembles fine crumbs. This can also be done in a bowl with a pastry blender if you don't have a food processor.

2. In a small bowl, whisk together the eggs and cream. Set aside 2 tablespoons of the mixture for glazing the tops of the scones. Stir the egg mixture into the dry ingredients until a stiff dough forms, adding more cream if the dough is dry and crumbly.

3. Turn the dough out onto a lightly floured board and knead just until the dough holds together. Divide the dough in half and shape each into a disc about 6 inches in diameter. Place the discs on an ungreased baking sheet and cut through each one to make 4 wedges but leave the wedges in place. Brush the tops with the reserved egg mixture and sprinkle with the remaining sugar.

4. Bake until golden, 15 to 18 minutes. Let cool on a rack. Serve warm. Cool completely to wrap for freezing. To warm frozen scones, remove from the freezer, unwrap, and let stand at room temperature until thawed.

Chilled Melon Soup
(WITH) Blueberry Banana Bread

CHILLED MELON SOUP

Chilled fruit soups are a great vehicle for leftover bits of fruit. I use melon here, but almost any combination of fruits can be used. Buttermilk or plain yogurt gives the soup a pleasant zing—the perfect pick-me-up on a hot day. **MAKES 4 TO 6 SERVINGS**

6 CUPS VERY COLD SEEDED WATERMELON (OR OTHER MELON) CHUNKS, PLUS SMALL MELON BALLS FOR GARNISH

1¾ CUPS BUTTERMILK OR PLAIN GREEK YOGURT (1% OR WHOLE MILK)

1 TABLESPOON GIN (OPTIONAL)

½ TEASPOON ROSE WATER (OPTIONAL)

SALT

MINT SPRIGS OR CHOPPED MINT

1. In a blender, combine the melon, buttermilk or yogurt, gin (if using), and rose water (if using) and blend until smooth. Cover and refrigerate for several hours, until thoroughly chilled. Season with salt to taste.

2. Ladle the soup into chilled bowls or iced-tea glasses, and garnish with melon balls and mint.

BLUEBERRY BANANA BREAD

I seem to always have a loaf of this versatile bread in the freezer. It comes in handy when friends stop by unexpectedly. As bananas go beyond their peak, I default to making it, and I make it the lazy way—in the food processor. I prefer to bake the bread in three small loaves rather than one big loaf, so I can freeze the other two.

MAKES ONE 9 × 5-INCH LOAF OR THREE 4½ × 2½-INCH LOAVES

1½ CUPS ALL-PURPOSE FLOUR

¾ CUP SUGAR

8 TABLESPOONS (1 STICK) PLUS
 2 TABLESPOONS BUTTER

⅓ CUP WHOLE OR 2% MILK

2 LARGE EGGS

2 RIPE MEDIUM BANANAS, SLICED (OR
 MASHED IF MIXING BY HAND)

1 TABLESPOON LEMON JUICE OR
 WINE VINEGAR

1 TEASPOON BAKING SODA

½ TEASPOON SALT

½ CUP WALNUTS OR PECANS, CHOPPED

1 CUP FRESH BLUEBERRIES

1. Preheat the oven to 350°F. Lightly grease a 9 × 5-inch loaf pan or three 4½ × 2½-inch mini loaf pans.

2. In a food processor, combine the flour, sugar, butter, milk, eggs, bananas, lemon juice, baking soda, and salt and process until the batter is smooth and well blended. (Alternatively, stir the ingredients by hand in a large bowl.) Stir in the nuts and blueberries.

3. Spoon the batter into the loaf pan(s). Bake until a wooden skewer inserted into the center of a loaf comes out clean and dry, about 1 hour 15 minutes for the large loaf, 45 to 55 minutes for the smaller loaves.

4. Transfer to a rack to cool. To freeze, double-wrap in foil and place in resealable freezer bags. To warm frozen loaves, remove from the freezer, unwrap, and let stand at room temperature until thawed.

Spanish Gazpacho ⬤WITH⬤ Skillet-Toasted Parmesan Flatbread

SPANISH GAZPACHO

Very traditional recipes for this soup call for bread layered into the soup. Today, popular versions leave the bread out. My version includes crispy, dry-toasted croutons. Despite this, I still like to serve hot flatbread on the side. **MAKES 6 SERVINGS**

4 LARGE TOMATOES, CHOPPED

1 LARGE CUCUMBER, PEELED
    AND CHOPPED

1 MEDIUM SWEET RED ONION,
    FINELY MINCED

1 GREEN OR RED BELL PEPPER, MINCED

2 SMALL CLOVES GARLIC, MINCED

3 TABLESPOONS EXTRA-VIRGIN OLIVE OIL,
    PLUS ADDITIONAL FOR SERVING

2 TABLESPOONS SHERRY VINEGAR,
    PLUS ADDITIONAL FOR SERVING

2 TABLESPOONS FINELY MINCED CHIVES

SALT AND GROUND BLACK PEPPER

1 CUP TOASTED CROUTONS, HOMEMADE
    (SEE BOX) OR STORE-BOUGHT

1. In a large bowl, combine the tomatoes, cucumber, onion, bell pepper, garlic, oil, vinegar, and chives. Season to taste with salt and pepper. Cover and refrigerate until icy cold.

2. Place an ice cube in each of 6 glasses. Spoon the soup over and top with a few toasted croutons. The gazpacho can be stored in an airtight container in the refrigerator for up to 3 days.

Toasted Croutons

To make your own toasted croutons, cut the crusts off sliced white or wheat bread and dice the slices to about ½-inch cubes. Spread on a baking sheet and toast in a 300°F oven until lightly browned and crisp, 10 to 15 minutes.

SKILLET-TOASTED PARMESAN FLATBREAD

These flatbreads are best served hot, straight from the pan. They can also be served cooled and spread with hummus or baba ghanoush. To serve as a dipper, just rip off portions of the hot breads and use the pieces as scoops. **MAKES 6**

1 PACKAGE (¼ OUNCE) OR 1 SCANT
   TABLESPOON ACTIVE DRY YEAST
1 CUP WARM WATER (105°F TO 115°F)
1 TEASPOON SUGAR
4 TEASPOONS EXTRA-VIRGIN OLIVE OIL,
   PLUS ADDITIONAL FOR THE BOWL

1½ TO 2 CUPS ALL-PURPOSE FLOUR
1 CUP WHOLE WHEAT FLOUR
¾ CUP FINELY GRATED PARMESAN CHEESE
1¼ TEASPOONS SALT

1. In a large bowl, sprinkle the yeast over the warm water and stir in the sugar. Let stand until the mixture begins to foam, about 5 minutes. Stir in the oil.

2. In a bowl, combine 1½ cups of the all-purpose flour, the whole wheat flour, Parmesan, and salt. Gradually add the dry ingredients to the yeast mixture, stirring, to make a stiff but still soft dough. Let stand for 15 minutes to allow the flour to absorb more liquid.

3. Sprinkle a clean work surface or cutting board lightly with some of the remaining all-purpose flour. Turn the dough out onto the board and knead for about 5 minutes. Wash the bowl and coat with olive oil. Place the dough in the bowl and turn it over to coat lightly with oil. Cover with plastic wrap and let sit in a warm place for 1 to 1½ hours.

4. Punch the dough down and divide into 6 equal portions. Form each portion into a ball. On a floured board, roll each ball to a 7-inch round using a rolling pin.

5. Preheat a nonstick skillet over medium-high heat until it is very hot. Place a round of dough into the pan and cook until it starts to bubble up, about 45 seconds to 1 minute per side. Adjust the heat as needed. Transfer to a plate or a rack and repeat with the remaining dough. Serve warm.

Chilled Avocado–Potato Soup
🅦 Bacon Parmesan Crackers

CHILLED AVOCADO-POTATO SOUP

Avocado, potato, and bacon make an unbeatable trio—they come together here in this refreshing, filling soup and crispy crackers. Both can be made ahead and stored in airtight containers. **MAKES 6 SERVINGS**

2 AVOCADOS

JUICE OF 1 LEMON (ABOUT
   3 TABLESPOONS)

1½ POUNDS YELLOW POTATOES,
   PEELED AND CHOPPED

4 CUPS BASIC CHICKEN STOCK (PAGE 6)
   OR LOW-SODIUM STORE-BOUGHT

½ TEASPOON GROUND CUMIN

SALT AND GROUND BLACK PEPPER

FRESH CILANTRO LEAVES

1. Scoop the avocado flesh into a small bowl and toss with the lemon juice. Set aside.

2. In a soup pot, combine the potatoes and stock and bring to a boil. Cook until the potatoes are tender, about 20 minutes.

3. Transfer the potatoes and stock to a blender. Add the lemon-soaked avocados and blend until smooth. Add the cumin and salt and pepper to taste. Refrigerate until well chilled. Serve garnished with cilantro.

BACON PARMESAN CRACKERS

You can serve these savory, crispy bacon-topped crackers as appetizers as well as an accompaniment to almost any soup. My sister, Betty Mae, takes these crunchy treats to every potluck she attends. **MAKES ABOUT 7 DOZEN**

1 BOX (16 OUNCES) BUTTER CRACKERS, SUCH AS CLUB CRACKERS

1 POUND THINLY SLICED HICKORY SMOKED BACON, CUT INTO 1-INCH PIECES

1 CUP GRATED PARMESAN CHEESE

ABOUT 1 TEASPOON CHILI POWDER (CHILI SEASONING)

1. Preheat the oven to 250°F.

2. Spread the crackers in a single layer on a rimmed baking sheet, side by side. Top each cracker with a piece of bacon. Sprinkle with the cheese and chili powder. Bake just until the bacon is browned and crisp, about 1 hour. Let cool. Store in an airtight container, refrigerated or frozen.

Thai Fresh Pea Soup
(WITH) Red Curry and Coconut Bread

THAI FRESH PEA SOUP

The flavor of this soup is most delicate in the spring and early summer, when fresh peas are in the garden or at the farmers' market. If you opt to make it any other time of year, use frozen sweet peas. **MAKES 6 SERVINGS**

4 CUPS BASIC VEGETABLE BROTH (PAGE 12) OR LOW-SODIUM STORE-BOUGHT

2 MEDIUM BOILING POTATOES, PEELED AND DICED

1 CUP CHOPPED SWEET ONION

4 CLOVES GARLIC, FINELY CHOPPED

2 TEASPOONS THAI RED CURRY PASTE

1 CUP CANNED UNSWEETENED COCONUT MILK

5 CUPS FRESH OR FROZEN BABY GREEN PEAS

SALT AND GROUND BLACK PEPPER

1 TEASPOON MUSTARD SEEDS, TOASTED (SEE BOX)

CHOPPED FRESH MINT

1. Pour 2 cups of the broth into a 4-quart soup pot and bring to a simmer. Add the potatoes, onion, garlic, and curry paste. Cook, stirring frequently, until the onions are softened and translucent. Add the remaining 2 cups broth, increase the heat, and bring to a boil.

2. Add the coconut milk and peas and simmer until the peas are cooked, about 10 minutes. Working in batches, transfer the soup to a blender and process until pureed. Add salt and pepper to taste.

3. Serve with a sprinkling of mustard seeds and garnish with mint.

Toasting Mustard Seeds

To toast mustard seeds, set a small skillet over medium-high heat. Add the seeds, cover, and toast for about 30 seconds. Mustard seeds will pop. Remove from the heat and spread on paper towels to cool.

RED CURRY AND COCONUT BREAD

Thai red curry paste in the dough gives this bread a pinkish hue and a mildly herbal flavor. Be sure to stir coconut milk well, as it tends to separate in the can.

MAKES 2 LOAVES

1 PACKAGE (¼ OUNCE) OR 1 SCANT TABLESPOON ACTIVE DRY YEAST

1¼ CUPS WARM WATER (105°F TO 115°F)

1 TABLESPOON SUGAR

⅔ CUP CANNED UNSWEETENED COCONUT MILK, WELL STIRRED

4 TABLESPOONS THAI RED CURRY PASTE

1½ TEASPOONS SALT

3 CUPS UNBLEACHED BREAD FLOUR

1. In a large bowl, sprinkle the yeast over the warm water. Stir in the sugar and let stand until the yeast begins to foam, about 5 minutes. Add the coconut milk, curry paste, and salt and mix until well blended. Add the flour, ½ cup at a time, beating until a stiff dough forms. Let the dough rest, covered, for 15 minutes.

2. Turn the dough out onto a floured surface and knead to make a smooth and satiny dough, about 10 minutes. Alternatively, place the dough in the bowl of a stand mixer fitted with the dough hook and knead for 5 minutes. Lightly grease a bowl and place the dough in it. Turn the dough over to grease the top. Cover the bowl and let rise until doubled in bulk, about 1 hour.

3. Turn the dough out onto a lightly oiled surface and divide in half. Shape each half into a narrow 12-inch-long loaf. Place the loaves on a lightly greased baking sheet, cover, and let rise until almost doubled in bulk, about 45 minutes. Preheat the oven to 425°F.

4. Using a razor blade or French *lame,* slash the tops of the loaves 4 or 5 times on the diagonal and spray with water. Bake until the loaves are golden, about 25 minutes. Transfer to a rack to cool.

Parsnip and Tahini Soup
(WITH) Pita Crisps

PARSNIP AND TAHINI SOUP

Tahini is a paste of ground sesame seeds used in Middle Eastern cooking. Its flavor blends well with parsnips as well as any other root vegetable. **MAKES 4 TO 6 SERVINGS**

2 TABLESPOONS CANOLA OIL

1 LARGE SWEET ONION, CHOPPED

6 CLOVES GARLIC, MINCED

1 TEASPOON KOSHER SALT

½ TEASPOON GROUND BLACK PEPPER

½ TEASPOON GROUND CORIANDER

¼ TEASPOON TURMERIC

PINCH OF CAYENNE PEPPER

1½ POUNDS PARSNIPS, PEELED AND
    CUT INTO ½-INCH SLICES

4 CUPS BASIC VEGETABLE BROTH
    (PAGE 12) OR LOW-SODIUM
    STORE-BOUGHT

2 CUPS WATER

2 SPRIGS THYME (OPTIONAL)

⅓ CUP TAHINI

LEMON JUICE

GRATED LEMON ZEST

⅓ CUP CHOPPED FRESH CILANTRO
    OR MINT

1. Heat the oil in a soup pot over medium heat. Add the onion and cook until translucent, about 4 minutes. Add the garlic, salt, black pepper, coriander, turmeric, and cayenne, and cook until the garlic is fragrant, about 1 minute.

2. Add the parsnips and cook, stirring, for 3 minutes. Add the broth, water, and thyme (if using). Bring to a simmer, partially cover, and cook until the parsnips are very tender, about 25 minutes. Remove from the heat and let cool for 10 minutes.

3. Remove the sprigs of thyme and stir in the tahini. Using either an immersion blender, standard blender, or food processor, puree the soup until smooth. Return it to the pot and reheat if necessary. Season with lemon juice to taste and add more salt if desired. Serve garnished with the lemon zest and cilantro.

PITA CRISPS

Prepare home-baked pita bread (page 92) or buy a good-quality packaged version from a local bakery to make these savory toasts. **MAKES 4 TO 6 SERVINGS**

4 SANDWICH PITAS (6 INCHES IN
    DIAMETER), EACH CUT INTO 8
    WEDGES, AND EACH WEDGE
    SEPARATED INTO TWO PIECES

OLIVE OIL

SALT

1. Preheat the oven to 400°F.

2. Brush the pita wedges with oil and sprinkle with salt. Spread on a baking sheet and bake until browned and crisp, 10 to 12 minutes. Let cool.

Spiced Zucchini Soup ⬤ₜₕ Sun-Dried Tomato and Pesto Bread

SPICED ZUCCHINI SOUP

Here's one way to use up those giant zucchini that seem to overtake the garden. This soup is delicious hot or cold with a nice swirl of my homemade version of crème fraîche on top. You can use light sour cream or a dollop of low-fat plain yogurt as a topping as well. **MAKES 4 TO 6 SERVINGS**

2 TABLESPOONS BUTTER

1 TEASPOON GROUND CUMIN

1 TEASPOON GROUND CORIANDER

1 LARGE SWEET ONION, CUT INTO CHUNKS

3 CLOVES GARLIC, CHOPPED

2 POUNDS ZUCCHINI, CUT INTO CHUNKS (ABOUT 8 CUPS)

1 LARGE THIN-SKINNED BOILING POTATO, SCRUBBED AND CUT INTO CHUNKS

2 CUPS BASIC CHICKEN STOCK OR BASIC VEGETABLE BROTH (PAGE 6 OR 12) OR LOW-SODIUM STORE-BOUGHT

SALT AND GROUND BLACK PEPPER

FRESH HERBS, SUCH AS PARSLEY, BASIL, CHERVIL, OR CHIVES

CREAM TOPPING (SEE RECIPE)

1. Melt the butter in a soup pot. Add the cumin, coriander, onion, garlic, zucchini, potato, and stock or broth. Cover and cook over medium heat for 2 minutes, reduce the heat, and simmer until the vegetables are tender, about 30 minutes.

2. Puree in batches in a blender until smooth. Season to taste with salt and pepper. Return to the pot and add the fresh herbs. Serve hot or refrigerate until thoroughly chilled. Top with the Cream Topping, sour cream, or yogurt.

Cream Topping

Bring 1 cup heavy (whipping) cream to room temperature. Stir in 1 heaping tablespoon lemon juice. The cream will thicken in a few minutes. Use as a garnish for soup, or as a topping for fresh berries or steamed vegetables. **MAKES ABOUT 1 CUP**

SUN-DRIED TOMATO AND PESTO BREAD

I like to mix this dough in the bread machine set on the "dough" cycle (see "Bread Machine Method" on this page) and shape the loaf into baguettes, but it can also be made by hand. **MAKES 6 SERVINGS**

1 CUP WARM WATER (105°F TO 115°F)

1 PACKAGE (¼ OUNCE) OR 1 SCANT
    TABLESPOON ACTIVE DRY YEAST

⅓ CUP PESTO

⅓ CUP CHOPPED SUN-DRIED TOMATOES

2 TABLESPOONS SUGAR

1½ TEASPOONS SALT

2½ CUPS UNBLEACHED BREAD FLOUR

1. In a large bowl, combine the warm water, yeast, pesto, sun-dried tomatoes, sugar, and salt. Stir in the bread flour to make a stiff dough. Let stand until the dough becomes puffy, 15 minutes. Turn out onto a floured board and knead until the dough is smooth. Place it in the bowl, cover, and let rise for 45 minutes.

2. Punch down the dough and shape into an oval loaf. Place on a lightly greased baking sheet. Cover and let rise until almost doubled in bulk, 45 minutes to 1 hour.

3. Preheat the oven to 375°F. Bake until golden and a wooden skewer inserted into the loaf comes out dry, about 30 minutes. Serve warm.

VARIATION

Bread Machine Method

In a bread machine, combine the warm water, yeast, bread flour, pesto, sun-dried tomatoes, sugar, and salt. Program the bread machine to "dough." When the machine stops, proceed with shaping and baking as described in the main recipe.

Zucchini and Macaroni Soup WITH Herbed Toasts

ZUCCHINI AND MACARONI SOUP

Here's one way to encourage kids to eat their vegetables. Any small pasta shape will do here—the idea is for every spoonful to include a few small pieces of both pasta and zucchini. **MAKES 6 SERVINGS**

6 CUPS BASIC CHICKEN STOCK (PAGE 6) OR LOW-SODIUM STORE-BOUGHT

1 CUP SMALL PASTA SHAPES, SUCH AS ORECCHIETTE OR RADIATORE

1 POUND ZUCCHINI (ABOUT 2 MEDIUM), CUT INTO ⅓-INCH CUBES

3 LARGE EGG YOLKS

1 LARGE EGG

¼ CUP LEMON JUICE

SALT AND GROUND BLACK PEPPER

MINCED FRESH PARSLEY

1. Bring the stock to a boil in a 5-quart soup pot. Add the pasta, return to a boil, and cook for 5 minutes. Add the zucchini and cook until the pasta is al dente, about 3 minutes, depending on the size of the pasta.

2. Meanwhile, in a small bowl, whisk together the egg yolks and whole egg. Whisk in the lemon juice.

3. Whisk 1 cup of the hot stock into the egg mixture, whisking vigorously, and then whisk the mixture back into the soup, cooking until it is slightly thickened. Season to taste with salt and pepper. Ladle the soup into hot soup mugs or bowls and garnish with parsley.

HERBED TOASTS

I prefer dill and parsley on these, but any soft herb will do. Bake up a Fresh Baguette (page 17) or purchase a good-quality one at a local bakery. **MAKES 40**

8 TABLESPOONS (1 STICK) BUTTER, AT ROOM TEMPERATURE

1 TABLESPOON SNIPPED FRESH DILL

1 TABLESPOON MINCED FRESH PARSLEY

1 TEASPOON DIJON MUSTARD

SALT AND GROUND BLACK PEPPER

1 FRESH BAGUETTE (PAGE 17) OR GOOD-QUALITY STORE-BOUGHT, CUT ON THE DIAGONAL INTO ½-INCH SLICES

1. Preheat the oven to 400°F.

2. In a small bowl, cream the butter with the dill, parsley, mustard, and salt and pepper to taste. Spread the bread slices with the herb butter and place, buttered side up, on a baking sheet. Bake until the toasts are golden brown, about 5 minutes, and transfer to a serving plate.

Ten-Minute Chickpea–Tomato Soup <small>WITH</small> Parmesan–Basil Baguette Toasts

TEN-MINUTE CHICKPEA-TOMATO SOUP

With a few ingredients in the cupboard, you can whip up this soup quickly. I like to cook dried chickpeas in one-pound batches and freeze them in resealable plastic bags to make fast work of this soup. **MAKES 4 TO 6 SERVINGS**

2 CUPS COOKED OR CANNED CHICKPEAS (DRAINED AND RINSED IF CANNED)

2 CLOVES GARLIC, SMASHED

2 CUPS DICED FRESH TOMATOES

1 CUP WHOLE DAIRY MILK, SOY MILK, OR RICE MILK

2 TABLESPOONS LEMON JUICE

1 TEASPOON GROUND CUMIN

SALT

CAYENNE PEPPER

2 TABLESPOONS MINCED FRESH PARSLEY OR CILANTRO

1. In a blender, combine the chickpeas and garlic and process until minced. Add the tomatoes, ½ cup of the milk, the lemon juice, cumin, and salt and cayenne to taste. Blend until smooth. Add the remaining ½ cup milk and blend until smooth and creamy. Taste and adjust the seasonings, if needed.

2. Transfer the soup to a large saucepan and cook over medium heat, stirring, until hot, about 5 minutes. Ladle into bowls and top with parsley or cilantro.

PARMESAN-BASIL BAGUETTE TOASTS

These crispy toasts are an excellent way to use up slightly stale baguettes. Slice them thinly for best results. They make great last-minute snacks. **MAKES ABOUT 24**

1 FRESH BAGUETTE (PAGE 17) OR GOOD-QUALITY STORE-BOUGHT, CUT ON THE DIAGONAL INTO ¼-INCH SLICES

OLIVE OIL

SHREDDED PARMESAN CHEESE

CRUSHED DRIED BASIL

1. Preheat the oven to 350°F. Brush both sides of the bread slices lightly with the oil and arrange on a baking sheet. Bake until golden and crisp, 10 to 15 minutes.

2. Turn over and sprinkle with the Parmesan and basil. Bake a few minutes longer, watching them closely, until lightly toasted. Serve warm.

Summer Vegetable Soup
⬤ Easy Refrigerator Rolls

SUMMER VEGETABLE SOUP

I like to make this soup in the early summer, when succulent young vegetables are ready in the garden or in the farmers' market. **MAKES 4 TO 6 SERVINGS**

15 TINY NEW CARROTS (OR 2 OR 3 LARGER CARROTS), SCRUBBED AND CUT INTO 1-INCH PIECES

2 CUPS TINY NEW POTATOES, THIN SKINS SCRUBBED OFF

1 CUP SWEET NEW PEAS

2 CUPS TINY SNAP BEANS, CUT INTO 2-INCH PIECES

3 GREEN ONIONS (SCALLIONS), WHITE AND LIGHT GREEN PARTS ONLY, CHOPPED

2 TABLESPOONS ALL-PURPOSE FLOUR

1 TABLESPOON SUGAR

1 TEASPOON SALT

4 CUPS WHOLE MILK OR HALF-AND-HALF

2 TABLESPOONS BUTTER

CHOPPED PARSLEY

1. In a 3-quart soup pot, combine the carrots, potatoes, peas, beans, and green onions. Add boiling water just to cover. Cook over medium heat until the vegetables are almost tender, about 5 minutes.

2. In another pot, combine the flour, sugar, and salt. Stir in the milk and bring to a boil, whisking to keep the mixture smooth. Pour the liquid into the pot of cooked vegetables, bring to a simmer, and cook for 10 minutes longer.

3. Pour into a soup tureen, dot with the butter, and sprinkle with parsley. Serve hot.

EASY REFRIGERATOR ROLLS

This chilled yeast dough is the easiest way to make freshly baked bread and requires no special bread-baking skills. You just stir up the dough, cover and refrigerate it, and take out what you need to bake when you need it. The dough can be refrigerated for up to four days. Use this basic recipe to make several different flavored rolls or bread according to the variations on page 118. **MAKES 24**

2 PACKAGES (¼ OUNCE EACH) OR
    2 SCANT TABLESPOONS ACTIVE
    DRY YEAST
1¼ CUPS WARM WATER (105°F TO 115°F)
8 TABLESPOONS (1 STICK)
    BUTTER, MELTED

¼ CUP SUGAR
3 LARGE EGGS
1 TEASPOON SALT
ABOUT 4 CUPS BREAD FLOUR

1. In a large bowl, preferably one that has a cover, sprinkle the yeast over the warm water. Stir and let stand until the yeast looks foamy, about 5 minutes.

2. Stir in the butter, sugar, eggs, and salt. Beat in the flour, 1 cup at a time, until the dough is too stiff to mix, which may be before all of the flour is added. Cover and refrigerate for 2 hours or up to 4 days.

3. To bake the rolls, remove the dough from the refrigerator. Grease as many regular muffin cups as you need (as many as 24). Scoop the dough into the cups using an ice-cream scoop. Cover with a towel and allow to rise until doubled in bulk, about 1 hour.

4. Preheat the oven to 350°F. Bake until lightly browned, 20 to 25 minutes. Transfer to a rack to cool.

CONTINUED ▶

VARIATIONS

Old-Fashioned Parker House Rolls

Roll out the dough to a ½-inch thickness. Cut out rounds with a 2½-inch cutter. Dip each round in melted butter, fold in half (with buttered side inside), and place on a baking sheet, with one flat side down. Press lightly to seal. Bake as directed in the basic recipe.

Cloverleaf Rolls

Pinch off small pieces of dough and roll into balls slightly larger than 1 inch in diameter. This recipe should make 72 dough balls. Brush a muffin tin with melted butter; then add 3 dough balls to each tin. Bake as directed in the basic recipe.

Caraway Rye Rolls

Replace the sugar with molasses, add 1 tablespoon caraway seeds to the basic dough, and replace 1 cup of the bread flour with rye flour.

Whole Wheat Rolls

Replace the granulated sugar with light brown sugar. Replace half the bread flour with whole wheat flour.

Raisin-Cranberry Rolls

Add ½ cup raisins and ½ cup dried cranberries to the bowl when you add the butter, sugar, eggs, and salt.

Smooth Spiced Broccoli Soup
⬤WITH No-Knead Focaccia

SMOOTH SPICED BROCCOLI SOUP
....

This creamy soup has no cream in it, even though it tastes rich and is quite filling. Fragrant cumin intensifies the earthy flavor of the broccoli. **MAKES 6 SERVINGS**

3 TABLESPOONS CANOLA OIL

½ CUP SHORT-GRAIN RICE

2 MEDIUM CARROTS, CHOPPED

2 RIBS CELERY, CHOPPED

1 MEDIUM ONION, CHOPPED

2 TEASPOONS GROUND CUMIN

4 CUPS BASIC CHICKEN STOCK (PAGE 6) OR LOW-SODIUM STORE-BOUGHT

½ TEASPOON GROUND BLACK PEPPER

2 SMALL BUNCHES BROCCOLI (ABOUT 1 POUND), TRIMMED

2 CUPS WHOLE OR 2% MILK

¼ CUP SHREDDED PARMESAN CHEESE

1. Heat the oil in a large heavy-bottomed pot over medium-high heat. Add the rice and cook, stirring to coat, for 5 minutes. Add the carrots, celery, onion, and cumin. Stir over medium-high heat for 5 minutes. Add the stock and pepper and bring to a boil, stirring occasionally. Reduce to a simmer and cook 10 minutes. Add the broccoli and simmer until the vegetables and rice are tender, 5 to 10 minutes more.

2. Working in batches, ladle the soup into a blender and blend until pureed. Return to the pot and stir in the milk and Parmesan. Cook until heated through.

CONTINUED ▶

NO-KNEAD FOCACCIA

This hassle-free recipe yields a golden, tender focaccia. Top it with parmesan cheese or fresh herbs, garlic, sun-dried tomatoes, or cherry tomatoes.

MAKES 6 SERVINGS

1 PACKAGE (¼ OUNCE) OR 1 SCANT TABLESPOON ACTIVE DRY YEAST

¼ CUP WARM WATER (105°F TO 115°F)

1 CUP WARM WHOLE MILK (105°F TO 115°F)

1 TABLESPOON SUGAR

ABOUT 3 CUPS ALL-PURPOSE FLOUR

1½ TEASPOONS SALT

1 LARGE EGG

2 TABLESPOONS OLIVE OIL, PLUS ADDITIONAL FOR THE PAN AND DRIZZLING

TOPPINGS (USE ANY OR ALL): ¼ CUP CHOPPED FRESH HERBS (THYME, BASIL, OREGANO, MARJORAM); ¼ CUP DICED SUN-DRIED TOMATOES; 1 CUP HALVED CHERRY TOMATOES

¼ CUP FRESHLY GRATED PARMESAN CHEESE

1. In a large bowl, sprinkle the yeast over the warm water, stir in the warm milk and sugar, and let stand until the yeast begins to foam, about 5 minutes.

2. Stir in 1 cup of the flour, the salt, and egg and beat with a wooden spoon until the batter is very smooth. Add the oil and slowly add enough of the remaining 2 cups flour to form a smooth, soft dough. Cover and let rise until doubled in bulk, about 1 hour.

3. Generously oil a 10 × 15-inch rimmed baking sheet. Punch the dough down and spread evenly into the pan. Let rise until doubled again, 45 minutes to 1 hour.

4. Preheat the oven to 400°F.

5. With your fingers, poke indentations all over the top of the dough. Sprinkle with your choice of toppings, pressing them into the dough. Bake until golden, 25 to 30 minutes. Drizzle with olive oil and sprinkle with the Parmesan while still warm. Cut into 6 rectangles to serve.

Quick Summer Squash Soup with Pesto (WITH) Kale Crostini

QUICK SUMMER SQUASH SOUP WITH PESTO

Think of this soup when time is short, the day has been busy and hot, and the garden or the farmers' market is abundant with squash. **MAKES 4 SERVINGS**

2 TABLESPOONS OLIVE OIL

1 LARGE SWEET ONION, CHOPPED

2 SMALL ZUCCHINI, DICED

2 SMALL YELLOW CROOKNECK
    SQUASH, DICED

3 CANS (15 OUNCES EACH) CANNELLINI
    BEANS, UNDRAINED

4 CUPS BASIC CHICKEN STOCK (PAGE 6)
    OR LOW-SODIUM STORE-BOUGHT

2 MEDIUM TOMATOES, CHOPPED

BASIL PESTO (SEE RECIPE) OR
    STORE-BOUGHT

½ CUP LIGHT SOUR CREAM

Heat the oil in a large heavy soup pot over medium heat. Add the onion and cook until translucent, about 8 minutes. Add the zucchini and yellow squash and cook, stirring occasionally, until crisp-tender, about 10 minutes. Add the beans (and their liquid), stock, and tomatoes and bring to a simmer. Cook until heated through. Serve with a dollop of pesto and sour cream in each bowl.

Basil Pesto

In a food processor, combine 1 cup tightly packed fresh basil leaves, ⅓ cup grated Parmesan cheese, and 3 tablespoons olive oil. Pulse until the basil is finely chopped. Add 3 tablespoons lemon juice and process until smooth. **MAKES 1 SCANT CUP**

CONTINUED ▶

KALE CROSTINI
. . . .

Sautéed kale makes a tasty topping for crostini. The kale can be cooked a day ahead and stored in the refrigerator in a container with a tight-fitting lid. Rewarm in a skillet over medium heat until heated through. **MAKES 4 SERVINGS**

1 FRESH BAGUETTE (PAGE 17) OR
    GOOD-QUALITY STORE-BOUGHT, CUT
    ON THE DIAGONAL INTO 12 SLICES
8 TABLESPOONS OLIVE OIL
5 CLOVES GARLIC—1 HALVED, 4 MINCED
½ TEASPOON RED-PEPPER FLAKES

1 POUND KALE, THICK STEMS TRIMMED
    AND DISCARDED
1 CUP BASIC CHICKEN STOCK (PAGE 6) OR
    LOW-SODIUM STORE-BOUGHT
SALT AND GROUND BLACK PEPPER

1. Preheat the oven to 375°F. Brush the bread slices on both sides with 4 tablespoons of the oil and place on a baking sheet. Bake until golden, about 6 minutes. Rub the toasts with the halved garlic.

2. Heat 3 tablespoons of the oil in a large pot over medium heat. Add the minced garlic and pepper flakes and cook, stirring, until fragrant. Add the kale and stock and bring to a boil. Reduce to a simmer, cover, and cook until the kale is tender and the stock has evaporated, about 15 minutes. Season to taste with salt and black pepper.

3. Top the toasts with the sautéed kale and drizzle with the remaining 1 tablespoon oil. Serve warm.

Roma Tomato Soup with Basil
WITH Mexican-Style Cornbread

ROMA TOMATO SOUP WITH BASIL

My husband and I enjoyed a version of this flavorful soup in Cabo San Lucas. In true Mexican style, the addition of red chiles there can be heavy-handed, so use your own discretion when adding them as they can be a bit fiery. Meaty Roma tomatoes are ideal for this soup, which simmers slowly over low heat for two hours. This gives you time to stir up and bake fresh Mexican-style cornbread. Rainy days inspire me to prepare this combination. **MAKES 4 SERVINGS**

3 TABLESPOONS OLIVE OIL

5 CLOVES GARLIC, SLICED

2 SMALL DRIED RED CHILE PEPPERS, FINELY CHOPPED, OR 2 TO 4 TEASPOONS RED-PEPPER FLAKES (**CAUTION** *USE PLASTIC GLOVES WHEN HANDLING CHILE PEPPERS.*)

2 POUNDS ROMA (PLUM) TOMATOES, ROUGHLY DICED

2 CUPS BASIC CHICKEN STOCK (PAGE 6) OR LOW-SODIUM STORE-BOUGHT

SALT AND GROUND BLACK PEPPER

¼ CUP PACKED FRESH BASIL LEAVES

½ CUP HEAVY (WHIPPING) CREAM

⅓ CUP SOUR CREAM

2 CUPS CUBED (½-INCH) DAY-OLD BAGUETTE, INCLUDING THE CRUSTS

1. Heat the oil in a heavy soup pot over medium heat until hot but not smoking. Add the garlic, half of the chiles, the tomatoes, and stock. Increase the heat to high and bring to a boil, stirring. Reduce to a low simmer, cover, and cook for 2 hours.

2. Using an immersion blender, process the soup until almost fully pureed. Season to taste with salt and black pepper. Taste and add the remaining chiles as desired. Sprinkle with half of the basil.

3. Meanwhile, mix together the heavy cream and sour cream.

4. Add the bread to the soup. Ladle the soup into bowls, drizzle the cream mixture onto each serving (about 3 tablespoons each), and garnish with the remaining basil.

CONTINUED ▶

MEXICAN-STYLE CORNBREAD

When cooking with chile peppers, be especially careful handling the ribs and seeds. This recipe makes nine squares of cornbread, which is two squares per person, plus one for good measure. **MAKES 9 SQUARES**

8 TABLESPOONS (1 STICK)
 BUTTER, MELTED
⅓ CUP SUGAR
2 LARGE EGGS
⅓ CUP MILK
2 TABLESPOONS CHOPPED GREEN
 CHILE PEPPERS, MILD OR HOT,
 SEEDS REMOVED (**CAUTION** USE
 PLASTIC GLOVES WHEN HANDLING
 CHILE PEPPERS.)

⅔ CUP SHREDDED CHEDDAR CHEESE
⅔ CUP ALL-PURPOSE FLOUR
⅔ CUP YELLOW CORNMEAL
1 TABLESPOON BAKING POWDER
⅛ TEASPOON SALT

1. Preheat the oven to 350°F. Lightly coat an 8 × 8-inch baking dish with cooking spray. In a large bowl, stir together the butter and sugar. Beat in the eggs and milk. Stir in the chiles and cheddar.

2. In a separate bowl, whisk together the flour, cornmeal, baking powder, and salt. Add the flour mixture to the cheese mixture and stir until smooth. Pour the batter into the prepared pan.

3. Bake until a skewer or cake tester inserted into the center of the cornbread comes out clean, 35 to 40 minutes. Cut into 9 squares and serve warm.

Brown Rivel Soup
with Amish White Bread

BROWN RIVEL SOUP

This old-fashioned soup highlights the creativity of the Pennsylvania Dutch, who are masters at thrifty cooking. "Rivels" are a cross between a dumpling and fresh pasta, not unlike German spaetzle. **MAKES 6 SERVINGS**

2 CUPS ALL-PURPOSE FLOUR

½ TEASPOON SALT

1 LARGE EGG, BEATEN

MILK OR WATER (OPTIONAL)

6 CUPS BASIC CHICKEN STOCK (PAGE 6) OR LOW-SODIUM STORE-BOUGHT

CHOPPED FRESH PARSLEY

1. Set a heavy skillet over medium heat. Add the flour and stir until it is toasted to a golden brown, about 10 minutes.

2. Transfer the browned flour to a medium bowl and stir in the salt and egg until a stiff dough forms. Add 1 or 2 teaspoons of milk or water, if necessary. Turn the dough out onto a floured surface and divide into quarters. Roll each quarter into a long rope. Cut into ½-inch pieces to make the rivels.

3. Pour the stock into a soup pot and bring to a simmer. Drop the rivels into the soup pot, cover, and simmer until the rivels are cooked through, about 15 minutes. Ladle into serving bowls and garnish with the parsley.

CONTINUED ▶

AMISH WHITE BREAD

To make this simple bread even easier, you can use a bread machine for the first rise (although the Amish would not use the machine method). **MAKES ONE 9 × 5-INCH LOAF**

1 PACKAGE (¼ OUNCE) OR 1 SCANT
    TABLESPOON ACTIVE DRY YEAST
1¼ CUPS WARM WATER (105°F TO 115°F)
3 TABLESPOONS SUGAR
1 TEASPOON SALT

2 TABLESPOONS VEGETABLE OIL, PLUS
    ADDITIONAL FOR OILING THE BOWL
3 TO 3½ CUPS UNBLEACHED
    BREAD FLOUR

1. In a large bowl, sprinkle the yeast over the warm water and stir in the sugar. Let stand until the yeast foams, about 5 minutes. Stir in the salt and oil. Add the flour ½ cup at a time to make a smooth but soft dough. Turn out onto a floured surface and knead until smooth. Place the dough in a well-oiled bowl and turn to coat. Cover and let rise until doubled in bulk, about 1 hour.

2. Punch the dough down. Shape into a loaf and place in a lightly greased 9 × 5-inch loaf pan. Cover with a cloth and let rise until almost doubled in bulk, about 30 minutes.

3. Preheat the oven to 350°F.

4. Brush the top of the loaf generously with water and sprinkle with flour. Bake until a wooden skewer inserted into the center comes out clean and dry, 30 to 40 minutes.

VARIATION

Bread Machine Method

In a bread machine, combine the yeast, warm water, sugar, salt, oil, and bread flour. Program the bread machine to "dough." When the machine stops, proceed with shaping and baking as described in the main recipe.

Cranberry Bean and Pasta Soup
⬤ Crusty Tuscan Bread

CRANBERRY BEAN AND PASTA SOUP

Late summer brings a crop of pretty pink-speckled cranberry beans. They are also available dried. When dried, they require the same soaking and cooking as any dried bean. Unfortunately, they lose their color when cooked, but they do retain all their nutritional value and their nutty flavor. You can substitute any cooked or canned white beans in this recipe. **MAKES 6 SERVINGS**

½ LARGE SWEET ONION, FINELY CHOPPED (ABOUT 1 CUP)

1 RIB CELERY, FINELY CHOPPED

2 CLOVES GARLIC, MINCED

⅛ TEASPOON RED-PEPPER FLAKES (OR MORE TO TASTE)

¼ CUP CANOLA OIL

6 ROMA (PLUM) TOMATOES, CHOPPED

1½ POUNDS FRESH CRANBERRY BEANS OR 2½ CUPS DRIED WHITE BEANS, COOKED (SEE "COOKING DRIED BEANS," PAGE 196)

2 TEASPOONS SALT

6 CUPS BASIC VEGETABLE BROTH OR BASIC CHICKEN STOCK (PAGE 12 OR 6) OR LOW-SODIUM STORE-BOUGHT

¾ CUP SMALL SHELL PASTA

FRESHLY GRATED PARMESAN CHEESE

1. In a 5-quart soup pot, combine the onion, celery, garlic, pepper flakes, and oil. Cook over medium-low heat, stirring occasionally, until the vegetables are softened, about 10 minutes.

2. Add the tomatoes, beans, salt, and broth or stock and simmer for 1 hour. Add the pasta during the last 15 minutes of cooking (or for the amount of time the pasta needs to be al dente). The pasta will thicken the soup too much if it cooks too long.

3. Ladle into soup bowls and top with Parmesan.

CONTINUED ▶

CRUSTY TUSCAN BREAD

Yeast, flour, and water are all you need to make this ancient, classic bread. It's a perfect example of what salt (or the lack of it) does to yeast, as this loaf has an airy texture. Tuscans eat it with salty food like prosciutto or strong flavors like mashed garlic. It's a perfect partner to Cranberry Bean and Pasta Soup. I often add even more pepper flakes than the soup recipe calls for to amp up the broth's flavor. This makes it perfect for sopping up with thick slices of this bread. To intensify the bread's wheat flavor, refrigerate the dough overnight. **MAKES 1 LARGE LOAF**

1 PACKAGE (¼ OUNCE) OR 1 SCANT
  TABLESPOON ACTIVE DRY YEAST
2 CUPS WARM WATER (105°F TO 115°F)
2 CUPS UNBLEACHED BREAD FLOUR

2 TO 2½ CUPS UNBLEACHED
  ALL-PURPOSE FLOUR
CORNMEAL

1. In a large bowl or the bowl of a stand mixer, sprinkle the yeast over the warm water. Let stand until it looks foamy, about 5 minutes. Stir in the bread flour and 2 cups of the all-purpose flour. Turn the dough out onto a floured surface and knead by hand for 5 to 10 minutes, adding more flour as needed. Alternatively, in a stand mixer, knead with a dough hook until the dough is springy and pulls cleanly away from the sides of the bowl, about 10 minutes. Place the dough in a greased bowl, cover with plastic wrap, and refrigerate overnight.

2. Turn the cold dough out onto a floured surface. Shape into a ball, pulling the top surface under until smooth. Place on a baking pan or pizza peel generously dusted with cornmeal. Brush the loaf with water and dust with flour. Cover with a cloth or towel and let rise until doubled in bulk. This can take up to 2 hours because the dough is starting from cold.

3. Meanwhile, place a baking stone on the center rack of the oven and preheat the oven to 475°F for at least 30 minutes. Slide the loaf off the pan or peel and onto the stone. Spray the oven with water. Bake until lightly browned, 20 to 25 minutes. Transfer to a rack to cool.

Red Kidney Bean Soup
WITH Cheese Pupusas

RED KIDNEY BEAN SOUP
....

This soup is elegant in its simplicity. Start with canned beans to make it swiftly. A perfect accompaniment is freshly made *pupusas,* a widely popular snack in El Salvador. **MAKES 4 SERVINGS**

6 SLICES BACON, CHOPPED

2 TABLESPOONS CHOPPED ONION

2 CUPS COOKED RED KIDNEY BEANS

2 CUPS TWO-FOR-ONE BEEF STOCK
    (PAGE 9) OR LOW-SODIUM
    STORE-BOUGHT

½ CUP HEAVY (WHIPPING) CREAM

1 TABLESPOON WORCESTERSHIRE SAUCE

CHOPPED FRESH CILANTRO

1. Cook the bacon in a saucepan until crisp. Transfer to a plate lined with paper towels and set aside.

2. Scoop out all but 1 tablespoon of the bacon fat from the pan. Add the onion to the pan and cook over medium heat until soft. Add the beans and stock. Cook, covered, for 10 minutes.

3. Puree the soup in a blender and return to the saucepan. Just before serving, whisk in the cream and Worcestershire sauce. Ladle into bowls and garnish with the bacon bits and cilantro.

CONTINUED ▶

CHEESE PUPUSAS

Pupusas are made like fresh corn tortillas, ideally with a tortilla press. They are cooked in a dry skillet and taste wonderful when eaten hot straight out of the pan. Pupusas are generally served with a coleslaw-like relish called *curtido*.

MAKES 4 SERVINGS

1 CUP MASA HARINA
½ TO ¾ CUP HOT WATER
½ TEASPOON SALT

4 TABLESPOONS SHREDDED MONTEREY JACK CHEESE
CURTIDO (SEE RECIPE)

1. In a medium bowl, mix together the masa harina, ½ cup hot water, and ½ teaspoon salt. Knead well, adding more water 1 tablespoon at a time, if needed, to make a moist yet firm dough. (It should not crack at the edges when you press down on it.) Cover and set aside to rest for 5 to 10 minutes.

2. Roll the dough into a log and cut it into 4 equal portions. Roll each portion into a ball. Press an indentation in each ball with your thumb. Put 1 tablespoon of the cheese into each indentation and fold the dough over to completely enclose it. Press the ball with your palms to form a disc, taking care that the filling doesn't spill out.

3. Line a tortilla press with plastic wrap and press out each ball to 5 to 6 inches wide and about ¼ inch thick. If you don't have a tortilla press, place the dough between two pieces of plastic wrap or waxed paper and roll it out with a rolling pin.

4. Heat an ungreased skillet over medium-high heat. Cook each pupusa for 1 to 2 minutes on each side, until lightly browned and blistered. Make all the pupusas, stacking them on top of each other and keeping them covered. Serve hot with the *curtido*.

5. To reheat pupusas, heat a cast-iron griddle or skillet over medium-high heat. When it is really hot, slap on as many pupusas as it will hold in a single layer and heat them for about 30 seconds on each side. You could also wrap all of them in foil and put the whole bundle into a preheated 350°F oven for 15 minutes.

Curtido
....

1 CUP FINELY CHOPPED GREEN CABBAGE

½ CUP SHREDDED ICEBERG LETTUCE

½ CUP SHREDDED CARROT

2 GREEN ONIONS (SCALLIONS),
    FINELY SLICED

2 TABLESPOONS LIGHT BROWN SUGAR

1 TEASPOON DRIED OREGANO

½ TEASPOON CAYENNE PEPPER

½ TEASPOON SALT

3 TABLESPOONS RED WINE VINEGAR

3 TABLESPOONS OLIVE OIL

In a large bowl, combine the cabbage, lettuce, carrot, green onions, brown sugar, oregano, cayenne, salt, vinegar, and oil and toss to mix. Taste and adjust the
seasonings as desired. Serve with the pupusas as a relish. The slaw will keep, tightly
covered, in the refrigerator up to three days. **MAKES ABOUT 2 CUPS**

Southwestern Chicken Tortilla Soup
WITH Cowboy Beer and Cheddar Bread

SOUTHWESTERN CHICKEN TORTILLA SOUP

You can find dried ancho chiles in the international section of most supermarkets. The chile itself is mild, but the seeds are spicy. The flavor of ancho chiles rounds out the distinctive flavor of this soup. **MAKES 8 SERVINGS**

2 TABLESPOONS VEGETABLE OIL

1 RED BELL PEPPER, DICED

½ CUP FINELY CHOPPED ONION

6 CLOVES GARLIC, MINCED

2 TEASPOONS ANCHO CHILE POWDER (SEE BOX)

2 TEASPOONS GROUND CUMIN

4 CUPS BASIC CHICKEN STOCK (PAGE 6) OR LOW-SODIUM STORE-BOUGHT

1 DRIED ANCHO CHILE

4 CUPS DICED FRESH TOMATOES OR 2 CANS (14.5 OUNCES EACH) DICED TOMATOES

SALT AND GROUND BLACK PEPPER

1 POUND BONELESS, SKINLESS CHICKEN BREASTS, COOKED AND SHREDDED

3 CUPS FRESH OR THAWED FROZEN WHOLE-KERNEL CORN

1. Heat the oil in a 4-quart soup pot over medium-high heat. Add the bell pepper, onion, garlic, chile powder, and cumin and cook, stirring, until the vegetables are tender and fragrant, about 5 minutes. Add the stock and whole ancho chile and cook until the chile softens, about 15 minutes.

2. Remove the chile from the soup, pull off the stem, and discard the seeds. (If you prefer a spicier soup, leave the seeds in.) In a blender, combine the softened chile and diced tomatoes and process until smooth. Add the tomato mixture to the soup pot and simmer 1 hour. Season to taste with salt and black pepper.

3. Just before serving, add the chicken and corn and cook until heated through. Ladle the soup into bowls and serve with the garnishes arranged in separate bowls.

Garnishes

2 AVOCADOS, DICED

TORTILLA CHIPS OR STRIPS

2 TOMATOES, DICED

CHOPPED FRESH CILANTRO

SHREDDED JACK OR CHEDDAR CHEESE

SOUR CREAM

COWBOY BEER AND CHEDDAR BREAD

Beer breads like this one are popular because they are simple to mix together, require no rising time, and have an irresistible texture and flavor. It's nice served with a slice of cheddar cheese. **MAKES ONE 9 × 5-INCH LOAF**

3 CUPS ALL-PURPOSE FLOUR

1 CUP SHREDDED SHARP
   CHEDDAR CHEESE

½ CUP SUGAR

4 TEASPOONS BAKING POWDER

1 TEASPOON SALT

1 BOTTLE (12 OUNCES) BEER,
   ANY KIND WILL DO—EVEN
   NONALCOHOLIC BRANDS

BUTTER

1. Preheat the oven to 350°F. Grease a 9 × 5-inch loaf pan.

2. In a large bowl, combine the flour, cheese, sugar, baking powder, and salt. Add the beer and mix with a fork until all the dry ingredients are moistened. Do not overmix.

3. Spread the dough into the prepared pan. Bake until a wooden skewer inserted into the center of the loaf comes out clean and dry, 40 to 55 minutes. Brush the top of the hot loaf with butter. Transfer to a rack to cool; then cut into thick slices.

Chile Basics

Ancho chile powder is a pantry staple in Mexican cuisine. It is used in everything from mole sauce, stews, rice, and bean dishes to chocolate desserts. Indeed, a bit of it added to chocolate cake or brownie batter enhances the chocolate flavor. Dried whole ancho chiles can be found in the Hispanic section of your supermarket if they aren't hanging in bags in the produce section. They are a dried, deep reddish brown chile pepper about 3 inches wide and 4 inches long with a sweet hot flavor. When fresh, they are referred to as poblanos. Anchos are flat, wrinkled, and heart shaped. The ancho is the sweetest of the dried chiles. It is most commonly used in authentic Mexican cooking and is a staple in red chili and tamales. Ground ancho chile pepper can be purchased online from *www.penzeys.com* if you cannot find it in your market.

AUTUMN

A loaf of bread, a jug of wine, and thou.

–OMAR KHAYYÁM

Autumn is my favorite time of year, not least because it's harvest time. Beets, carrots, onions, leeks, celeriac, potatoes of all kinds, rutabagas, turnips, parsnips, sweet potatoes, yams, garlic, broccoli, brussels sprouts, cabbage, cauliflower, celery, chard, eggplant, fennel, kale, wild mushrooms, okra, pumpkins, spinach, winter squash—the list goes on and on. With so many colorful, nutritious, and flavorful vegetables plucked fresh from the earth, there's no time like the fall for making soup. It's also the season for partaking in one of my favorite activities—foraging for the golden chanterelles that grow in the forest surrounding our home. When my husband and I have collected enough to feed several people, we invite friends over to sample them—sautéed in butter with fried sage to start, followed by a creamy chanterelle soup with crisp croutons. For a larger gathering, our annual Harvest Soup Party is the perfect, low-stress way to celebrate the season's bounty. The instructions on the invitations are simple: "Bring 1 cup chopped pot-ready vegetables." When the guests arrive, I ask them to dump their vegetables into the pot of broth boiling on the stove. We've had as many as fifty university students at a party at one time, and there is always plenty of soup to go around. I bake several breads and set out spreads, cheeses, and drinks. Admittedly, this is a direct take on the classic Stone Soup as described in the folktale of the same name. But it works, and not just with a gathering at home but for neighborhood-wide parties, church dinners, and

extended family gatherings as well. Fall is also a great time to pour soup into a thermos, pack a blanket and a warm loaf of bread, and take a drive through the colorful countryside, or chase away the chill at a football game or tailgate party, or seize the moment and picnic under a tree at the peak of foliage. There's no better way to appreciate the simple, soulful pleasure of soup and bread.

Stone Soup ⬤ Country Hearth Bread

STONE SOUP

This is the ideal potluck soup, in which you ask each guest to contribute at least 1 cup of cut-up vegetables to the pot. It's inspired by the classic folktale, which is always nice to tell while the soup simmers. **MAKES 10 SERVINGS**

1 STONE, SUCH AS A SMOOTH GRANITE OR BASALT, 3 TO 4 INCHES IN DIAMETER, SCRUBBED CLEAN

4 QUARTS BASIC VEGETABLE BROTH, TWO-FOR-ONE CHICKEN STOCK, OR TWO-FOR-ONE BEEF STOCK (PAGE 12, 7, OR 9) OR WATER

10 CUPS CHOPPED VEGETABLES SUCH AS POTATOES, ONIONS, CARROTS, PARSNIPS, RUTABAGA, OR CELERY

SALT AND GROUND BLACK PEPPER

CHOPPED HERBS

SHREDDED CHEESE

1. Place the stone in the pot. Add the broth, stock, or water and bring to a boil. Reduce the heat to a simmer, add the vegetables as guests arrive, and cover. Cook until all of the vegetables are fork-tender, the "magic moment" when the soup comes together and all the vegetables are done, between 1 and 2 hours.

2. Season to taste with salt and pepper. Ladle the soup into bowls and invite guests to sprinkle on herbs and cheese.

CONTINUED ▶

The Stone Soup Story

There are many versions of the Stone Soup story that date back in history. All of them emphasize that people working together can accomplish great things. The following is how the story of Stone Soup was told in the 1905 edition of *Brewer's Dictionary of Phrase and Fable,* written by Ebenezer Cobham Brewer and published in England.

> **Stone Soup, or St. Bernard's Soup.** A beggar asked alms at a lordly mansion but was told by the servants they had nothing to give him. "Sorry for it," said the man, "but will you let me boil a little water to make some soup of this stone?" This was so novel an idea that the curiosity of the servants was aroused, and the man was readily furnished with saucepan, water, and a spoon. In he popped the stone, and he begged for a little salt and pepper for flavoring. Stirring the water and tasting it, he said it would be the better for any fragments of meat and any vegetables they might happen to have. These were supplied, and ultimately he asked for a little catsup or other sauce. When fully boiled and fit, each of the servants tasted it, and declared that stone soup was excellent.

Other stories tell of a poor man who comes into town carrying just a stone. Having been turned down when he asked for food, he tells the villagers that he will make soup using his stone. He builds a fire, adds the stone to a pot of water, and declares that an onion would make it taste much better. A villager soon produces it, and then other vegetables are offered to the soup along with bits of meat, salt, pepper, and other flavorings. After the villagers add their bits to the soup, he finally offers the soup to them, and they declare that it is excellent. Further stories are based on the same idea. In a Scandinavian version, nails are used instead of the stone. In an Estonian version, an axe is the magic ingredient that turns water into soup.

COUNTRY HEARTH BREAD

Breads like this were historically baked on flat stones over an open fire. Of course, if you are lucky enough to have an outdoor brick oven, go for it! This is a large free-form loaf with an earthy wheat flavor. **MAKES 1 LARGE LOAF**

¼ CUP HONEY

1 PACKAGE (¼ OUNCE) OR 1 SCANT
    TABLESPOON ACTIVE DRY YEAST

2 CUPS WARM WATER (105°F TO 115°F)

¼ CUP WHEAT GERM

2 TABLESPOONS BUTTER, MELTED

2 TEASPOONS SALT

1 CUP WHOLE WHEAT FLOUR

3 TO 3½ CUPS UNBLEACHED
    BREAD FLOUR

1. In a large bowl, preferably the bowl of a stand mixer fitted with the dough hook, combine the honey and yeast with the warm water. Let stand until the yeast begins to foam, about 5 minutes. Stir in the wheat germ, butter, salt, and whole wheat flour. Let stand for 15 minutes.

2. With the mixer running, gradually add the bread flour and mix until the dough cleans the sides of the bowl, about 5 minutes. Alternatively, knead by hand for 10 minutes. Cover and let rise in a lightly greased bowl until doubled in bulk, about 1 hour.

3. Turn the dough out onto a lightly floured surface and knead a few times to punch down. Shape into a ball and place on a lightly greased baking sheet. Cover loosely with a towel and let rise until almost doubled in bulk, about 45 minutes.

4. Preheat the oven to 350°F. Bake until a wooden skewer inserted into the center of the loaf comes out clean and dry, 35 to 40 minutes. Transfer to a rack to cool.

Autumn Root Vegetable Chowder
WITH Chive Batter Bread

AUTUMN ROOT VEGETABLE CHOWDER

Hearty by nature, fall's root vegetables make an excellent chowder, flavored here with smoky bacon and cheddar cheese. This soup always tastes good after an afternoon spent outdoors in the brisk air. **MAKES 8 SERVINGS**

6 SLICES BACON, CHOPPED

1 CUP CHOPPED ONION

2 CUPS BASIC VEGETABLE BROTH, BASIC CHICKEN STOCK, OR TWO-FOR-ONE BEEF STOCK (PAGES 12, 6, OR 9) OR LOW-SODIUM STORE-BOUGHT

2½ CUPS PEELED, DICED POTATOES

1 CUP CHOPPED CARROTS

1 CUP PEELED, CHOPPED PARSNIPS

4 CUPS FRESH OR THAWED FROZEN CORN KERNELS

3 CUPS MILK

3 CUPS SHREDDED CHEDDAR CHEESE

3 TABLESPOONS ALL-PURPOSE FLOUR

1. Cook the bacon in a 4-quart soup pot or Dutch oven over medium-high heat until crisp. Transfer to a plate lined with paper towels to drain.

2. Remove all but 1 tablespoon of the bacon drippings from the pan. Add the onion and cook until it is softened. Add the broth or stock, potatoes, carrots, and parsnips. Bring to a boil; then reduce to a simmer and cook until the vegetables are tender, 15 to 20 minutes. Add the corn and milk and return to a simmer.

3. Meanwhile, in a small bowl, combine the cheese and flour.

4. Stir the cheese mixture into the soup, stirring constantly until the cheese is melted. Ladle into bowls and garnish with the bacon.

CONTINUED ▶

CHIVE BATTER BREAD

This rich, moist bread features sour cream and an egg and is baked in a pie plate. **MAKES ONE 9-INCH LOAF**

1 PACKAGE (¼ OUNCE) OR 1 SCANT
    TABLESPOON ACTIVE DRY YEAST
1 CUP WARM WATER (105°F TO 115°F)
2⅓ CUPS UNBLEACHED
    ALL-PURPOSE FLOUR
2 TABLESPOONS SNIPPED FRESH CHIVES

2 TABLESPOONS SUGAR
1 TEASPOON SALT
1 CUP SOUR CREAM
1 EGG
1 TABLESPOON BUTTER, MELTED

1. In the bowl of a stand mixer fitted with the paddle attachment, sprinkle the yeast over the warm water. Let stand until the yeast looks foamy, about 5 minutes. Stir in 1⅓ cups of the flour, the chives, sugar, salt, sour cream, and egg. Beat on low speed, scraping the bowl constantly. Once all of the ingredients are combined, beat on high speed for 2 minutes.

2. Stir in the remaining 1 cup flour to make a thick, soft batter. Spread evenly in a greased 9-inch pie plate. Cover and let rise until slightly, but not quite doubled, 45 minutes to 1 hour.

3. Preheat the oven to 350°F.

4. Brush the top of the dough with the melted butter. Bake the bread until golden brown, 40 to 45 minutes.

Colombian Chicken and Potato Soup with Corn ● Almojábanas (Colombian Cheese Rolls)

COLOMBIAN CHICKEN AND POTATO SOUP WITH CORN

In Colombia, this soup, which is called *ajiaco*, is served in rustic black pottery bowls nested in individual baskets. It is customary to pick up the chunks of corncob with your hands, so an additional supply of napkins is good to have on hand. *Guascas* is a seasoning that gives ajiaco its special flavor. Reportedly, it is a weed that grows almost everywhere, but unless you know what you are looking for, it is next to impossible to find it except in markets in Colombia. It can be ordered online at *www.amigofoods.com*. You can substitute dried basil leaves, but the flavor, of course, will be somewhat different. **MAKES 4 SERVINGS**

4 BONELESS, SKINLESS CHICKEN BREAST HALVES (1 TO 1¼ POUNDS TOTAL), QUARTERED

1 MEDIUM YAM OR SWEET POTATO (ABOUT ½ POUND), PEELED AND CUT INTO 8 PIECES

1 MEDIUM ONION, CUT INTO CHUNKS

2 CLOVES GARLIC, QUARTERED

4 CUPS BASIC CHICKEN STOCK (PAGE 6) OR LOW-SODIUM STORE-BOUGHT

6 GREEN ONIONS (SCALLIONS), WHITE AND LIGHT GREEN PARTS, CHOPPED

2 MEDIUM POTATOES, PEELED AND THINLY SLICED (PREFERABLY YELLOW)

2 EARS CORN, EACH CUT INTO 4 PIECES

3 TABLESPOONS CAPERS, PLUS ADDITIONAL FOR SERVING

1 TEASPOON DRIED GUASCAS OR DRIED BASIL

½ TEASPOON GROUND CORIANDER

1 CUP FAT-FREE YOGURT

Garnishes

1 AVOCADO, SLICED

CREMA MEXICANA OR SOUR CREAM

CAPERS

CHOPPED FRESH CILANTRO

COOKED RICE

CONTINUED ▶

1. In a heavy pot or Dutch oven, combine the chicken, yam or sweet potato, onion, garlic, and stock. Bring to a boil over medium heat; then reduce to a simmer, cover, and cook until the chicken is cooked through, about 30 minutes.

2. Remove the chicken pieces, cut into 1-inch cubes, and set aside. Add the green onions, potatoes, corn, capers, guascas or basil, and coriander to the pot.

3. Cover, bring the mixture to a simmer, and cook until the potatoes are tender, about 30 minutes. Return the chicken cubes to the pot and cook until heated through. Reduce the heat to low and stir in the yogurt.

4. Scoop into deep soup bowls and top each serving with avocado, crema Mexicana or sour cream, capers, cilantro, and a spoonful of rice.

ALMOJÁBANAS (COLOMBIAN CHEESE ROLLS)

When I spent a few days in Colombia several years ago, I enjoyed eating *ajiaco* and these delicious cheese rolls. They are made with white cornmeal and a special cheese called *cuajada*, not an easy ingredient to find in U.S. supermarkets. However, a blend of ricotta and queso blanco, a fresh Mexican cheese available in the cheese section of most supermarkets, makes an excellent substitute. **MAKES 8**

1 CUP WHOLE MILK RICOTTA

1 CUP SHREDDED MONTEREY
    JACK CHEESE

½ CUP QUESO BLANCO

¼ CUP BUTTERMILK

2 LARGE EGGS

2 TABLESPOONS BUTTER, AT ROOM
    TEMPERATURE

1 TEASPOON BAKING POWDER

½ TEASPOON SALT

1 CUP MASA HARINA

1. In a food processor, combine the ricotta, Monterey Jack, queso blanco, buttermilk, eggs, and butter and process until smooth. Add the baking powder, salt, and masa harina and pulse to combine.

2. Preheat the oven to 350°F. Line a baking sheet with parchment. Let the mixture rest about 10 minutes while the oven preheats.

3. Divide the dough into 8 equal pieces, shape into smooth balls, and place on the baking sheet, evenly spaced apart. Bake until golden and puffed, 20 to 25 minutes. Serve warm.

Masa Harina: Twice-Dried Corn Flour

Masa harina is a very finely ground corn flour made from corn that has been dried, cooked, ground up, and dried again. Its unique flavor comes from the cooking water that contains calcium hydroxide or slaked lime, used in various food preparations. Dough made with masa harina can be easily shaped and is used for making fresh tortillas and other Mexican and South American breads.

Curried Chicken Wild Rice Soup
WITH Oatmeal Batter Bread

CURRIED CHICKEN WILD RICE SOUP

Warm spices—curry, cumin, and coriander—season this earthy soup, perfect for serving on a chilly fall afternoon. Oatmeal Batter Bread makes an ideal partner, with its rustic free-form shape and dense texture. **MAKES 8 SERVINGS**

2 TABLESPOONS BUTTER

½ POUND MUSHROOMS, SLICED

1 SWEET ONION, FINELY CHOPPED

½ CUP CHOPPED CELERY

½ CUP SLICED CARROTS

6 CUPS BASIC CHICKEN STOCK (PAGE 6)
    OR LOW-SODIUM STORE-BOUGHT

2 CUPS COOKED WILD RICE

1 POUND BONELESS, SKINLESS CHICKEN
    BREASTS, COOKED AND CUBED

1 TEASPOON CURRY POWDER

1 TEASPOON GROUND CORIANDER

1 TEASPOON GROUND CUMIN

½ TEASPOON SALT

½ TEASPOON GROUND BLACK PEPPER

3 TABLESPOONS DRY SHERRY

2 CUPS HALF-AND-HALF OR LIGHT CREAM

1 CUP SLIVERED ALMONDS, TOASTED

1. Melt the butter in a large saucepan over medium heat. Stir in the mushrooms, onion, celery, and carrots and cook for 5 minutes. Gradually add the stock, stirring constantly. Bring to a gentle boil, reduce to a simmer, and cook until the vegetables are tender, about 20 minutes.

2. Add the wild rice, chicken, curry powder, coriander, cumin, salt, pepper, and sherry. Simmer until heated through, about 15 minutes. Stir in the half-and-half or cream.

3. Ladle into soup bowls and serve hot, sprinkled with the toasted almonds.

OATMEAL BATTER BREAD

This is a thick, flat bread studded with pepitas (hulled pumpkin seeds, a popular Mexican snack) as well as dried apricots and sunflower seeds. The combination gives this bread a delightful texture. You can buy already roasted pepitas and sunflower seeds in the whole foods section of most supermarkets. **MAKES 1 LOAF**

2 TO 2½ CUPS BREAD FLOUR

¾ CUP QUICK COOKING OR
 OLD-FASHIONED ROLLED OATS

1 TEASPOON SALT

1 PACKAGE (¼ OUNCE) OR 1 SCANT
 TABLESPOON ACTIVE DRY YEAST

1 CUP WATER

⅓ CUP HONEY

4 TABLESPOONS (½ STICK) BUTTER

1 EGG

¼ CUP ROASTED PEPITAS (HULLED
 PUMPKIN SEEDS)

¼ CUP ROASTED UNSALTED
 SUNFLOWER SEEDS

1 CUP CHOPPED DRIED APRICOTS

1. In a large bowl, combine 1 cup of the flour, the oats, salt, and yeast and mix well.

2. In a small saucepan, combine the water, honey, and butter and heat until very warm, about 120°F. Add to the flour mixture along with the egg, pepitas, sunflower seeds, and apricots and beat with a wooden spoon for 3 minutes. Stir in enough of the remaining flour to make a stiff batter. Cover and let rise until puffy, 25 to 30 minutes.

3. Stir the batter to bring it down and turn out onto a greased baking sheet to make a free-form shape. Cover and let rise until the batter is puffy, about 30 minutes.

4. Preheat the oven to 375°F.

5. Bake until the loaf sounds hollow when lightly tapped on the bottom, 35 to 40 minutes. Cut into thick slices and serve.

Chicken and Dumpling Soup
⬤ Dutch Raisin Bread

CHICKEN AND DUMPLING SOUP

These dumplings, also known as rivels, are a simple combination of eggs, flour, salt, and black pepper and are based on a traditional Eastern European dumpling. The soup is a classic of early Pennsylvania Dutch settlers, who were known for their expertise in raising chickens—and cooking the hens that had aged out of their egg-laying years at a long, slow simmer to make them palatable. Organic, range-fed hens, available in farmers' markets, are ideal for this soup. Preroasting the hen intensifies the flavor. **MAKES 8 SERVINGS**

Soup

1 FREE-RANGE CHICKEN
   (ABOUT 4 POUNDS)
1 TABLESPOON BUTTER, MELTED
1 LARGE ONION, CHOPPED

1½ TEASPOONS SALT
1 TEASPOON GROUND BLACK PEPPER
1 TEASPOON DRIED THYME
2 TO 3 SPRIGS PARSLEY

Dumplings

2 LARGE EGGS
1¼ CUPS ALL-PURPOSE FLOUR

½ TEASPOON SALT
⅛ TEASPOON GROUND BLACK PEPPER

Garnishes

MINCED FRESH PARSLEY
CRUMBLED COOKED BACON

CHOPPED HARD-COOKED EGG

1. To make the soup: Preheat the oven to 400°F. Wash the hen and pat dry with paper towels. Rub all over with the butter and place on a rack set in a roasting pan. Roast until the skin is golden and crackled, about 30 minutes.

2. Transfer the hen to a 6-quart soup pot and add the onion, salt, pepper, thyme, and parsley. Add water to cover and bring to a boil. Reduce to a simmer and cook until the meat is very tender and falls off the bones, 1 hour to 1 hour 30 minutes. Remove the hen from the pot and set aside until cool enough to handle.

3. Remove and discard the skin and bones. Skim off any accumulated fat from the broth and discard the parsley. Add the shredded meat to the broth and bring to a simmer over low heat.

4. To make the dumplings: Beat the eggs with a whisk or fork in a medium bowl. Blend in the flour, salt, and pepper until the mixture is moistened but still looks lumpy. Do not overmix.

5. Working with a portion of the dumpling mixture at a time, pinch off marble-size pieces and drop into the soup. Repeat until all of the dumpling mixture is used. Simmer until the dumplings rise to the surface, about 3 minutes. Taste and adjust seasonings, if necessary.

6. To serve, ladle the soup into bowls and garnish with parsley, bacon, and hard-cooked egg.

DUTCH RAISIN BREAD

This country-style bread is equally delicious made with whole wheat flour or rye flour. Raisins add a hint of sweetness. Cut the loaf into thick slices while still warm, spread with butter, and top with a thin slice of sharp cheddar cheese. **MAKES 1 LOAF**

1 PACKAGE (¼ OUNCE) OR 1 SCANT TABLESPOON ACTIVE DRY YEAST

1½ CUPS WARM WATER (105°F TO 115°F)

1½ TABLESPOONS LIGHT BROWN SUGAR

3 TABLESPOONS BUTTER, MELTED

1 CUP WHOLE WHEAT OR RYE FLOUR

½ CUP NONFAT DRY MILK POWDER

2 TEASPOONS SALT

2½ TO 3 CUPS BREAD FLOUR

1 CUP RAISINS

1 EGG WHITE, LIGHTLY BEATEN

1. In a large bowl, dissolve the yeast in the warm water and add the brown sugar. Set aside until the yeast begins to foam, about 5 minutes.

2. Stir in the butter, wheat or rye flour, dry milk, and salt and beat with a wooden spoon until no lumps remain. Set aside for 15 minutes.

3. Stir in the bread flour ½ cup at a time, keeping the mixture free of lumps after each addition. When the mixture is too thick to stir easily, cover and let rest another 15 minutes.

CONTINUED ▶

4. Turn the dough out onto a floured work surface and knead the dough until it holds together in a fat, round ball and has a "springy" touch. Cover and let rise until doubled in bulk, about 1 hour.

5. Knead in the raisins until evenly dispersed. Shape the dough into a smooth, round ball and place on a lightly greased baking sheet. Cover with a towel and let rise until almost doubled in bulk, 45 minutes to 1 hour.

6. Preheat the oven to 350°F.

7. Brush the risen loaf with the egg white. Using a razor blade, French *lame*, or sharp knife, score the top of the loaf with an "*x*" and bake until a skewer inserted into the center of the loaf comes out clean and dry, 45 to 50 minutes.

Green Cabbage and Hamburger Soup `WITH` Honey Whole Wheat Cranberry–Nut Bread

GREEN CABBAGE AND HAMBURGER SOUP

My friend Mary Boman, who insists she doesn't like to cook, calls this her favorite go-to meal. Whenever her kids and grandkids are around, she makes this slow-cook soup. If I am short on tomato paste, I use canned diced tomatoes instead. The results are not as "tomatoey" but still delicious. **MAKES 6 SERVINGS**

1 LARGE ONION, CHOPPED

6 CUPS SHREDDED CABBAGE
   (ABOUT ½ LARGE HEAD)

6 CUPS WATER

3 TABLESPOONS SUGAR

2 TABLESPOONS WORCESTERSHIRE SAUCE

1½ TEASPOON SALT

4 ALLSPICE BERRIES

3 BLACK PEPPERCORNS

1 BAY LEAF

1 POUND EXTRA-LEAN GROUND BEEF

2 CANS (6 OUNCES EACH) TOMATO
   PASTE OR 1 CAN (14.5 OUNCES)
   DICED TOMATOES

1. In a large soup pot, combine the onion, cabbage, water, sugar, Worcestershire sauce, salt, allspice, peppercorns, bay leaf, and ground beef and bring to a simmer. Cook over medium-low heat, covered, 1 hour, until the vegetables are well cooked and the soup comes together.

2. Stir in the tomato paste and cook until heated through. The soup can be served immediately but improves if simmered for 2 to 3 hours.

CONTINUED ▶

HONEY WHOLE WHEAT CRANBERRY-NUT BREAD

Sometimes I use a bread machine for the first rise when making this fruit and nut-studded bread (see variation). Depending on the climate and time of year, flour may contain more or less moisture. If the dough seems too dry, add water, a tablespoon at a time, to achieve a smooth, stiff dough. **MAKES 1 LOAF**

1 CUP WARM WATER (105°F TO 115°F)

1 PACKAGE (¼ OUNCE) OR 1 SCANT TABLESPOON ACTIVE DRY YEAST

½ CUP NONFAT DRY MILK POWDER

2 TABLESPOONS BUTTER, AT ROOM TEMPERATURE OR MELTED

1 TEASPOON SALT

1 LARGE EGG

3 TABLESPOONS HONEY

1 CUP DRIED CRANBERRIES

1 CUP CHOPPED WALNUTS OR PECANS (OPTIONAL)

1 CUP STONE-GROUND WHOLE WHEAT FLOUR

1½ TO 2 CUPS BREAD FLOUR

1. In a large bowl, combine the warm water, yeast, dry milk, butter, salt, egg, and honey and stir to blend well. Set aside until the mixture begins to foam, about 10 minutes. Stir in the cranberries and nuts (if using). Stir in the whole wheat flour. Gradually add enough bread flour to make a stiff dough. You may not need to use it all.

2. Turn the dough out onto a floured work surface. Invert the bowl over the dough and let rise for 15 minutes. During this time, the dough will come together and be easier to handle.

3. With floured hands, knead the dough until the ingredients are well mixed and the dough holds together in a smooth ball. Clean and lightly grease the bowl. Place the dough in the bowl and turn to coat. Cover with a cloth and let rise until doubled in bulk, about 1 hour.

4. Shape the dough into a round loaf and place on a greased baking sheet. Let rise until almost doubled in bulk, 30 to 45 minutes.

5. Preheat the oven to 350°F.

6. Bake until a wooden skewer inserted into the center of the loaf comes out clean and dry, 35 to 40 minutes. Transfer to a rack to cool.

VARIATION

Bread Machine Method

Throw all the ingredients into the bread machine and set the machine to "dough," but add the cranberries last of all to prevent them from getting mashed into the dough and becoming unrecognizable. When the machine stops, proceed with shaping and baking as described in the main recipe.

Maine Corn Chowder
⬤ Whole Wheat Raisin Muffins

MAINE CORN CHOWDER

A touch of cumin warms this classic New England soup, made hearty with the addition of potatoes. **MAKES 4 TO 6 SERVINGS**

2 TABLESPOONS BUTTER

1 LARGE SWEET ONION, CHOPPED

1 TEASPOON GROUND CUMIN

4 LARGE YUKON GOLD POTATOES, PEELED AND CUBED

2 CUPS FRESH OR THAWED FROZEN CORN KERNELS

1½ CUPS HALF-AND-HALF OR WHOLE MILK, OR 1 CAN (12 OUNCES) EVAPORATED MILK

½ TEASPOON GROUND WHITE PEPPER

SALT

1. Heat the butter in a soup pot over medium heat. Add the onion and cook until soft, about 10 minutes. Do not let the onion brown. Stir in the cumin.

2. Add the potatoes and just enough water to cover. Cover and simmer until the potatoes are cooked, 20 to 25 minutes. Using a potato masher, mash the potatoes into small chunks but not pureed. Add the corn, half-and-half or milk, white pepper, and salt to taste. Serve hot.

WHOLE WHEAT RAISIN MUFFINS

Whole wheat flour gives these muffins a slightly nutty flavor. I coat paper muffin liners with cooking spray so the muffins can be removed more easily, but I have found that the natural brown muffin liners do not need to be coated. **MAKES 12**

¾ CUP ALL-PURPOSE FLOUR

¾ CUP WHOLE WHEAT FLOUR

2 TEASPOONS BAKING POWDER

1 CUP RAISINS

½ CUP CHOPPED WALNUTS OR PECANS (OPTIONAL)

½ TEASPOON SALT

1 EGG

½ CUP MILK

¼ CUP CANOLA OR VEGETABLE OIL

¼ CUP PACKED LIGHT BROWN SUGAR

1. Preheat the oven to 375°F. Line 12 muffin cups with paper liners. Coat with cooking spray.

2. In a large bowl, stir together the all-purpose and wheat flours, baking powder, raisins, nuts (if using), and salt. Set aside.

3. In a small bowl, whisk together the egg, milk, oil, and brown sugar. Stir into the flour mixture just until moistened. Do not overmix.

4. Spoon the batter into the muffin cups, filling each about two-thirds full. Bake until a wooden skewer inserted into the center of a muffin comes out clean and dry, about 20 minutes.

Brie and Apple Soup ⬤ Fougasse

BRIE AND APPLE SOUP

Inspired by the classic cheese and fruit combination, this soup brings together the two in a different way for a lovely appetizer. The riper the brie, the more intense the flavor. **MAKES 4 SERVINGS**

2 TABLESPOONS BUTTER

1 MEDIUM SWEET ONION, CHOPPED

2 RIBS CELERY, CHOPPED

2 GRANNY SMITH APPLES, PEELED
    AND CHOPPED

2 TABLESPOONS ALL-PURPOSE FLOUR

3 CUPS BASIC CHICKEN STOCK (PAGE 6)
    OR LOW-SODIUM STORE-BOUGHT

8-OUNCE ROUND BRIE, CUT INTO
    1-INCH CUBES

¼ CUP HEAVY (WHIPPING) CREAM

SALT AND GROUND BLACK PEPPER

SLICED ALMONDS, TOASTED

1. Melt the butter in a medium saucepan over low heat. Add the onion, celery, and apples and cook, stirring often, until the onion and celery are soft, about 10 minutes. Stir in the flour and cook, stirring, for 2 minutes. Whisk in 1 cup of the stock. Stir in the remaining 2 cups stock and bring to a boil. Reduce to a simmer, cover, and simmer until the onion, celery, and apples are cooked, about 20 minutes.

2. Transfer the soup to a food processor or blender and puree until smooth. Return the soup to the saucepan.

3. Just before serving, stir the brie and cream into the hot soup. Stir until the brie is melted. Taste and add salt and pepper, as needed. Ladle into soup bowls and garnish with almonds.

Herbes de Provence at Home

Combine equal parts dried savory, rosemary, thyme, oregano, basil, marjoram, fennel seed, and lavender. Store in a cool, dry place in an airtight container for up to six months.

FOUGASSE

Fougasse is the French version of focaccia, the Italian yeasted flatbread flavored with herbs and drizzled with olive oil. From start to finish, this bread takes less than 2 hours, very little of it active time. It's best served straight from the oven. Herbes de Provence is a classic mix of dried herbs commonly used in its namesake locale. It is available in most grocery stores, or you can make your own (see page 154). **MAKES 1 FLATBREAD, ABOUT 4 SERVINGS**

1 PACKAGE (¼ OUNCE) OR 1 SCANT
    TABLESPOON ACTIVE DRY YEAST
1 CUP WARM WATER (105°F TO 115°F)
1 TEASPOON SUGAR
2 CUPS ALL-PURPOSE FLOUR
1 TEASPOON SALT

1 TABLESPOON HERBES DE PROVENCE,
    OR 1 TEASPOON EACH DRIED BASIL,
    OREGANO, AND ROSEMARY
¼ CUP OLIVE OIL, PLUS ADDITIONAL
    FOR SERVING

1. In a small bowl, combine the yeast, warm water, and sugar. Let stand until the yeast begins to foam, about 5 minutes.

2. In a large bowl or in a food processor, combine the flour and salt. Add the yeast mixture and stir or process until a soft dough forms. Let stand until the dough begins to rise, about 20 minutes.

3. Stir in the herbs and oil and mix until blended. Turn the dough out onto a floured surface and, with oiled hands, shape into a ball. Place on a baking sheet and press the dough out to make an oval leaf shape, about 10 inches long and 1 inch thick.

4. Preheat the oven to 400°F.

5. Let rise until puffy, about 30 minutes. Using a razor blade or French *lame*, make diagonal slashes down the center and along the length of both sides of the dough. Pull each slash out gently to open the holes to somewhat resemble the veins on a leaf.

6. Bake until crisp and golden brown, 15 to 20 minutes. Transfer to a rack to cool. Tear apart to make individual servings. Serve warm with olive oil for dipping.

Spiced Parsnip and Carrot Soup WITH Lavash

SPICED PARSNIP AND CARROT SOUP
....

Silky and smooth, this pureed soup looks and tastes great with a crunchy garnish of finely cut matchsticks of fresh parsnip and carrot. **MAKES 6 SERVINGS**

1 POUND PARSNIPS	1½ TEASPOONS SALT
1 POUND CARROTS	1 TEASPOON GROUND CINNAMON
1 TABLESPOON VEGETABLE OIL	⅛ TEASPOON CAYENNE PEPPER
1 LARGE LEEK, HALVED LENGTHWISE, WELL WASHED AND SLICED CROSSWISE INTO ½-INCH PIECES	⅓ CUP QUICK-COOKING OATS
	6 CUPS WATER
	REDUCED-FAT SOUR CREAM
2 TEASPOONS CURRY POWDER	CHOPPED FRESH CILANTRO

1. Peel the parsnips and carrots. Cut half of the parsnips and half of the carrots into very thin matchsticks and set aside for garnish. Slice the remaining parsnips and carrots.

2. Heat the oil in a heavy Dutch oven or soup pot over medium heat. Add the leek, curry powder, salt, cinnamon, and cayenne. Cook, stirring, until the leek is soft-ened, about 5 minutes. Add the parsnips, carrots, oats, and water and simmer until the parsnips and carrots are softened, about 30 minutes.

3. Working in batches, transfer the mixture to a blender and puree until smooth. Taste and adjust seasonings if necessary.

4. Ladle into serving bowls and top with a dollop of sour cream. Garnish with cilantro and parsnip and carrot matchsticks.

LAVASH

This classic Armenian flatbread is among my favorites. This is a soft, thin flatbread in a rectangular shape and is often topped with flavorful seeds. It is sometimes used as a wrap. **MAKES 6**

1 PACKAGE (¼ OUNCE) OR 1 SCANT
    TABLESPOON ACTIVE DRY YEAST
1½ CUPS WARM WATER (105°F TO 115°F)
½ TEASPOON SUGAR
3½ CUPS BREAD FLOUR
2 TEASPOONS SALT

1 LARGE EGG, BEATEN WITH
    1 TABLESPOON WATER
TOPPINGS (ANY OR ALL): SESAME
    SEEDS, POPPY SEEDS, PAPRIKA,
    CUMIN, OR SALT

1. Preheat the oven to 375°F.

2. In a medium bowl, sprinkle the yeast over the warm water. Add the sugar and let stand until the yeast begins to foam, about 5 minutes. Add the flour, ½ cup at a time, and salt and mix until a moist, pliable dough, almost like Silly Putty, forms. Knead by hand, or in a stand mixer fitted with a dough hook, until the dough becomes elastic and stretchy, which might be as soon as 5 minutes if you are using a stand mixer or 10 minutes if kneading by hand.

3. Turn the dough out onto a lightly floured surface. Divide into 6 pieces. Let the dough relax for 10 minutes. Shape each piece of dough by stretching or rolling to make rectangular pieces about 8 inches by 3 inches. If the dough pulls back, let it rest 5 minutes to allow the gluten strands to relax—this will allow you to roll it out thinner.

4. Place three lavash on each of two nonstick baking sheets or on baking sheets lined with parchment paper. Brush the breads with the egg wash, leaving some parts unbrushed to provide a color contrast. Sprinkle with any or all of the toppings. Bake for 10 to 15 minutes until golden brown.

Cream of Fresh Mushroom Soup
WITH Avocado–Tomato Wraps

CREAM OF FRESH MUSHROOM SOUP

Once you get a taste of fresh homemade mushroom soup, it is hard to imagine ever opening a can of it again. Best of all, you control what goes into it and avoid thickeners and preservatives. **MAKES 6 SERVINGS**

4 TABLESPOONS (½ STICK) BUTTER

1 SMALL ONION, QUARTERED

1 POUND MUSHROOMS, BUTTON, CREMINI, OR SHIITAKE, CLEANED AND QUARTERED

4 CUPS BASIC VEGETABLE BROTH OR BASIC CHICKEN STOCK (PAGE 12 OR 6) OR LOW-SODIUM STORE-BOUGHT

2 SPRIGS PARSLEY

1 SMALL BAY LEAF

⅛ TEASPOON DRIED THYME

2 TABLESPOONS POTATO STARCH OR CORNSTARCH

3 TABLESPOONS WATER

SALT AND GROUND BLACK PEPPER

1 CUP HEAVY (WHIPPING) CREAM

1. Heat the butter in a soup pot over medium heat. Add the onion and mushrooms and cook until soft and fragrant, about 5 minutes. Add the broth or stock, parsley, bay leaf, and thyme. Simmer until aromatic, 20 minutes.

2. Discard the bay leaf. Transfer the mixture to a blender and puree. Return to the pot and bring to a boil.

3. Meanwhile, combine the starch with the water and stir until dissolved.

4. Whisk the starch mixture into the soup. Cook the soup until thickened. Season to taste with salt and pepper. Just before serving, stir in the cream.

AVOCADO-TOMATO WRAPS

Have the ingredients for filling the tortillas ready and fill them just before serving, to prevent the wraps from getting soggy. Use spinach or sun-dried tomato tortillas for color and flavor contrast. **MAKES 6 SERVINGS**

2 AVOCADOS, THINLY SLICED

2 TABLESPOONS LOW-FAT YOGURT

3 FLOUR TORTILLAS (10-INCH DIAMETER)

6 BUTTER LETTUCE LEAVES

2 MEDIUM TOMATOES, THINLY SLICED

2 TABLESPOONS SHREDDED PARMESAN CHEESE

¼ CUP SHREDDED MONTEREY JACK CHEESE

1. In a small bowl, combine 1 of the avocados with the yogurt and mash with a fork. Spread the mixture over the tortillas. Then layer the tortillas with the lettuce, tomatoes, remaining avocado, and the cheeses and roll them up.

2. Cut each roll-up in half on a diagonal and serve right away.

Easy Cream of Tomato Soup
WITH Old-Fashioned Grilled Cheese, Apple, and Basil Sandwiches

EASY CREAM OF TOMATO SOUP

Cream of tomato soup always reminds me of the standard Friday fare in the school cafeteria. It was my favorite hot lunch day of all, although I am sure the soup wasn't made from scratch! There's nothing quite as homespun as a bowl of cream of tomato soup with a classic grilled cheese sandwich. **MAKES 4 SERVINGS**

2 CUPS BASIC VEGETABLE BROTH (PAGE 12) OR LOW-SODIUM STORE-BOUGHT

2 TABLESPOONS ALL-PURPOSE FLOUR

4 CUPS CRUSHED FRESH TOMATOES, OR 1 CAN (28 OUNCES) CRUSHED TOMATOES

1 CAN (6 OUNCES) TOMATO PASTE

¾ CUP HEAVY (WHIPPING) CREAM

SALT AND GROUND BLACK PEPPER

In a soup pot, whisk together the broth, flour, tomatoes, and tomato paste and bring to a simmer over medium heat, stirring until slightly thickened. Using an immersion blender or a standard blender, puree the soup. Stir in the cream and season to taste with salt and pepper. Serve hot.

OLD-FASHIONED GRILLED CHEESE, APPLE, AND BASIL SANDWICHES

Slices of crisp fall apples and fresh basil leaves lend a whiff of the season to this classic sandwich. **MAKES 4 SERVINGS**

8 SLICES BASIC HOME-BAKED BREAD (PAGE 20), WHITE OR WHEAT, OR GOOD-QUALITY STORE-BOUGHT

8 THIN SLICES EXTRA-SHARP CHEDDAR CHEESE

1 FUJI, GALA, OR GRANNY SMITH APPLE, THINLY SLICED

4 LARGE FRESH BASIL LEAVES

1 TO 2 TABLESPOONS BUTTER, AT ROOM TEMPERATURE

1. Arrange 4 of the bread slices on a work surface and place a slice of cheese on each. Top each with the apple slices and a basil leaf. Top with the remaining cheese and the remaining 4 slices of bread.

2. Spread both sides of each sandwich with a little butter. Preheat a skillet, griddle, or panini press over medium heat. Toast the sandwiches over medium heat until golden and the cheese is melted, about 1 minute per side. Cut on the diagonal and serve.

Butternut Squash Soup with Pecan Cream ⬤ Quick Yeast Buns

BUTTERNUT SQUASH SOUP WITH PECAN CREAM

Roasting any vegetable intensifies its flavor, but butternut squash and onions seem to take particularly kindly to it. They act as the base of this soup, which is also flavored with ginger and fennel. Heavy cream spiked with hazelnut oil, cayenne, and toasted pecans add luscious layers of flavors. **MAKES 8 SERVINGS**

2 LARGE BUTTERNUT SQUASH
(3½ POUNDS TOTAL), HALVED
LENGTHWISE AND SEEDED

1 LARGE SWEET ONION, PEELED
AND HALVED

1 LARGE YELLOW POTATO, SCRUBBED
AND HALVED

1 TABLESPOON OLIVE OIL

¾ CUP PECANS

2 TABLESPOONS UNSALTED BUTTER

1 SMALL FENNEL BULB, CUT INTO
½-INCH DICE

1½-INCH FRESH GINGER, PEELED AND
FINELY CHOPPED

6 CUPS BASIC CHICKEN STOCK (PAGE 6)
OR LOW-SODIUM STORE-BOUGHT

1½ CUPS MILK

¾ CUP HEAVY (WHIPPING) CREAM

1 TEASPOON HAZELNUT, VEGETABLE,
OR CANOLA OIL

⅛ TEASPOON CAYENNE PEPPER

KOSHER SALT

1½ TABLESPOONS LEMON JUICE

1. Preheat the oven to 350°F. Rub the cut sides of the squash, onion, and potato with the olive oil and set them, cut side down, on a large rimmed baking sheet. Roast until the vegetables are soft, about 1 hour. Remove from the oven (but leave the oven on) and let stand until cool enough to handle. Scrape the flesh from the squash and transfer to a large bowl; discard the skins. Chop the onion and potato.

2. Spread the pecans on a small baking sheet and toast until fragrant and golden, about 8 minutes. Remove from the oven and set aside to cool. (If you're making the Quick Yeast Buns to go with this soup, leave the oven on and increase the temperature to 425°F.)

3. Meanwhile, melt the butter in a large lidded pot. Add the fennel and ginger and cook over medium heat until fragrant, about 8 minutes. Add the squash, onion, potato, and stock. Cover and simmer for 20 minutes, stirring occasionally. Uncover the pot and continue cooking until all of the vegetables are soft, about 10 minutes longer. Remove from the heat and stir in the milk.

4. Meanwhile, in a food processor, pulse the pecans until they are finely chopped. In a medium bowl, with an electric mixer, beat the cream until soft peaks form. Fold in the pecans, hazelnut oil, and cayenne pepper and season to taste with salt. Cover and refrigerate.

5. Working in batches, puree the soup in a blender until smooth. Stir in the lemon juice and season with salt. Ladle the soup into bowls, top with a dollop of the pecan cream, and serve hot.

QUICK YEAST BUNS

While the squash and onion roast for the Butternut Squash Soup, stir up this simple dough. Drop it into muffin cups, allowing enough time for the buns to rise. Bake them after the vegetables are roasted, at which point you will need to increase the oven temperature to 425°F. **MAKES 12**

3 TABLESPOONS SUGAR
2 TABLESPOONS BUTTER, MELTED
1 PACKAGE (¼ OUNCE) OR 1 SCANT
    TABLESPOON ACTIVE DRY YEAST

1 CUP WARM WATER (105°F TO 115°F)
1 EGG, BEATEN
2¼ CUPS ALL-PURPOSE FLOUR
1 TEASPOON SALT

1. Preheat the oven to 425°F. Coat 12 muffin cups with cooking spray.

2. In a large bowl, combine the sugar, butter, yeast, and warm water. Mix in the egg, flour, and salt to make a smooth, soft dough. Allow the dough to rise until doubled in bulk, about 1 hour (while the veggies roast).

3. Drop the dough into the muffin cups, cover with a towel, and let rise until doubled in bulk, about 30 minutes. Bake until a skewer inserted in the center of a bun comes out clean, 10 to 15 minutes.

Moroccan Vegetable Soup with Couscous (WITH) Olive Flatbread

MOROCCAN VEGETABLE SOUP WITH COUSCOUS

Cinnamon, coriander, and cumin perfume this chunky vegetarian soup. If you prefer, use chicken stock in place of the vegetable broth and add diced, cooked chicken. **MAKES 12 SERVINGS**

3 CUPS BASIC VEGETABLE BROTH (PAGE 12) OR LOW-SODIUM STORE-BOUGHT

4 CUPS CUT-UP (¾-INCH SQUARES) BELL PEPPERS (A MIX OF RED, GREEN, AND YELLOW)

3 CUPS DICED RED POTATOES

2 CUPS SLICED CARROTS

3 CUPS DICED TOMATOES

2 CUPS COARSELY CHOPPED ONIONS

1 CAN (8 OUNCES) TOMATO SAUCE

3 LARGE CLOVES GARLIC, MINCED

2 TEASPOONS GROUND CINNAMON

2 TEASPOONS GROUND CORIANDER

1 TEASPOON GROUND CUMIN

1 TEASPOON SALT

½ TEASPOON GROUND BLACK PEPPER

½ TEASPOON SUGAR

DASH OF CAYENNE PEPPER

2 CUPS BROCCOLI FLORETS

2 CUPS CAULIFLOWER FLORETS

1 CAN (15 OUNCES) CHICKPEAS, RINSED AND DRAINED

1 CUP DICED ZUCCHINI

2 TABLESPOONS LEMON JUICE

For Serving

6 CUPS COOKED COUSCOUS

CHOPPED FRESH MINT

1. In a large pot, combine the broth, bell peppers, potatoes, carrots, tomatoes, onions, tomato sauce, garlic, cinnamon, coriander, cumin, salt, black pepper, sugar, and cayenne. Bring to a boil. Reduce to a simmer and cook, partially covered, until the potatoes and carrots are tender, about 30 minutes.

2. Stir in the broccoli, cauliflower, chickpeas, zucchini, and lemon juice. Return to a boil. Reduce to a simmer, partially cover, and cook until the vegetables are fork-tender but not mushy.

3. Meanwhile, prepare the couscous according to package directions.

4. To serve, spoon ½ cup couscous into each serving bowl. Top with the cooked vegetables and some of the broth. Sprinkle with some mint.

OLIVE FLATBREAD

This simple dough, baked into a free-form loaf and studded with olives, is a staple on Middle Eastern tables. **MAKES 12 PIECES**

1 CUP WARM WATER (105°F TO 115°F)
1 PACKAGE (¼ OUNCE) OR 1 SCANT
    TABLESPOON ACTIVE DRY YEAST
1 TEASPOON SUGAR
2½ CUPS ALL-PURPOSE FLOUR

1 TEASPOON SALT
1 TABLESPOON ANISE SEEDS
1 CUP PITTED KALAMATA OLIVES, HALVED
OLIVE OIL

1. In a bowl, combine the warm water with the yeast, sugar, and 1¼ cups of the flour. Stir with a wooden spoon until blended. Add the remaining 1¼ cups flour, the salt, and anise seeds and mix to make a soft, smooth dough.

2. Turn the dough out onto a lightly floured surface, cover with an inverted bowl, and let rise until the dough has doubled in bulk, about 1 hour.

3. Place the dough on a greased baking sheet and pat or roll out to make a rectangle about 15 × 11 inches. Let rise about 30 minutes.

4. Preheat the oven to 450°F.

5. With fingers, make indentations in the dough about 1 inch apart and poke the halved olives, cut sides down, into the indentations. Drizzle with olive oil.

6. Bake until well browned at the edges, about 15 minutes. Halve lengthwise; then cut each half into 6 pieces.

French Onion Soup
WITH Crunchy Breadsticks

FRENCH ONION SOUP

On a chilly day, a bowl of this steaming hot soup hits the spot unlike any other. I like to use sweet onions because they produce a more succulent soup. Look for Vidalias, Walla Wallas, Texas sweets, or Mauis. If you make the soup in a slow cooker, it can simmer away unattended. But it is almost as unfussy to make on the stove top set over low heat. **MAKES 6 SERVINGS**

6 LARGE SWEET ONIONS
    (ABOUT 3 POUNDS), HALVED
    AND SLICED INTO HALF-MOONS
2 TABLESPOONS BUTTER
1 TABLESPOON SUGAR
1 TEASPOON SALT
1 TEASPOON CRACKED BLACK
    PEPPERCORNS
8 CUPS TWO-FOR-ONE BEEF STOCK
    OR BASIC VEGETABLE BROTH
    (PAGE 9 OR 12) OR LOW-SODIUM
    STORE-BOUGHT

2 TABLESPOONS BRANDY, COGNAC,
    OR DRY SHERRY (OPTIONAL)
12 SLICES FRESH BAGUETTE (PAGE 17)
    OR GOOD-QUALITY STORE-BOUGHT,
    CUT INTO ½-INCH-THICK SLICES
2 CUPS SHREDDED SWISS, GRUYÈRE,
    OR JARLSBERG CHEESE, PLUS
    ADDITIONAL FOR SERVING

1. In a soup pot, combine the onions and butter and cook over low heat, stirring to coat the onions thoroughly, until softened, about 30 minutes. (If using a slow cooker, cover and cook on high until the onions are softened, about 1 hour.)

2. Add the sugar, salt, and peppercorns and stir well. Increase the heat to medium-low, cover, and cook for 2 hours. (Cook on high for 4 hours in the slow cooker.) Add the stock or broth and brandy (if using). Cook for 2 hours longer (or 2 hours in the slow cooker).

3. Preheat the broiler. Ladle the soup into 6 ovenproof bowls and place 2 slices of the baguette in each bowl. Sprinkle liberally with cheese and broil for 2 to 3 minutes, until the top is bubbling and brown. Serve immediately. Pass extra cheese at the table.

CRUNCHY BREADSTICKS

Sometimes I snip one end of the dough for each of these breadsticks to simulate stalks of wheat, as they curve slightly when they bake. I arrange them in a crock and set them in the center of the table for an attractive, edible centerpiece. Other times, I just run the dough through the fettuccine blade of the pasta maker to make pencil-thin sticks (see Sesame Sunflower Breadsticks, page 45). **MAKES 20**

3 TO 3½ CUPS ALL-PURPOSE FLOUR

2 PACKAGES (¼ OUNCE EACH) OR
   2 SCANT TABLESPOONS ACTIVE
   DRY YEAST

1 TABLESPOON SUGAR

1 TEASPOON SALT

1⅔ CUPS WARM WATER (105°F TO 115°F)

¼ CUP OLIVE OIL OR VEGETABLE OIL,
   PLUS ADDITIONAL FOR COATING
   THE BREADSTICKS

KOSHER SALT, SESAME SEEDS, OR
   POPPY SEEDS (OPTIONAL)

1. In a food processor or in a large bowl, combine 3 cups of the flour, the yeast, sugar, salt, and warm water. Add the oil and process or mix until the dough is smooth and satiny and the flour has been incorporated. Add more flour, if necessary, to make a soft dough that will pull away from the sides of the food processor or bowl.

2. Preheat the oven to 300°F. Shape the dough into a rough log. Using a sharp knife, cut it crosswise into 20 pieces. Roll each piece of dough until it is 16 to 20 inches long or as long as your baking sheet. Coat each stick generously with oil and place side by side about 1 inch apart on 2 baking sheets. Sprinkle with salt or seeds (if using). Bake until lightly browned and crispy, 40 to 50 minutes. Cool on racks.

Leek, Sweet Onion, and Potato Soup with Spinach WITH Stir-It-Up-and-Bake-It Many-Seed Bread

LEEK, SWEET ONION, AND POTATO SOUP WITH SPINACH

The gentle flavor of sweet onions lends depth to the classic combination of leek and potato. **MAKES 6 SERVINGS**

3 TABLESPOONS BUTTER

1 LARGE LEEK (WHITE AND PALE-GREEN PARTS ONLY), WELL WASHED AND CUT INTO 1-INCH PIECES

2 LARGE SWEET ONIONS, SLICED

LARGE PINCH OF KOSHER SALT, PLUS ADDITIONAL FOR SEASONING

2 POUNDS YUKON GOLD POTATOES (ABOUT 5 MEDIUM), PEELED AND CUT INTO SMALL DICE

2 CUPS PACKED SPINACH LEAVES, RINSED

4 CUPS BASIC VEGETABLE BROTH (PAGE 12) OR LOW-SODIUM STORE-BOUGHT

1 CUP HEAVY (WHIPPING) CREAM

1 CUP BUTTERMILK

½ TEASPOON GROUND WHITE PEPPER

2 TABLESPOONS CHOPPED FRESH CHIVES

1. Melt the butter in a 6- to 8-quart pot over medium heat. Add the leek and onions and cook until softened, about 5 minutes. Reduce the heat to medium-low and cook, stirring occasionally, until the leeks are tender, about 25 minutes. Add a pinch of salt.

2. Add the potatoes, spinach, and broth and bring to a boil. Reduce to a simmer, cover, and cook gently until the potatoes are soft, about 45 minutes.

3. Using an immersion blender, or a standard blender working in batches, puree until smooth. Stir in the cream, buttermilk, and white pepper. Taste and adjust seasoning, if needed. Sprinkle with the chives and serve immediately. This soup is also delicious chilled.

STIR-IT-UP-AND-BAKE-IT MANY-SEED BREAD

I am a big fan of "stir and pour" breads, not only because they're a cinch to make, but also because they lend themselves to so many variations. If baking yeast breads intimidates you, this one will bolster your confidence. Just turn the mixed batter out onto a baking sheet and let rise until puffy. **MAKES 1 LOAF**

2 CUPS ALL-PURPOSE FLOUR

1 PACKAGE (¼ OUNCE) OR 1 SCANT
    TABLESPOON ACTIVE DRY YEAST

1 TABLESPOON SUGAR

1 TABLESPOON OLIVE OR VEGETABLE OIL

1 CUP WARM WATER (120°F TO 130°F)

1 TEASPOON SALT

1 TABLESPOON POPPY SEEDS

1 TABLESPOON SESAME SEEDS

2 TABLESPOONS SUNFLOWER SEEDS

2 TABLESPOONS HULLED PUMPKIN
    SEEDS, RAW OR ROASTED

4 TABLESPOONS (½ STICK)
    BUTTER, MELTED

1 TABLESPOON FRESH OR DRIED
    ROSEMARY

1. Grease a baking sheet and set aside. In a large bowl, stir 1 cup of the flour, the yeast, sugar, oil, and warm water together until a "sloppy" wet dough is formed. Add the remaining 1 cup flour, the salt, poppy seeds, sesame seeds, sunflower seeds, and pumpkin seeds and mix until smooth. Add a few more tablespoons of water if the dough gets too dry.

2. Turn the dough out onto the prepared baking sheet. Let rise in a warm place, uncovered, until puffy, 30 minutes to 1 hour.

3. Preheat the oven to 400°F.

4. Poke holes deep into the bread with your fingers and drizzle with the melted butter. Sprinkle with the rosemary. Bake until nicely browned, 15 to 20 minutes. Serve hot or at room temperature.

Acorn Squash Soup ⬤ Granola Loaf

ACORN SQUASH SOUP

Serve this as a first course when you're entertaining or as a main lunch course. The creamy, smooth texture appeals to young and old alike. Sweet carrots and a tart Granny Smith apple round out the flavors. **MAKES 6 SERVINGS**

3 ACORN SQUASH, HALVED AND SEEDED

2 TABLESPOONS BUTTER

2 CARROTS, CHOPPED

1 GRANNY SMITH APPLE, PEELED
    AND CHOPPED

1 YELLOW ONION, CHOPPED

1 YUKON GOLD POTATO, PEELED AND
    CHOPPED

1 TABLESPOON SWEET PAPRIKA

3 CUPS BASIC CHICKEN STOCK (PAGE 6)
    OR LOW-SODIUM STORE-BOUGHT

1 CUP WHOLE MILK

SALT AND GROUND BLACK PEPPER

HEAVY (WHIPPING) CREAM

1. Preheat the oven to 400°F. Line a baking sheet with foil and lightly grease it. Place the squash, cut side down, on the prepared baking sheet and bake until soft, 40 minutes to 1 hour. When cool enough to handle, scoop out the flesh.

2. Heat the butter in a soup pot over medium heat. Add the carrots, apple, onion, potato, and squash and cook, stirring, until all of the vegetables are soft and fragrant, 30 minutes. Add the paprika and stock and bring to a boil. Reduce the heat to bring the soup down to a simmer. When the vegetables are cooked, remove the pot from the heat and puree the soup using an immersion blender, a standard blender, or a food processor. Stir in the milk and season to taste with salt and pepper.

3. Ladle into soup bowls, drizzle in a little heavy cream, and serve hot.

GRANOLA LOAF

Granola that includes raisins, dates, wheat flakes, oat flakes, apples, apricots, and nuts is perfect for this loaf. The amount of flour needed may vary a little, depending on the granola you are using. **MAKES 1 LOAF**

1 PACKAGE (¼ OUNCE) OR 1 SCANT TABLESPOON ACTIVE DRY YEAST

¾ CUP WARM WATER (105°F TO 115°F)

1 CUP WARM MILK (105°F TO 115°F)

1 TABLESPOON HONEY

2 TABLESPOONS CANOLA OR VEGETABLE OIL

1 CUP WHOLE WHEAT FLOUR

1½ CUPS UNSWEETENED GRANOLA

2 TEASPOONS SALT

3 CUPS BREAD FLOUR

1. In a large bowl, or in the bowl of a stand mixer fitted with the dough hook, sprinkle the yeast over the warm water. Stir in the warm milk and honey and let stand until the yeast begins to foam, about 5 minutes.

2. Stir in the oil, whole wheat flour, granola, and salt. Stir in enough of the bread flour to make a firm dough. Let the dough stand for 15 minutes to come together.

3. Knead in the mixer for 5 minutes, or turn the dough out onto a lightly floured surface and knead by hand for 10 minutes, adding flour as needed to keep the dough from sticking. Place the dough in a lightly greased bowl and turn to coat. Cover and let rise until doubled in bulk, 1 to 1½ hours.

4. Turn the dough out onto an oiled surface and shape into a round loaf about 8 inches in diameter. Place on a lightly greased baking sheet. Using a razor blade, French *lame*, or sharp kitchen knife, score the loaf to about a ½-inch depth marking 8 wedges. Cover and let rise until almost doubled in bulk, about 1 hour.

5. Preheat the oven to 375°F. Bake until a wooden skewer inserted into the center of the loaf comes out clean and dry, 30 to 40 minutes. Transfer to a rack to cool. Break into wedges to serve.

Broccoli and Cauliflower Cheddar Soup ⬤WITH Soft Rye Pretzels

BROCCOLI AND CAULIFLOWER CHEDDAR SOUP

Broccoli and cauliflower are loaded with vitamins, minerals, and fiber—putting them into the "super vegetable" category. I leave them in tiny florets in this soup, which is traditionally creamy. **MAKES 6 SERVINGS**

2 TABLESPOONS BUTTER

2 MEDIUM ONIONS, CHOPPED

1 TEASPOON CARAWAY SEEDS, CRUSHED

6 MEDIUM RUSSET (BAKING) POTATOES (ABOUT 2 POUNDS), PEELED AND CUT INTO 1-INCH CHUNKS

4 CUPS BASIC CHICKEN STOCK (PAGE 6) OR LOW-SODIUM STORE-BOUGHT

1 BAY LEAF

3 CUPS BITE-SIZE BROCCOLI FLORETS

3 CUPS BITE-SIZE CAULIFLOWER FLORETS

½ CUP HEAVY (WHIPPING) CREAM OR EVAPORATED MILK

6 OUNCES SHARP CHEDDAR CHEESE, SHREDDED

1. Melt the butter in a soup pot over medium heat. Add the onions and caraway seeds and cook until the onions are tender, about 5 minutes. Add the potatoes, stock, and bay leaf and simmer until the potatoes are tender, about 30 minutes.

2. Add the broccoli and cauliflower and simmer until just tender, about 10 minutes. Add the cream or milk and cheddar and stir until blended. Discard the bay leaf. Ladle into soup bowls and serve hot.

SOFT RYE PRETZELS

These fresh, chewy pretzels are fun to make and even better to eat. Lift the pretzels off the baking sheet gently before slipping them into the boiling water, as they can easily lose their shape. Interesting fact: the baking soda is what gives the pretzels their mahogany hue. **MAKES 12**

2½ CUPS ALL-PURPOSE FLOUR

½ CUP RYE FLOUR

1 TABLESPOON SUGAR

1 PACKAGE (¼ OUNCE) OR 1 SCANT
    TABLESPOON ACTIVE DRY YEAST

1 CUP WARM WATER (105°F TO 115°F)

1 TEASPOON SALT

¼ CUP BAKING SODA

COARSE SALT

1. In a bowl, combine ½ cup of the all-purpose flour, the rye flour, sugar, yeast, and warm water. Mix with a spoon until smooth. Let stand 15 minutes to proof the yeast.

2. In a food processor, combine the remaining 2 cups all-purpose flour and the salt. Pulse one or two times just to mix. Add the yeast mixture to the flour mixture and process until the dough spins around the bowl about 25 times. Add ¼ to ½ cup more water if necessary to make a soft and supple dough.

3. Turn the dough out onto a lightly greased work surface, shape into a ball, cover with an inverted bowl, and let rise until puffy, 15 to 30 minutes.

4. Line a baking sheet with parchment paper. Divide the dough into 12 equal parts. Shape each into a strand about 20 inches long and twist into a pretzel shape. Place on the prepared baking sheet. Let rise until puffy, about 30 minutes.

5. Preheat the oven to 400°F.

6. Combine the baking soda with 6 cups water in a large skillet and bring to a boil. Using a pancake turner, carefully lift the pretzels, one at a time, off the baking sheet and lower into the boiling water. Cook about 15 seconds. Using a slotted spoon, lift the pretzels from the water and return them to the parchment-lined baking sheet. Sprinkle lightly with coarse salt.

7. Bake the pretzels until golden, about 20 minutes. Transfer to a rack to cool. Serve warm.

Yam and Sweet Onion Soup
(WITH) Buttermilk Corn Muffins

YAM AND SWEET ONION SOUP

This smooth, simple soup can be vegetarian if you use vegetable broth in place of the chicken stock. If you use cooked yams, it is even quicker to make. I avoid using canned yams, as their flavor doesn't come close to fresh ones. Though they hail from different botanical families, yams or sweet potatoes will yield similar results here.

MAKES 6 SERVINGS

1 TABLESPOON BUTTER

1 TABLESPOON CURRY POWDER

¼ TEASPOON GROUND BLACK PEPPER

1 LARGE SWEET ONION, DICED

2 MEDIUM YAMS OR SWEET POTATOES, PEELED AND DICED

3 CUPS BASIC CHICKEN STOCK OR BASIC VEGETABLE BROTH (PAGE 6 OR 12) OR LOW-SODIUM STORE-BOUGHT

½ CUP HEAVY (WHIPPING) CREAM OR EVAPORATED MILK

1. Melt the butter in a large saucepan over medium heat. Add the curry powder, pepper, and onion. Stir until the spices are aromatic, about 5 minutes. Add the yams and stock or broth. Simmer until the vegetables are fork-tender, about 30 minutes.

2. Working in batches, transfer the soup to a blender and blend until smooth. Return to the pan. Stir in the cream or milk until thoroughly mixed. Serve hot.

BUTTERMILK CORN MUFFINS

These are definitely "Northern" corn bread muffins, as they have less cornmeal and more flour than their Southern counterparts. This proportion produces a denser, less crumbly muffin. To make a fruited corn muffin, add one cup chopped apple or one cup blueberries to the batter. **MAKES 12**

1⅓ CUPS ALL-PURPOSE FLOUR

1 CUP YELLOW CORNMEAL

2 TABLESPOONS SUGAR

1 TEASPOON BAKING SODA

½ TEASPOON SALT

1¾ CUPS BUTTERMILK OR 1¾ CUPS MILK
PLUS 2 TABLESPOONS WHITE VINEGAR

2 TABLESPOONS VEGETABLE OIL

1 EGG, BEATEN

1. Preheat the oven to 425°F. Coat 12 muffin cups with cooking spray.

2. In a large bowl, combine the flour, cornmeal, sugar, baking soda, and salt. In a small bowl, whisk together the buttermilk, oil, and egg. Add the liquid ingredients to the dry ingredients and stir just until moistened.

3. Divide the batter evenly among the muffin cups. Bake until the edges begin to brown, about 15 minutes.

Finnish Chanterelle Soup
⬤ Rye and Barley Bread

FINNISH CHANTERELLE SOUP

My husband is an avid mushroomer, having learned the art in Finland. When brilliant yellow chanterelles begin popping up in the forest near our home, we eat them almost every evening. We clean and slice them, then toss with flour and cook them in butter. Fresh sage leaves from the garden add a subtle peppery flavor, and a pinch each of ground cumin and ground coriander underscore the fragrance of the sage. There's no need for salt. Butter-and-sage-fried chanterelles go well with a chilled Chardonnay, as does this soup. **MAKES 4 SERVINGS**

½ POUND CHANTERELLES, CLEANED
    AND CHOPPED
3 TABLESPOONS ALL-PURPOSE FLOUR
2 TABLESPOONS BUTTER
1 TEASPOON SWEET PAPRIKA
4 CUPS BASIC CHICKEN STOCK (PAGE 6)
    OR LOW-SODIUM STORE-BOUGHT

1 TEASPOON DIJON MUSTARD
1 TEASPOON SZECHUAN PEPPERCORNS,
    CRUSHED (OPTIONAL)
2 TABLESPOONS ARMAGNAC, BRANDY,
    OR SHERRY
¼ CUP HEAVY (WHIPPING) CREAM

1. In a medium bowl, toss together the chanterelles and flour. Melt the butter in a heavy-bottomed 2- to 3-quart saucepan over medium heat. Add the chanterelles and cook, stirring, until they are aromatic and slightly crisp on the edges, about 2 minutes. Add the paprika and stock, increase the heat to high, and bring to a simmer. Cook, stirring occasionally, until the broth is thickened. Whisk in the mustard, peppercorns (if using), and Armagnac.

2. Using an immersion blender or a regular blender, puree the soup, leaving small chunks for texture. Add the cream and warm before serving.

RYE AND BARLEY BREAD

This is a Finnish favorite and just the right complement to the chanterelle soup. **MAKES TWO 9-INCH ROUND LOAVES**

2 PACKAGES (¼ OUNCE EACH)
    OR 2 SCANT TABLESPOONS
    ACTIVE DRY YEAST
½ CUP WARM WATER (105°F TO 115°F)
2 CUPS WARM MILK (105°F TO 115°F)
2 TABLESPOONS BUTTER, MELTED, PLUS
    ADDITIONAL MELTED BUTTER FOR
    BRUSHING THE BAKED LOAF

1 TABLESPOON MOLASSES
1½ TEASPOONS SALT
1½ TEASPOONS CRUSHED ANISE SEEDS
1½ TEASPOONS CRUSHED FENNEL SEEDS
1 CUP STONE-GROUND RYE FLOUR
1 CUP BARLEY FLOUR
2½ TO 3 CUPS UNBLEACHED
    BREAD FLOUR

1. In a large bowl, sprinkle the yeast over the warm water. Stir and let stand until the yeast looks foamy, about 5 minutes. Add the milk, butter, molasses, salt, anise seeds, and fennel seeds.

2. Gradually stir in the rye and barley flours, mixing well after each addition. Stir in the bread flour, ½ cup at a time, until the dough is stiff but still feels soft. Let the dough rest for 10 to 15 minutes. Turn the dough out onto a floured surface and knead about 10 minutes until smooth.

3. Alternatively, combine all the ingredients and mix the dough in the bowl of a stand mixer fitted with the dough hook and knead until very smooth, about 10 minutes.

4. Place the dough in a lightly greased bowl and turn to coat. Cover and let rise until doubled in bulk, 1 to 2 hours. Divide the dough into 2 equal parts and shape each into a ball. Place on a greased baking sheet or in two lightly greased 9-inch round cake pans, smooth side up. Flatten slightly and let rise again until almost doubled in bulk, about 45 minutes.

5. Preheat the oven to 375°F.

6. Prick the loaves all over with a fork. Bake until light golden brown, 40 to 45 minutes. Brush with butter while hot. Transfer to a rack to cool. Serve warm.

Ginger–Carrot Shooters
(WITH) Mini Scones

GINGER-CARROT SHOOTERS

I serve this soup as an appetizer at my annual kickoff-to-autumn party. Serve in two-ounce heatproof glasses that can be warmed before pouring the soup into them. **MAKES ABOUT 12 SHOOTER SERVINGS**

1 TABLESPOON BUTTER

1 MEDIUM CARROT, CHOPPED

2 CUPS BASIC VEGETABLE BROTH (PAGE 12) OR LOW-SODIUM STORE-BOUGHT

1 TABLESPOON ORANGE JUICE

2 TEASPOONS GRATED FRESH GINGER

SALT AND GROUND BLACK PEPPER

1. Melt the butter in a medium saucepan over low heat. Add the carrot and cook, stirring, until it begins to soften, about 8 minutes.

2. Add the broth, orange juice, and ginger and increase the heat to medium to bring the mixture to a simmer. Reduce to a low simmer and cook until the carrot is very soft, about 30 minutes.

3. Transfer the soup to a blender and puree until smooth. Season to taste with salt and pepper. Serve hot.

MINI SCONES

These little savory bites are perfect served with sips of gingery soup. **MAKES 12**

2 CUPS ALL-PURPOSE FLOUR

1 TABLESPOON BAKING POWDER

½ TEASPOON SALT

2 TABLESPOONS FINELY CHOPPED
    FRESH PARSLEY

1 TABLESPOON FINELY CHOPPED
    FRESH CHIVES

8 TABLESPOONS (1 STICK) COLD
    BUTTER, CUT INTO SMALL PIECES

⅓ TO ½ CUP MILK, PLUS ADDITIONAL
    FOR BRUSHING THE DOUGH

1. Preheat the oven to 400°F. Line a baking sheet with parchment paper.

2. In a large bowl or in a food processor, combine the flour, baking powder, salt, parsley, and chives. Add the butter to the flour mixture and pulse until the mixture resembles coarse bread crumbs. Turn the crumbs into a bowl and, stirring with a fork, gradually add enough milk to make a moist, biscuit-like dough.

3. On a floured surface, roll or pat the dough to a 2-inch thickness. Using a 1½-inch biscuit cutter, cut the dough into rounds. Or, using a vegetable cutter, cut into 12 small squares. Reroll the scraps and cut out more rounds or squares. Place on the baking sheet and brush with milk to glaze the tops. Bake until golden, 10 to 12 minutes. Serve warm.

Potato–Leek Soup
🄦 Rosemary Baguette

POTATO-LEEK SOUP
....

Serve this classic soup hot or chilled with a freshly baked Rosemary Baguette, set out with olive oil and balsamic vinegar for dipping. **MAKES 6 SERVINGS**

1 POUND LEEKS

2 BAY LEAVES

20 BLACK PEPPERCORNS

4 SPRIGS THYME

2 TABLESPOONS BUTTER

½ CUP DRY WHITE WINE

4 CUPS BASIC CHICKEN STOCK (PAGE 6)
    OR LOW-SODIUM STORE-BOUGHT

6 MEDIUM BOILING POTATOES (ABOUT
    1½ POUNDS), PEELED AND DICED

1½ TEASPOONS SALT

¾ TEASPOON GROUND WHITE PEPPER

½ CUP HEAVY (WHIPPING) CREAM

2 TABLESPOONS SNIPPED FRESH CHIVES

1. Wash and trim the dark green portions of the leeks. Using two of the largest and longest leek leaves, make a bouquet garni by folding the two leaves crisscrossed around the bay leaves, peppercorns, and thyme. Tie into a bundle with kitchen twine and set aside.

2. With a sharp knife, cut the white part of the leeks lengthwise and rinse well under cold running water to remove grit and sand. Slice thinly and set aside.

3. Melt the butter in a large soup pot over medium heat. Add the sliced leeks and cook until wilted, about 5 minutes. Add the wine and bring to a boil. Add the bouquet garni, stock, potatoes, salt, and white pepper. Bring to a boil; then reduce to a simmer and cook until the potatoes are fork-tender, about 30 minutes.

4. Remove the bouquet garni and, using an immersion blender or working in batches in a regular blender, puree the soup. Stir in the cream and taste and adjust the seasoning. Serve garnished with the chives.

ROSEMARY BAGUETTE

To get a nice, crisp crust on your baguette, spray the risen loaf with water before baking. If the dough is dry and "hard," add water one tablespoon at a time until the dough is soft and smooth. **MAKES 2 LOAVES**

3 CUPS BREAD FLOUR

1 PACKAGE (¼ OUNCE) OR 1 SCANT
    TABLESPOON ACTIVE DRY YEAST

1¼ CUPS WARM WATER (120°F TO 130°F)

1½ TEASPOONS SALT

2 TABLESPOONS FRESH
    ROSEMARY LEAVES

1. In a medium bowl, combine 1½ cups of the flour, the yeast, and the warm water. Stir until smooth. Set aside until the mixture begins to proof and bubble, about 10 minutes.

2. In a food processor, combine the remaining 1½ cups flour and the salt and pulse just to blend. Add the proofed dough to the bowl and process until the dough spins around about 25 times. Add the rosemary and process just until the leaves are mixed into the dough.

3. Turn the dough (it should be fairly soft) out onto a floured work surface. Invert a bowl over the dough and let rise until doubled in bulk, about 1 hour.

4. Preheat the oven to 475°F.

5. Dust two baking sheets with flour. Divide the dough into two pieces and shape each into a 19- to 20-inch-long baguette. Place the loaves diagonally on the baking sheets. Using a razor blade, French *lame*, or sharp knife, slash the loaves diagonally along the length of the baguette 5 or 6 times. Spray generously with water. Bake each loaf, one at a time, until golden, about 20 minutes.

Sweet Corn–Onion Shooters ⓦ Pine Nut and Anise Seed Breadsticks

SWEET CORN-ONION SHOOTERS

Instead of finger foods and appetizers, serve this creamy sweet corn soup in two-ounce shot glasses and pass a tray of aromatic breadsticks. You can make the soup a day in advance and heat or bring it to room temperature just before serving. It is also delicious chilled. **MAKES 24 SHOOTER SERVINGS**

1 TABLESPOON OLIVE OIL

1 LARGE SWEET ONION, COARSELY CHOPPED (ABOUT 2 CUPS)

2½ CUPS FRESH OR THAWED FROZEN WHOLE-KERNEL CORN

6 CUPS WATER

SALT

FRESHLY GRATED NUTMEG

1. Place a 4- to 5-quart soup pot over medium-low heat and add the oil. Add the onion and cook, stirring occasionally, until the onion is softened but not browned, about 10 minutes.

2. Add the corn and water. Increase the heat to medium and stir occasionally until the soup is simmering. Cover and cook until the onion and corn are soft, about 30 minutes.

3. Working in batches, transfer the soup to a blender and process until extremely smooth. For an even finer texture, pass the soup through a fine-mesh sieve. Season to taste with salt. Ladle the soup into small cups or shot glasses, sprinkle on the nutmeg, and serve.

PINE NUT AND ANISE SEED BREADSTICKS

A food processor makes fast work of this dough, which produces beautiful sticks studded throughout with rich pine nuts. **MAKES 32**

1 PACKAGE (¼ OUNCE) OR 1 SCANT
    TABLESPOON ACTIVE DRY YEAST
1 TABLESPOON SUGAR
½ TEASPOON ANISE SEEDS
1 CUP WARM WATER (105°F TO 115°F)
2¼ CUPS ALL-PURPOSE FLOUR

1 TEASPOON SALT
¼ CUP EXTRA-VIRGIN OLIVE OIL
⅔ CUP PINE NUTS OR SLIVERED ALMONDS
1 EGG, BEATEN
2 TABLESPOONS KOSHER SALT

1. In a small bowl, combine the yeast, sugar, anise seeds, and warm water and let stand until bubbly, about 5 minutes.

2. In a food processor, combine the flour, salt, and oil. Pulse until mixed, 4 to 5 times. Add the yeast mixture and process until the dough comes together in a ball and spins around the bowl 25 times. Add the nuts and process just until the nuts are incorporated into the dough. Let the dough stand, covered, in the work bowl for about 30 minutes.

3. Turn the dough out onto a floured work surface and divide in half. Divide each half into 16 equal parts and shape each part into a rope about 6 inches long. Place the ropes about 1 inch apart on greased baking sheets. Cover loosely with a towel and let stand in a warm place until doubled in bulk, about 30 minutes.

4. Preheat the oven to 300°F.

5. Brush the breadsticks with the beaten egg and sprinkle with the kosher salt. Bake until crisp, 25 to 30 minutes. Transfer to racks to cool.

Curried Pumpkin Soup
WITH Peppered Cheese Bread

CURRIED PUMPKIN SOUP

This soup looks pretty served in a hollowed-out pumpkin shell, especially if you can find mini pumpkins for individual servings. **MAKES 6 SERVINGS**

2 TABLESPOONS BUTTER

2 TEASPOONS CURRY POWDER

1 LARGE ONION, CHOPPED

1 LARGE CARROT, SHREDDED

2 CUPS BASIC CHICKEN STOCK (PAGE 6)
OR LOW-SODIUM STORE-BOUGHT

2 CUPS HOMEMADE PUMPKIN PUREE
(SEE RECIPE) OR 1 CAN (15 OUNCES)
UNSWEETENED PUMPKIN PUREE

2 CUPS HALF-AND-HALF

½ TEASPOON SALT

¼ TEASPOON GROUND WHITE PEPPER

¼ CUP SOUR CREAM

TOASTED SUNFLOWER SEEDS

1. Heat the butter in a heavy soup pot over medium heat. Add the curry powder, onion, and carrot. Cook, stirring, until the vegetables are soft, about 10 minutes. Add the stock and simmer, uncovered, for 10 minutes. Transfer to a blender or food processor and process until smooth.

2. Return the mixture to the soup pot and stir in the pumpkin, half-and-half, salt, and white pepper. Heat over medium heat to serving temperature. Scoop into soup bowls or pumpkin shells. Top with sour cream and sunflower seeds.

Cooking Fresh Pumpkin

To cook fresh pumpkin, split a pumpkin in half and scoop out the seeds and fiber. Preheat the oven to 350°F. Cover a rimmed baking sheet with foil and coat with cooking spray. Place the seeded pumpkin halves cut side down on the pan. Bake until the pumpkin is tender enough to pierce with a fork, about 1 hour. Remove from the oven and cool. Scoop the flesh out of the pumpkin and puree in a food processor. Measure out what you need to use and freeze the remainder in 2-cup amounts in resealable freezer bags.

PEPPERED CHEESE BREAD

This bread, while perfect as an accompaniment to the soup, can double as an hors d'oeuvre, topped with hummus or small pieces of meat or cheese. **MAKES 2 LOAVES**

3 CUPS ALL-PURPOSE FLOUR

1 PACKAGE (¼ OUNCE) OR 1 SCANT TABLESPOON ACTIVE DRY YEAST

1 TABLESPOON SUGAR

1¼ CUPS WARM WATER (120°F TO 130°F)

⅓ CUP SHREDDED SHARP CHEDDAR CHEESE

2 TABLESPOONS FRESHLY GRATED PARMESAN CHEESE

2 TABLESPOONS BUTTER, AT ROOM TEMPERATURE

1 TEASPOON SALT

½ TEASPOON TABASCO SAUCE

¼ TEASPOON CAYENNE OR BLACK PEPPER

OLIVE OR VEGETABLE OIL

1. In a small bowl, combine 1 cup of the flour, the yeast, sugar, and warm water. Stir until blended and set aside until the mixture has begun to bubble and rise, about 10 minutes.

2. In a food processor, combine the remaining flour, cheddar cheese, Parmesan cheese, butter, salt, Tabasco sauce, and pepper and pulse just until blended. Add the yeast mixture and process until the dough comes together in a ball and spins around the bowl 25 times. If the dough seems very firm, add water 1 tablespoon at a time to make a soft and smooth dough. If the dough is too sticky, add more flour 1 tablespoon at a time.

3. Turn the dough out onto a lightly oiled board or countertop. Cover with an inverted bowl and let rise for 15 minutes.

4. Lightly grease a baking sheet. Divide the dough in half. Shape each half into a baguette 12 inches long. Place the loaves on the baking sheet 4 inches apart and brush with the oil. Let stand, covered with a towel, in a warm place until almost doubled in bulk, about 45 minutes.

5. Preheat the oven to 375°F.

6. Bake the loaves until they are golden, 20 to 22 minutes. Transfer to a rack to cool.

Mushroom Barley Soup ⬤ Cinnamon Raisin Walnut Wheat Bread

MUSHROOM BARLEY SOUP

Simple and satisfying, this earthy soup becomes vegetarian if you use water instead of the beef stock. **MAKES 8 SERVINGS**

½ CUP PEARL BARLEY

8 CUPS TWO-FOR-ONE BEEF STOCK (PAGE 9) OR LOW-SODIUM STORE-BOUGHT, OR WATER

½ TO 1 TEASPOON SALT

3 TO 4 TABLESPOONS TAMARI OR SOY SAUCE

3 TO 4 TABLESPOONS SHERRY

3 TABLESPOONS BUTTER

1 POUND MUSHROOMS, CHOPPED

1 CUP FINELY CHOPPED ONIONS

2 CLOVES GARLIC, MINCED

GROUND BLACK PEPPER

1. In a saucepan, combine the barley and stock or water and cook over medium heat until tender, 45 to 50 minutes. Add the salt, tamari, and sherry.

2. Melt the butter in a skillet over medium heat. Add the mushrooms, onions, and garlic and cook, stirring, until the onions are tender and the mixture is aromatic, about 15 minutes. Add the vegetable mixture, including the liquid, to the barley. Add the pepper, cover, and simmer over the lowest possible heat until the barley is cooked and the mushrooms are tender, about 20 minutes. Taste and adjust the seasoning, as desired. Serve hot.

CINNAMON RAISIN WALNUT WHEAT BREAD

Cinnamon enhances the whole wheat flavor in this bread, while raisins and walnuts add sweetness and texture. This is great with a sharp white cheddar cheese and also makes excellent French toast. **MAKES 1 LOAF**

2 TABLESPOONS LIGHT BROWN SUGAR

1 PACKAGE (¼ OUNCE) OR 1 SCANT
    TABLESPOON ACTIVE DRY YEAST

1 TEASPOON GROUND CINNAMON

1¼ CUPS WARM WATER (105°F TO 115°F)

½ CUP WHOLE WHEAT FLOUR

1½ TEASPOONS SALT

1 TABLESPOON BUTTER,
    AT ROOM TEMPERATURE

2½ CUPS BREAD FLOUR

½ CUP RAISINS

½ CUP COARSELY CHOPPED WALNUTS

1. In the bowl of a stand mixer, combine the brown sugar, yeast, cinnamon, and warm water. Let stand until the yeast bubbles, about 5 minutes. Add the whole wheat flour, salt, and butter and mix until smooth.

2. With the mixer on low speed, gradually add the bread flour until incorporated. Turn the mixer to medium speed and knead until the dough pulls away from the sides of the bowl and feels soft, pliable, and smooth, about 10 minutes. Add the raisins and nuts and mix until just incorporated.

3. Place the dough in a large greased bowl, turn to coat, cover, and let rise until doubled in bulk, about 1 hour.

4. Punch the dough down and shape into a round loaf. Place on a lightly greased baking sheet. Cover and let rise until almost doubled in bulk, about 45 minutes.

5. Preheat the oven to 375°F.

6. Brush or spray the loaf with water and dust lightly with additional flour. Using a razor blade, French *lame,* or sharp knife, slash across the top of the loaf in two or three places. Bake until a wooden skewer inserted into the center of the loaf comes out clean and dry, about 40 minutes. Transfer to a rack to cool.

Wild Rice and Mushroom Soup
(WITH) No-Knead Whole Wheat Bread

WILD RICE AND MUSHROOM SOUP

Wild rice is actually not rice at all but the seed of a grass that grows in the water-flooded paddies of Minnesota's northern lakes, where it is a staple in the diet of the Native Americans who live there. It is probably more closely related to barley than to rice. To make this a vegetarian soup, replace the chicken stock with vegetable broth.

MAKES 6 SERVINGS

½ CUP WILD RICE

1½ CUPS WATER

3 TABLESPOONS BUTTER

1 SMALL LEEK, WELL WASHED AND CHOPPED

½ POUND MUSHROOMS, PREFERABLY CREMINI, SLICED

¼ CUP ALL-PURPOSE FLOUR

4 CUPS BASIC CHICKEN STOCK (PAGE 6) OR LOW-SODIUM STORE-BOUGHT

1 CUP HEAVY (WHIPPING) CREAM

2 TABLESPOONS DRY SHERRY

3 ROMA (PLUM) TOMATOES, DICED

6 TABLESPOONS CHOPPED FRESH CILANTRO OR PARSLEY

1. Rinse the wild rice in hot tap water three times. In a medium saucepan, combine the rice and water. Bring to a boil, reduce to a simmer, cover, and cook until the rice is tender, 35 to 45 minutes.

2. Melt the butter in a medium saucepan over medium heat. Add the leek and mushrooms and cook until the leek is soft, 3 to 5 minutes. Add the flour and cook, stirring, for 2 minutes. Stir in the stock, increase the heat, and bring to a boil, stirring until thickened.

3. Add the cooked wild rice, cream, and sherry, stirring until heated through. Serve hot, topped with the tomatoes and cilantro or parsley.

NO-KNEAD WHOLE WHEAT BREAD

Honey brings out the grainy flavor of whole wheat flour. To serve, cut the loaf into wedges and split the wedges horizontally. This bread makes great sandwiches too.

MAKES 1 LOAF

1 PACKAGE (¼ OUNCE) OR 1 SCANT
TABLESPOON ACTIVE DRY YEAST
1¼ CUPS WARM WATER (105°F TO 115°F)
2 TABLESPOONS HONEY

1 TABLESPOON SOFT BUTTER OR OIL,
PLUS ADDITIONAL MELTED BUTTER
TO BRUSH ON THE BAKED LOAF
½ CUP WHOLE WHEAT FLOUR
1 TEASPOON SALT
1½ CUPS UNBLEACHED BREAD FLOUR

1. In a large bowl, sprinkle the yeast over the warm water and stir in the honey. Let stand until the mixture begins to foam, about 5 minutes.

2. Stir in the butter or oil, whole wheat flour, and salt and beat until well blended. Stir in the bread flour, ½ cup at a time, and beat with a wooden spoon until smooth.

3. Lightly grease a baking sheet. Turn the dough out onto the sheet and shape into a round about 8 inches in diameter. Let rise for 30 minutes.

4. Preheat the oven to 400°F.

5. Bake until the center of the loaf springs back when touched or until a wooden skewer inserted into the center comes out clean and dry, 20 to 25 minutes. Brush the top of the loaf with melted butter. Transfer to a rack to cool. Serve warm.

Roasted Parsnip Root Vegetable Soup WITH Whole Grain Crackers

ROASTED PARSNIP ROOT VEGETABLE SOUP

I am quite fond of root vegetables, likely because I grew up eating them. They grow well in cold climates, so they were abundant in Minnesota. This is a perfect soup for a chilly autumn evening and is perfect paired with toothsome whole-grain rye crackers. **MAKES 8 SERVINGS**

1 POUND PARSNIPS, PEELED AND CUT
   INTO ½-INCH PIECES

1½ POUNDS CELERIAC (CELERY ROOT),
   PEELED AND CUT INTO
   ½-INCH CUBES

1 LARGE YELLOW POTATO, SCRUBBED
   AND CUT INTO 1-INCH CUBES

2 LARGE CARROTS, CUT INTO
   1-INCH PIECES

2 LEEKS (WHITE PARTS ONLY), WELL
   WASHED AND THINLY SLICED

2 CLOVES GARLIC, MINCED

1 LARGE ONION, THINLY SLICED

1 TABLESPOON CANOLA OR OLIVE OIL

1 CUP PEARL BARLEY

8 CUPS BASIC VEGETABLE BROTH OR
   BASIC CHICKEN STOCK (PAGE 12 OR 6)
   OR LOW-SODIUM STORE-BOUGHT

4 CUPS WATER

2 BAY LEAVES

12 OUNCES FRESH BABY SPINACH LEAVES

FRESHLY GRATED NUTMEG TO TASTE

SALT AND GROUND BLACK PEPPER

1. Preheat the oven to 375°F.

2. In a large bowl, toss the parsnips, celeriac, potato, carrots, leeks, garlic, and onion with the oil. Spread on a rimmed baking sheet and roast until the vegetables are tender, about 20 minutes.

3. In a large soup pot, combine the roasted vegetables, barley, broth or stock, water, and bay leaves. Simmer until the barley is cooked, 1½ to 2 hours. Stir in the spinach and nutmeg and simmer for 5 minutes longer. Season to taste with salt and pepper and more nutmeg, if desired.

WHOLE GRAIN CRACKERS

I like to keep a supply of these crackers on hand for a quick snack topped with a slice of Emmentaler or Swiss cheese. **MAKES 24**

1 PACKAGE (¼ OUNCE) OR 1 SCANT
    TABLESPOON ACTIVE DRY YEAST

1 TEASPOON SUGAR

¼ CUP WARM WATER (105°F TO 115°F)

1 CUP ALL-PURPOSE FLOUR

½ CUP MILK

1 CUP COARSE RYE FLOUR OR WHOLE
    WHEAT FLOUR

½ CUP ROLLED OATS, PLUS ADDITIONAL
    FOR COATING

½ TEASPOON SALT

2 TEASPOONS UNSALTED BUTTER,
    AT ROOM TEMPERATURE

MELTED BUTTER, FOR BRUSHING

1. In a medium bowl, sprinkle the yeast and sugar over the warm water. Stir and let stand until foamy, about 5 minutes. Stir in the all-purpose flour and milk and beat until smooth. Add the rye or whole wheat flour, oats, salt, and soft butter. Mix until a stiff but pliable dough forms.

2. Place the dough in a lightly greased bowl, turn to coat, cover with a towel, and let rise in a warm place until doubled in bulk, about 1 hour.

3. Preheat the oven to 400°F. Lightly oil two baking sheets.

4. Divide the dough in half and shape each into a ball. Roll the ball in oats to coat. Place a ball of dough on each of the prepared baking sheets and, with a rolling pin, roll each into a rectangle about 15 × 12 inches.

5. Using a pizza cutter, score each rectangle of dough into 5 × 3-inch rectangles. Pierce each rectangle about 3 times with a fork. Bake until lightly browned and crisp, 12 to 15 minutes. Remove from the oven and brush with melted butter. Return any rectangles to the oven if they are not crisp, watching carefully so they do not get too brown. Transfer to racks to cool.

WINTER

**To feel safe and warm on a cold wet night,
all you really need is soup.**

–LAURIE COLWIN

Here in northern Minnesota, winter begins with the first snow, which can be as early as late October. Although the season officially starts in late December, there's nothing like a soft blanket of the white stuff to fuel a desire to get cozy by a fire while a pot of soup simmers on the stove and a fragrant loaf of bread bakes in the oven. Because the cold months extend beyond a calendar winter here, we have had to learn to embrace the snow and cold. Minnesotans partake in every ice and snow sport imaginable: ice fishing, racing, hockey, skating, and sculpture as well as cross-country skiing. In fact, the wonderful network of trails near our home features a little warming hut where anyone can take a break and sip something hot to warm up. For me, that little cabin in the woods sums up everything that is great about winter soups and breads: They invite casual, cozy gatherings. Indeed, they can easily form relaxing menus for the red-letter winter holidays. For this chapter, I've drawn inspiration from just about everywhere and feature ingredients that are true to the season: root vegetables, dried beans, peas, and grains augmented by ingredients tucked away in the freezer or preserved from summer's haul and set on the pantry shelf. On Christmas Eve, the Swedes serve a "dip in the kettle" soup along with rye dipping bread. Traditionally, it was served as an early afternoon snack while the

Christmas ham baked in the oven. The family gathered in the kitchen and swabbed chunks of bread into the roasting pan juices. Today it is more likely to be served as a first course with Christmas dinner. In some Scandinavian families, Christmas Eve is a time for a very simple meal of fruit soup served over rice pudding.

In New England, oyster stew is traditionally served on Christmas Eve. I've included my version here, an Oyster Soup (page 202) served with Brown Bread Muffins (page 203), another twist on a classic New England offering, brown bread. Indeed, many of the combinations in this chapter are inspired by holiday traditions. In Europe and South America, lentils symbolize wealth and prosperity because of their coinlike appearance, so lentil soup, often with sausage, is common on the New Year's Day menu. It is served with Ezekiel bread, which its namesake lived on while he was in the desert for two years, and the combination seems an auspicious way to celebrate new beginnings. In the South, the New Year's menu must include black-eyed peas, greens, and cornbread for similar reasons: The gold of the corn represents wealth. With that tradition in mind, I have included a menu for Southern Prosperity Soup (page 206) served with Johnnycake (page 207). But don't wait for the last day of December to make it. A hearty, warm soup makes any winter day a red-letter day.

Spicy Black Bean Soup
⬤ High-Protein Health Bread

SPICY BLACK BEAN SOUP
....

This delicious, healthy combination is low in fat and high in protein—perfect for lunch or supper following an afternoon in the cold. Consider this soup and bread combination for a casual winter party. I tend to make it a day in advance. It tastes better the next day. **MAKES 12 TO 16 SERVINGS**

2 CUPS COOKED BLACK BEANS
    (SEE "COOKING DRIED BEANS,"
    PAGE 196)

1 TABLESPOON COCONUT OR
    CANOLA OIL

1 MEDIUM ONION, FINELY DICED

2 ANAHEIM OR POBLANO CHILES,
    SEEDED AND DICED (**CAUTION** USE
    PLASTIC GLOVES WHEN HANDLING
    CHILE PEPPERS.)

1 CUP FINELY DICED CELERY

1 TEASPOON RED-PEPPER FLAKES,
    OR TO TASTE

2 TEASPOONS GROUND CUMIN

1 TEASPOON DRIED ROSEMARY

1 CAN (14.5 OUNCES) DICED TOMATOES

2 CUPS TOMATO JUICE

3 QUARTS BASIC CHICKEN STOCK OR
    BASIC VEGETABLE BROTH
    (PAGE 6 OR 12) OR LOW-SODIUM
    STORE-BOUGHT

3 CUPS DICED VEGETABLES (GREEN
    PEPPER, RED PEPPER, SCALLIONS OR
    GREEN ONIONS, ZUCCHINI, CARROTS)

LEMON JUICE

SALT AND GROUND BLACK PEPPER

LIGHT SOUR CREAM

FRESH SALSA (MILD, MEDIUM, OR HOT)

CHOPPED FRESH CILANTRO

1. Mash the beans with a potato masher and set aside.

2. Heat the oil in a large, heavy soup pot over medium heat. Add the onion, chiles, and celery. Cook, stirring, until the vegetables are softened, about 15 minutes. Add the beans, pepper flakes, cumin, and rosemary. Stir in the tomatoes (with their juice), tomato juice, stock or broth, and diced vegetables. Bring to a simmer and cook for 30 minutes to meld the flavors.

3. Season to taste with lemon juice, salt, and black pepper. Ladle into soup bowls and garnish with the sour cream, salsa, and cilantro.

HIGH-PROTEIN HEALTH BREAD

A popular bread among dieters, this is delicious no matter what kind of regimen you follow. Cut it into thin slices and top with sharp cheddar or aged Gouda cheese. **MAKES TWO 8½ × 4½-INCH LOAVES**

¼ CUP HONEY

2 PACKAGES (¼ OUNCE EACH) OR
  2 SCANT TABLESPOONS ACTIVE
  DRY YEAST

3 CUPS WARM WATER (105°F TO 115°F)

3 CUPS WHOLE WHEAT FLOUR

¾ CUP NONFAT DRY MILK POWDER

½ CUP SOY FLOUR OR GARBANZO
  BEAN (CHICKPEA) FLOUR

¼ CUP WHEAT GERM

2 TEASPOONS SALT

2 TABLESPOONS CANOLA OIL

3 TO 4 CUPS UNBLEACHED BREAD
  FLOUR OR ALL-PURPOSE FLOUR

1. In a large bowl or in the bowl of a stand mixer, combine the honey, yeast, and warm water. Stir and let stand until the yeast foams, about 5 minutes. Add the whole wheat flour and beat well. Add the dry milk, soy or garbanzo bean flour, wheat germ, salt, and oil and stir to combine. Add the bread flour 1 cup at a time, beating well after each addition to make a soft but stiff dough. Turn out onto a lightly floured surface. Invert the bowl over the dough and let rest 15 minutes. During this time, the dough will come together, making it easier to knead.

2. Knead the dough about 15 minutes by hand, or transfer to the bowl of a stand mixer fitted with the dough hook and knead for 10 minutes. Place the dough in a lightly oiled bowl, turn to coat, cover, and let rise in a warm place until doubled in bulk, about 1 hour.

3. Coat a work surface lightly with oil or cooking spray. Turn the dough out onto the work surface, knead to punch out the air, and divide in half. Shape each into a loaf and place in greased 8½ × 4½-inch loaf pans. Let rise until almost doubled in bulk, about 45 minutes.

4. Preheat the oven to 350°F.

5. Bake until a wooden skewer inserted into the center of a loaf comes out clean and dry, 45 to 50 minutes. Transfer to racks to cool.

Cooking Dried Beans

Dried beans can be a bit off-putting to those of us who prefer to be spontaneous. And how best to cook them can be a polarizing topic. Some prefer to soak them overnight. Others use the quick soak method. And still others swear by the speed of the pressure cooker. To my mind, it depends on how much time you have. All the methods have virtues.

The Overnight Soak Method

Dried beans cook more evenly when they are soaked overnight. To do this, wash and pick over the beans, and cover with about 3 times their volume of cold water. Soak at least 8 hours. Drain and cook by adding fresh water to cover and simmering until the beans are tender, 2 to 2½ hours.

Quick Soak Method

Rinse beans in cold water, put them in a large pot with about 3 inches of cold water over them, and bring to a boil. Just as the beans come to a boil, remove from the heat and let sit for 1 hour. Drain. At this point, the beans are ready to cook.

Quick Cook Method

If you don't have time to soak the beans overnight, put them in a large soup pot and add 8 cups boiling water. Bring to a simmer and continue to simmer until the beans are tender, about 2 hours.

Pressure Cooker Method

If you're short on time, you can bypass the presoak by using a pressure cooker. Directions vary among pressure cookers, so follow the instructions that come with yours for best results.

Tips

- Despite their constitution, dried beans don't last forever. It's best to use them within a year. While older beans are okay to be cooked and eaten, the cooking times tend to be longer as they dry out more with age.
- A pound of uncooked dried beans measures about 2 cups.
- Use 3 cups of water per cup of dried beans for soaking.
- Beans triple in volume when soaked and cooked. So 1 cup dried beans yields 3 cups cooked, and 1 pound dried beans yields 6 cups cooked.
- One pound of dried beans makes about 12 servings of bean soup.
- A 16-ounce can of cooked beans yields about 2 cups.

Dutch Cheese Soup
WITH Oatmeal Rusks

DUTCH CHEESE SOUP

Deliciously rich, this Dutch soup is reminiscent of cheese fondue. The slightly unusual method of preparation here ensures a satiny-smooth texture. To reduce fat and calories, replace regular milk and cream with fat-free milk. You can substitute other well-aged semi-hard cheeses such as Gruyère, Swiss, or cheddar for the Gouda. **MAKES 6 SERVINGS**

2 CUPS SHREDDED AGED
  GOUDA CHEESE
¼ CUP ALL-PURPOSE FLOUR
4 TABLESPOONS (½ STICK) BUTTER
2 CUPS LIGHT CREAM, HEATED TO
  VERY WARM

2 CUPS WHOLE OR 2% MILK, HEATED
  TO VERY WARM
½ TEASPOON WORCESTERSHIRE SAUCE
3 DROPS OF TABASCO SAUCE
SALT
PAPRIKA

1. Put the cheese in a blender and set aside. In a 2-quart saucepan, stir the flour and butter together and cook over low heat for 2 minutes, stirring. Do not let the mixture brown. Slowly stir in the cream and milk and cook, covered, stirring occasionally, until the soup is the texture of heavy cream. Turn the blender on low and slowly pour the hot mixture into the cheese until the mixture begins to froth.

2. Pour the soup back into the saucepan and heat, stirring constantly, until it is hot but not boiling. Add the Worcestershire sauce, Tabasco sauce, and salt to taste. Pour into individual soup bowls or mugs and sprinkle with paprika. Serve right away.

OATMEAL RUSKS

Rusks are twice-baked breads, in this case oatmeal rolls that are split and baked a second time until crisp. You might wish to serve half of the fresh rolls at dinner and make the rest into dried rusks, which will keep for weeks if stored in an airtight container in a cool place. **MAKES 16**

1 PACKAGE (¼ OUNCE) OR 1 SCANT
   TABLESPOON ACTIVE DRY YEAST
¼ CUP WARM WATER (105°F TO 115°F)
½ CUP WHOLE OR 2% MILK, HEATED
   TO LUKEWARM
2 TABLESPOONS FIRMLY PACKED
   LIGHT BROWN SUGAR

½ TEASPOON SALT
2 TABLESPOONS BUTTER, AT ROOM
   TEMPERATURE
1 CUP QUICK-COOKING OATS, PLUS
   EXTRA FOR THE BAKING SHEET
1½ CUPS ALL-PURPOSE FLOUR

1. In a large bowl, sprinkle the yeast over the warm water. Stir and let stand until the yeast looks foamy, about 5 minutes. Stir in the milk, brown sugar, salt, butter, and oats. Gradually stir in the flour to make a stiff but soft dough.

2. Turn the dough out onto a floured surface and knead until smooth and no longer sticky, about 5 minutes. Place the dough in a greased bowl and turn to coat. Cover and let rise in a warm place until doubled in bulk, about 1 hour.

3. Punch the dough down and divide into 8 equal pieces. Shape each piece into a ball. Coat a baking sheet with cooking spray and sprinkle with rolled oats. Place the balls of dough 2 inches apart on the baking sheet. Press down on each with the palm of your hand to flatten lightly. Cover and let rise until doubled in bulk, about 45 minutes.

4. Meanwhile, position a rack in the middle of the oven and preheat to 425°F.

5. Brush the rolls with water and, using a razor blade, French *lame*, or sharp knife, slash the tops. Bake until lightly browned, about 10 minutes. Transfer to a rack to cool.

6. To make rusks, split the rolls in half horizontally. Arrange split side up on a baking sheet. Bake at 425°F until the breads are dry but not browned, about 5 minutes. Reduce the heat to 200°F and bake until light, dry, and crisp, about 45 minutes.

Swedish Christmas Eve Soup
⬤WITH Rye Dipping Bread

SWEDISH CHRISTMAS EVE SOUP

In the United States we mark the winter solstice on December 21, but many Scandinavians celebrate the official start to winter on December 24. In Sweden, this traditional soup and bread combination, known there as *doppa i grytan* or "dip in the pot," is meant to stave off hunger as family and guests await the Christmas Eve meal, often served after Christmas Eve church services. Guests dip chunks of bread into the savory juices that ooze out of the Christmas ham as it roasts. Today this soup is often served as a first course. I've changed it a bit to suit our modern lives. If you roast a Christmas ham, you will have broth in the roasting pan, which you can use instead of the beef stock called for in this recipe. **MAKES 6 SERVINGS**

6 CUPS TWO-FOR-ONE BEEF STOCK (PAGE 9)

SALT AND GROUND WHITE PEPPER

RYE DIPPING BREAD (PAGE 201), CUT INTO LARGE CUBES

MELTED BUTTER

THINLY SLICED LEMON

1. Pour the stock into a large saucepan. Season to taste with salt and white pepper. Bring to a boil.

2. Meanwhile, toast the bread on a baking sheet under the broiler and drizzle with melted butter. Place the toasted bread cubes into individual soup bowls and ladle the hot stock over them. Garnish with lemon slices and serve.

RYE DIPPING BREAD

This is the bread that Swedes use to dip into the Christmas ham broth. The secret to its success is to be stingy with flour and to knead the dough very well, preferably in a stand mixer fitted with a dough hook. The kneaded dough should be a little soft and sticky—with almost the same feeling as touching a freshly painted wall.

MAKES 2 LOAVES

1 PACKAGE (¼ OUNCE) OR 1 SCANT TABLESPOON ACTIVE DRY YEAST

¼ CUP WARM WATER (105°F TO 115°F)

2 CUPS LIGHT RYE FLOUR

1 TABLESPOON GROUND FENNEL SEEDS

1 TABLESPOON GROUND ANISE SEEDS

1 TEASPOON SALT

2 CUPS SCALDED AND COOLED WHOLE OR 2% MILK

2 TABLESPOONS DARK MOLASSES OR BROWN SUGAR

2 TABLESPOONS BUTTER, MELTED

4 TO 4½ CUPS UNBLEACHED BREAD FLOUR

1. In a large bowl, sprinkle the yeast over the warm water. Stir and let stand until the yeast looks foamy, about 5 minutes.

2. Add the rye flour, fennel seeds, anise seeds, salt, milk, molasses, and butter to the yeast mixture. Beat with a wooden spoon until smooth. Add the bread flour 1 cup at a time to make a stiff dough. Turn the dough out onto a lightly floured board. Invert the bowl over the dough and let rest for 15 minutes.

3. Knead, adding flour as necessary until the dough has a smooth surface, about 10 minutes. Place the dough in a lightly greased bowl and turn to coat. Cover and let rise in a warm place until doubled in bulk, about 2 hours.

4. Lightly coat a work surface with cooking spray or oil. Turn the dough out onto the work surface and cut the dough in half. Shape each half into a fat, round loaf. Place on a lightly greased baking sheet, cover, and let rise until doubled in bulk, 45 to 60 minutes.

5. Preheat the oven to 350°F.

6. Bake until a wooden skewer inserted into the center of the loaf comes out clean and dry, about 25 minutes. Transfer to a rack to cool.

Oyster Soup
⬤with Brown Bread Muffins

OYSTER SOUP

In New England, this soup is made with fresh oysters, which are easy to obtain there. But that's not always the case in other parts of the country, so I used canned oysters here. This soup takes no time to make, especially if you have all of the ingredients on hand. Use one quart of half-and-half in place of the milk and cream, if desired. **MAKES 4 TO 6 SERVINGS**

2 TABLESPOONS BUTTER

1 SMALL ONION, MINCED

2 CANS (8 OUNCES EACH) OYSTERS,
    LIQUID RESERVED

2 CUPS WHOLE OR 2% MILK

2 CUPS HEAVY (WHIPPING) CREAM

Melt the butter in a 4- to 5-quart pot over medium-high heat. Add the onion and cook until soft, about 5 minutes. Do not let the onion brown. Add the oysters with their juices, bring to a boil, and cook 3 minutes. Reduce to a simmer and stir in the milk and cream. Cook until heated completely through, 5 to 10 minutes.

BROWN BREAD MUFFINS

You can bake this batter in a 9 × 5-inch loaf pan and increase the baking time to 1 hour. Allow the bread to cool before slicing. **MAKES 12**

2 CUPS BUTTERMILK

2 CUPS WHOLE WHEAT FLOUR

⅔ CUP UNBLEACHED ALL-PURPOSE FLOUR

½ CUP PACKED LIGHT BROWN SUGAR

2 TEASPOONS BAKING SODA

1 TEASPOON GROUND CINNAMON

½ TEASPOON SALT

¾ CUP GOLDEN OR DARK RAISINS (OPTIONAL)

1. Preheat the oven to 350°F. Grease 12 cups of a muffin tin.

2. In a large bowl, combine the buttermilk, whole wheat and all-purpose flours, brown sugar, baking soda, cinnamon, salt, and raisins (if using) and stir until blended. Fill the muffin cups two-thirds full. Bake until a wooden pick inserted into the center of a muffin comes out clean, 25 to 30 minutes.

New Year's Good Luck Lentil Soup (WITH) Ezekiel Bread

NEW YEAR'S GOOD LUCK LENTIL SOUP

Ancient Egyptians used lentils as an aphrodisiac. In other cultures, they are considered symbols of longevity, wealth, and vision (in fact, the Latin word for *lentil* is lens). What a perfect soup to serve on the eve of a new year! **MAKES 8 TO 10 SERVINGS**

2 CUPS LENTILS, PREFERABLY PINK, RINSED AND PICKED OVER

8 CUPS WATER

4 SLICES BACON, CUT INTO ½-INCH PIECES

1 MEDIUM ONION, SLICED

½ CUP CHOPPED CELERY

¼ CUP CHOPPED CARROTS

3 TABLESPOONS CHOPPED FRESH PARSLEY

1 CLOVE GARLIC, MINCED

2 TEASPOONS SALT

1 TEASPOON DRIED OREGANO

¼ TEASPOON GROUND BLACK PEPPER

2 CUPS CHOPPED FRESH TOMATOES OR 1 CAN (14.5 OUNCES) DICED TOMATOES

2 TABLESPOONS RED WINE VINEGAR

1. In a 5-quart soup pot, combine the lentils, water, bacon, onion, celery, carrots, parsley, garlic, salt, oregano, and pepper. Cover and bring to a simmer over medium heat. Cook for 1½ hours.

2. Add the tomatoes and vinegar and simmer until the lentils are tender, about 30 minutes. Taste and adjust the seasoning, as desired. Serve hot.

EZEKIEL BREAD

The ingredients for this bread are described in the Bible in Ezekiel 4:9. It contains several whole grain flours, which are readily available at whole foods stores and in some supermarkets. While the original bread contains red kidney beans, I eliminated them here. I used to grind the lentils into flour, but in this version I cook them to make the bread a little easier to mix. **MAKES 2 LOAVES**

½ CUP GREEN, PINK, OR BROWN
    LENTILS, RINSED AND PICKED OVER
8 CUPS WATER
1 PACKAGE (¼ OUNCE) OR 1 SCANT
    TABLESPOON ACTIVE DRY YEAST
2¾ CUPS WARM WATER (105°F TO 115°F)
5 TABLESPOONS OLIVE OIL

1 TABLESPOON SALT
1 TABLESPOON HONEY
4 CUPS WHOLE WHEAT FLOUR
1 CUP BARLEY FLOUR
1 CUP SOY FLOUR
¼ CUP MILLET FLOUR
¼ CUP RYE FLOUR

1. In a saucepan, combine the lentils and water. Bring to a simmer over medium heat and cook until they are falling apart, about 2 hours. Drain and let cool. Mash with a fork and set aside.

2. In a large bowl, sprinkle the yeast over ¼ cup of the warm water. Stir and let stand until the yeast looks foamy, about 5 minutes. Add the remaining 2½ cups warm water to the yeast along with the oil, salt, honey, and 1 cup of the whole wheat flour. Mix in the mashed lentils, barley flour, soy flour, millet flour, and rye flour. Add more whole wheat flour, ½ cup at a time, beating well after each addition, until a stiff dough has formed.

3. Turn the dough out onto a lightly floured surface and knead until smooth, about 10 minutes. Place dough in an oiled bowl and turn to coat. Cover and let rise in a warm place until doubled in bulk, about 1 hour.

4. Turn the risen dough out onto a lightly floured surface and divide in half. Shape each half into a smooth, round loaf. Place on a lightly greased baking sheet, cover, and let rise until about doubled in bulk, 45 minutes to 1 hour.

5. Preheat the oven to 350°F.

6. Bake until a wooden skewer inserted into the center of a loaf comes out clean and dry, about 1 hour. Transfer to racks to cool.

Southern Prosperity Soup
WITH Johnnycake

SOUTHERN PROSPERITY SOUP

Follow Southern tradition and serve this soup on New Year's Day to ensure prosperity for the coming year. You can use canned beans in this recipe if you don't have the time to cook dried black-eyed peas or beans. **MAKES 8 SERVINGS**

1 TABLESPOON OLIVE OIL

1 LARGE ONION, FINELY DICED

2 CLOVES GARLIC, MINCED

2 RIBS CELERY, FINELY DICED

1 CUP CHOPPED SPINACH

2 CANS (15 OUNCES EACH) BLACK-EYED
   PEAS, RINSED AND DRAINED, OR
   4 CUPS COOKED DRIED BEANS (SEE
   "COOKING DRIED BEANS," PAGE 196)

4 CUPS BASIC CHICKEN STOCK (PAGE 6)
   OR LOW-SODIUM STORE-BOUGHT

2 CUPS CUBED COOKED CORNED BEEF

½ TEASPOON DRIED THYME

SALT AND GROUND BLACK PEPPER

1. Heat the oil in a 5-quart pot over medium heat. Add the onion, garlic, celery, and spinach and cook, stirring, until the onions are soft and the spinach wilts, about 15 minutes. Add the black-eyed peas or beans, stock, corned beef, and thyme. Bring to a boil; then reduce to a simmer, cover, and cook for 45 minutes to allow the flavors to blend.

2. Remove 2 cups of the soup and puree in a blender. Return the puree to the soup and stir. Season to taste with salt and pepper. Ladle into bowls and serve.

JOHNNYCAKE

The colonists are said to have learned how to make johnnycakes from the Native Americans and called them "shawnee cakes." At some point, the name transformed into "journey cake," because, according to popular belief, the cornbread was cooked over campfires during long trips into the wilderness. In Rhode Island, the bread is spelled jonnycake and is made with white cornmeal. Today, we might just call it cornbread! **MAKES 12 SERVINGS**

1½ CUPS STONE-GROUND CORNMEAL

1½ CUPS ALL-PURPOSE FLOUR

½ CUP SUGAR

1 TEASPOON BAKING SODA

1 TEASPOON SALT

1 CUP BUTTERMILK

¾ CUP VEGETABLE OIL

2 LARGE EGGS

1. Preheat the oven to 375°F. Lightly grease a 13 × 9-inch baking pan.

2. In a medium bowl, combine the cornmeal, flour, sugar, baking soda, and salt. Add the buttermilk, oil, and eggs and stir just until blended. Do not overmix.

3. Pour the batter into the baking pan and bake just until the cake springs back when touched in the center, 25 to 30 minutes.

4. Cool; then cut into 12 pieces.

Herbed White Bean and Sausage Soup (WITH) Beer Biscuits

HERBED WHITE BEAN AND SAUSAGE SOUP

You can start this hearty, country-style soup by cooking the beans in a slow cooker before you add any of the remaining ingredients. **MAKES 6 TO 8 SERVINGS**

1 POUND DRIED GREAT NORTHERN BEANS, RINSED AND PICKED OVER

8 CUPS BOILING WATER

2 TABLESPOONS OLIVE OIL, PLUS ADDITIONAL FOR SERVING

1 POUND SWEET ITALIAN SAUSAGE, SLICED ¾-INCH THICK

1 TABLESPOON TOMATO PASTE

½ TEASPOON GROUND CUMIN

2 MEDIUM CARROTS, FINELY DICED

2 RIBS CELERY, FINELY DICED

1 ONION, CHOPPED

2 CLOVES GARLIC, FINELY CHOPPED

2 TEASPOONS KOSHER SALT

2 SPRIGS THYME

1 LARGE SPRIG ROSEMARY

1 BAY LEAF

2 TEASPOONS BALSAMIC VINEGAR, PLUS ADDITIONAL FOR SERVING

½ TEASPOON GROUND BLACK PEPPER

1. Put the beans and boiling water into a 4-quart slow cooker. Cover and cook on high until the beans are tender, 2 to 3 hours. (Note, if the beans you are using are more than a year old, this may take longer.)

2. Heat the oil in a large skillet over medium-high heat. Add the sausage and cook, turning, until browned and cooked through, about 7 minutes. Using a slotted spoon, transfer to a plate lined with a paper towel. Add the sausage, tomato paste, cumin, carrots, celery, onion, garlic, salt, thyme, rosemary, and bay leaf to the cooked beans. Reduce the heat to low and cook 2 hours, adding more water if needed to make sure the beans remain submerged.

3. Stir in the vinegar and pepper. Taste and adjust the seasonings, as desired. Ladle into warm bowls and serve drizzled with additional vinegar and olive oil.

BEER BISCUITS

Beer adds tang to these rustic biscuits—a simple combination of just five ingredients.

MAKES 18

2 CUPS ALL-PURPOSE FLOUR

1 TABLESPOON BAKING POWDER

1 TEASPOON SALT

¼ CUP VEGETABLE OIL

¾ CUP LIGHT OR DARK BEER

1. Preheat the oven to 450°F.

2. In a medium bowl, combine the flour, baking powder, and salt. Stir in the oil and beer until a stiff dough forms.

3. Turn out onto a floured board. Roll the dough out to ½-inch thickness. Using a 2-inch biscuit cutter, cut into 18 rounds, gathering and rerolling the scraps. Place the rounds on an ungreased baking sheet and bake until golden brown, 10 to 12 minutes.

Cumin and Coriander Bean Soup
WITH Black Pepper Cracker Bread

CUMIN AND CORIANDER BEAN SOUP

Cumin, coriander, and black pepper are all assertive flavors. They're perfect for combining with the mild flavor of any bean—white navy, lima beans, chickpeas, kidney beans, black beans. **MAKES 8 SERVINGS**

2 CUPS DRIED BEANS, RINSED AND PICKED OVER

2 TABLESPOONS VEGETABLE OIL

1 LARGE ONION, CHOPPED

3 CLOVES GARLIC, MINCED

1 LARGE CARROT, DICED

1 RIB CELERY, DICED

2 TABLESPOONS DRY SHERRY

1 LARGE RED OR GREEN BELL PEPPER, DICED

1½ TEASPOONS GROUND CUMIN

1 TEASPOON GROUND CORIANDER

1 TEASPOON GRATED ORANGE ZEST

6 CUPS BASIC CHICKEN STOCK OR TWO-FOR-ONE BEEF STOCK (PAGE 6 OR 9) OR STORE-BOUGHT

¼ TEASPOON GROUND BLACK PEPPER

¼ TEASPOON RED-PEPPER FLAKES

SALT

HOT COOKED WHITE OR BROWN RICE

CHOPPED FRESH CILANTRO

YOGURT OR SOUR CREAM

1. Cook the dried beans using whatever method suits your schedule (see "Cooking Dried Beans," page 196).

2. Meanwhile, in a heavy skillet, heat the oil over medium-low heat. Add the onion, garlic, carrot, celery, sherry, bell pepper, cumin, coriander, orange zest, and stock. Reduce the heat to low, cover, and steam until the vegetables are tender, about 15 minutes. Add the vegetable mixture to the cooked beans.

3. Season with the black pepper, pepper flakes, and salt to taste. Serve over rice and top with cilantro and yogurt or sour cream.

BLACK PEPPER CRACKER BREAD

Don't let anyone know how easy this bread is to make—they'll think you toiled all day! Any combination of herbs works nicely here, or if you prefer none, that's fine too. The flatbread can be made two days ahead, cooled completely, and kept in an airtight container in a cool dark place. **MAKES 8 SERVINGS**

2 CUPS ALL-PURPOSE FLOUR

1 TABLESPOON DRIED HERBS (A SINGLE HERB OR A BLEND), SUCH AS ROSEMARY, THYME, TARRAGON, OR BASIL (OPTIONAL), PLUS ADDITIONAL HERBS TO SPRINKLE ON TOP

1 TABLESPOON COARSELY CRACKED BLACK PEPPER

1½ TEASPOONS BAKING POWDER

1 TEASPOON SALT

½ TO ¾ CUP WATER

⅓ CUP OLIVE OIL, PLUS ADDITIONAL FOR BRUSHING THE DOUGH

FLAKY OR COARSE SALT

1. Position a rack in the middle of the oven with a baking stone or heavy baking sheet and preheat the oven to 450°F.

2. In a large bowl, combine the flour, herbs (if using), pepper, baking powder, and salt. Add ½ cup of the water and the oil and stir until the dough comes together. Add up to ¼ cup more water 1 tablespoon at a time, if necessary, to get a soft but firm dough.

3. Turn the dough out onto a floured surface and knead a few times until the dough is well mixed. Cover the dough with plastic wrap and let rest for 15 minutes. This will make the dough easier to roll out.

4. Divide the dough into 3 pieces. Working with 1 piece at a time (keep the other 2 pieces covered with plastic wrap to prevent drying out), place the dough on a sheet of parchment paper and roll out to a very thin round about 10 inches across. Lightly brush the top with oil and scatter small clusters of additional herbs on top. Sprinkle with salt.

5. Slide the round on the parchment paper onto the preheated stone or baking sheet, and bake until pale golden and browned in spots, 8 to 10 minutes. Transfer (discarding the parchment) to a rack to cool; then make 2 more rounds, handling one at a time on fresh sheets of parchment. Break the cooked flatbread into pieces to serve.

Black Bean Soup
with Cheese Quesadillas

BLACK BEAN SOUP

For a vegetarian soup, use vegetable broth instead of chicken stock. To save money, soak one pound of black turtle beans overnight and cook them before adding them to this soup. To save time, use canned beans. **MAKES 6 SERVINGS**

6 CUPS COOKED DRIED BLACK BEANS (SEE "COOKING DRIED BEANS," PAGE 196) OR 3 CANS (15 OUNCES EACH), UNDRAINED

2 TABLESPOONS CANOLA OR OLIVE OIL

1 LARGE SWEET ONION, CHOPPED

2 CLOVES GARLIC, CHOPPED

1 TABLESPOON CHOPPED FRESH THYME

4 CUPS BASIC CHICKEN STOCK (PAGE 6) OR LOW-SODIUM STORE-BOUGHT

2 CANS (14.5 OUNCES EACH) DICED TOMATOES OR 4 LARGE FRESH TOMATOES, DICED

2 TEASPOONS GROUND CUMIN

1 TEASPOON GROUND CORIANDER

½ TEASPOON RED-PEPPER FLAKES

SALT AND GROUND BLACK PEPPER

YOGURT

CHOPPED FRESH CILANTRO

1. If using dried beans, cook the beans as directed on page 196, reserving 1 cup of the cooking liquid.

2. Heat the oil in a soup pot over medium heat. Add the onion, garlic, and thyme and cook, stirring, until the onion is golden, about 8 minutes.

3. Add the beans (and their liquid), stock, tomatoes (with juices), cumin, coriander, and pepper flakes. Simmer the soup for 25 minutes to thicken and blend the flavors.

4. Using an immersion blender or standard blender, puree the soup until smooth. Season to taste with salt and black pepper. Serve topped with a spoonful of yogurt and a sprinkling of cilantro.

CHEESE QUESADILLAS

These make a great snack as well as an accompaniment to soup. **MAKES 6 SERVINGS**

12 FLOUR TORTILLAS (6-INCH DIAMETER)

2 CUPS TOMATO SALSA (MILD, MEDIUM, OR HOT), PLUS ADDITIONAL FOR SERVING

6 TABLESPOONS CHOPPED FRESH CILANTRO

3 CUPS SHREDDED CHEDDAR CHEESE

CORN OIL

1. Place 6 tortillas on a work surface. Top each with some of the salsa, cilantro, cheese, and then another tortilla. Brush both sides of the tortillas with corn oil.

2. Heat a nonstick skillet over medium-high heat until a drop of water sizzles on the surface. Working with one at a time, place a quesadilla in the skillet and cook until golden brown on the bottom. Turn over and cook until the second side is golden.

3. Transfer the quesadilla onto a cutting board and cut into wedges. Serve with salsa for dipping.

Italian Bean and Swiss Chard Soup
WITH Easy Italian Loaf

ITALIAN BEAN AND SWISS CHARD SOUP

Swiss chard is delicious on its own, sautéed in butter, but it's also an excellent green to combine with flavors from Italy. Orzo is a small pasta shaped like grains of unhulled barley (though most people think it resembles rice) and cooks very quickly. Like any pasta, it will thicken the soup upon standing. **MAKES 4 TO 6 SERVINGS**

½ POUND SWISS CHARD, STEMS REMOVED, WELL WASHED

6 CUPS WATER

1 TEASPOON SALT

2 TABLESPOONS OLIVE OIL

2 CLOVES GARLIC, PEELED AND SMASHED

2 FLAT ANCHOVY FILLETS, CHOPPED

2- TO 3-INCH SPRIG ROSEMARY

2 CUPS COOKED CANNELLINI, GREAT NORTHERN, OR NAVY BEANS (SEE "COOKING DRIED BEANS," PAGE 196)

2 TABLESPOONS ORZO

SALT AND GROUND BLACK PEPPER

¼ CUP FRESHLY GRATED PARMESAN CHEESE

1. In a soup pot, combine the chard, 2 cups of the water, and the salt. Cover and bring to a boil; then reduce the heat to medium and cook until tender, about 10 minutes. Drain and reserve all the cooking liquid. Coarsely chop the chard and set aside.

2. Add the oil and garlic to the cooking pot and turn the heat to medium-high. Cook, stirring, until the garlic is pale gold. Add the anchovies and rosemary and cook until fragrant. Discard the garlic and rosemary sprig.

3. Add the chard to the pot and cook, stirring, until coated with oil. Add the beans, the reserved chard cooking liquid, and the remaining 4 cups water (or enough to cover all the ingredients). Bring to a boil. Add the orzo and cook to al dente, about 5 minutes. Season to taste with salt and pepper. Ladle into soup bowls and serve topped with the Parmesan.

EASY ITALIAN LOAF

This basic yeast dough makes great focaccia and pizza too. **MAKES 1 LOAF**

1 PACKAGE (¼ OUNCE) OR 1 SCANT
  TABLESPOON ACTIVE DRY YEAST
1 TEASPOON SUGAR
1 CUP WARM WATER (105°F TO 115°F)

2 TO 2½ CUPS BREAD FLOUR
2 TABLESPOONS OLIVE OIL
1 TEASPOON SALT

1. In a large bowl, combine the yeast, sugar, and water. Let stand until the yeast begins to bubble, about 5 minutes. Add 2 cups of the flour, the oil, and salt and stir until a shaggy dough forms.

2. Transfer the dough to a food processor fitted with either a dough blade or steel blade. Process, adding more flour if necessary, until the dough forms a ball that spins around the bowl 20 to 25 times. The dough should be soft to the touch.

3. Transfer the dough back to the first bowl, cover, and let rise until doubled in bulk, 30 to 45 minutes. Lightly grease a baking sheet.

4. Turn the dough out onto a lightly floured surface and shape into a 12-inch-long oblong loaf. Place on the baking sheet. Using a razor blade, French *lame*, or sharp knife, make ¼-inch-deep slashes along the top of the loaf. Cover and let rise until almost doubled in bulk, 45 minutes to 1 hour.

5. Preheat the oven to 400°F.

6. Brush the loaf with water and bake until golden brown, 18 to 20 minutes. Transfer to a rack to cool.

Senate Bean Soup
⬤ (WITH) Molasses Wheat Loaf

SENATE BEAN SOUP

A version of this classic bean soup has been served in the U.S. Senate dining room for more than one hundred years. It can be made with navy beans or Great Northern beans. The traditional recipe calls for a cup of mashed potatoes to thicken the soup, but ⅔ cup of instant mashed potato flakes does the job too. The meatier the ham hock, the better here. **MAKES 8 SERVINGS**

3 QUARTS BASIC CHICKEN STOCK
    (PAGE 6) OR LOW-SODIUM
    STORE-BOUGHT

1 POUND DRIED NAVY BEANS OR GREAT
    NORTHERN BEANS, COOKED AND
    DRAINED (SEE "COOKING DRIED
    BEANS," PAGE 196)

1 HAM HOCK

4 TABLESPOONS (½ STICK) BUTTER

2 LARGE ONIONS, COARSELY CHOPPED

4 LARGE RIBS CELERY, CHOPPED

4 CLOVES GARLIC, CHOPPED

½ CUP DRY WHITE WINE

½ CUP CHOPPED FRESH PARSLEY

1 CUP MASHED POTATOES OR ⅔ CUP
    INSTANT MASHED POTATO FLAKES

SALT AND GROUND WHITE PEPPER

1. In a heavy-bottomed soup pot, combine the stock, cooked beans, and ham hock. Bring to a boil; then reduce to a simmer, cover, and cook for 2 hours, occasionally skimming off any foam that forms on the surface.

2. Meanwhile, heat the butter in a saucepan over medium-low heat. Add the onions, celery, and garlic and cook until the onions are slightly translucent, stirring more or less continuously, 2 to 3 minutes. Add the wine and cook until it is reduced by about half, about 2 minutes.

3. When the beans have cooked for 2 hours, add the onion mixture, parsley, and potatoes or potato flakes to the pot and simmer until the beans are tender, about 1 hour longer.

4. Remove the ham hock. Pull the meat off the bone, chop it up, and return the meat to the soup. If necessary, add more stock or water to the soup if it is too thick. Season to taste with salt and white pepper and serve.

MOLASSES WHEAT LOAF

Baked in the round, this loaf offers plenty of sweet crust for everyone to enjoy.

MAKES 1 LOAF

1½ CUPS WARM WATER (105°F TO 115°F)
1 PACKAGE (¼ OUNCE) OR 1 SCANT
   TABLESPOON ACTIVE DRY YEAST
2 TABLESPOONS MOLASSES

1 TABLESPOON BUTTER,
   AT ROOM TEMPERATURE
1 TEASPOON SALT
½ CUP WHOLE WHEAT FLOUR
2 TO 2½ CUPS BREAD FLOUR

1. In a large bowl, combine the warm water, yeast, and molasses and let stand until the yeast begins to foam, about 5 minutes. Add the butter, salt, whole wheat flour, and 1 cup of the bread flour and mix until well blended. Gradually add enough of the remaining bread flour to make a stiff but smooth dough that is soft to the touch. Let the dough rest for 15 minutes.

2. Turn the dough out onto a floured surface. Invert a bowl over the dough and let rise until doubled in bulk, about 1 hour.

3. Punch the dough down and shape into a ball. Place on a lightly greased baking sheet and let rise until almost doubled in bulk, 45 minutes to 1 hour.

4. Preheat the oven to 350°F.

5. Bake the loaf until evenly browned and a wooden skewer inserted into the center comes out clean and dry. Transfer to a rack to cool.

German Lentil Soup
WITH Caraway Popovers

GERMAN LENTIL SOUP

This uncomplicated hearty soup tastes even better the day after it's made. **MAKES 6 SERVINGS**

1 CUP BROWN LENTILS, RINSED
   AND PICKED OVER
4½ CUPS WATER
1½ TEASPOONS SALT

½ TEASPOON GROUND BLACK PEPPER
3 TO 4 BRATWURST SAUSAGES
1½ CUPS COARSELY CHOPPED ONIONS

In a large soup pot, combine the lentils and water. Bring to a boil; then reduce to a simmer, cover, and cook for 30 minutes. Add the salt, pepper, sausages, and onions and cook until the soup comes together, about 1 hour.

CARAWAY POPOVERS

For convenience, mix up this batter several hours ahead or the day before. This even adds to the "pop" value! Caraway gives these a Germanic flavor. **MAKES 6 LARGE OR 12 SMALL POPOVERS**

1 CUP ALL-PURPOSE FLOUR

1 TABLESPOON CARAWAY SEEDS

1 CUP WHOLE OR 2% MILK

1 TABLESPOON BUTTER, AT ROOM TEMPERATURE

1 TEASPOON SALT

3 LARGE EGGS

1. Preheat the oven to 375°F. Grease and flour 12 muffin cups or six 6-ounce custard cups set on a baking sheet. Place in the oven to preheat along with the oven.

2. In a blender or food processor, combine the flour, caraway seeds, milk, butter, salt, and eggs. Process for 2½ minutes, scraping down the sides occasionally to be sure all the flour is incorporated.

3. Pour the batter into the preheated cups, filling each about three-quarters full. Bake until dark brown and crispy, 40 to 45 minutes for small popovers or 50 minutes for large popovers. Serve immediately.

VARIATION

Garlic Cheese Popovers

Add 2 cloves garlic to the batter and process for 2½ minutes as directed. Then add 2½ cups shredded sharp cheddar cheese to the batter and process using on/off pulses just to mix. Bake as directed.

Pea Soup and Spareribs
(WITH) Rustic Rye Bread

PEA SOUP AND SPARERIBS
. . . .

Spareribs, celery, carrots, and onion along with whole allspice and juniper berries add great flavor to this split pea soup. The ribs cook to fall-off-the-bone tenderness. A slow cooker is the ideal vessel, but you can slow simmer the soup on the stovetop in 4 to 5 hours. The split peas do not need to be soaked before adding to the pot.

MAKES 8 SERVINGS

3 POUNDS SPARERIBS, IN TWO PIECES

4 CUPS WATER

1 POUND (ABOUT 2 CUPS) GREEN SPLIT
   PEAS, RINSED AND PICKED OVER

2 RIBS CELERY, CUT UP

3 LARGE CARROTS, DICED

1 LARGE ONION, CHOPPED

1 TEASPOON SALT

8 ALLSPICE BERRIES

8 JUNIPER BERRIES

3 BAY LEAVES

1. Rinse and dry the ribs, and place in a large kettle or a large slow cooker. Add the water, peas, celery, carrots, onion, salt, allspice, juniper berries, and bay leaves. Cook on high for 1 hour. Reduce the heat to low and simmer until the soup is the consistency of thin porridge, about 4 hours. (If cooking on the stove, first heat to boiling; then reduce the heat to medium-low and continue cooking. Add more hot water if the soup cooks down too far and becomes thick.)

2. Remove the ribs from the soup, cut into individual ribs, and trim the meat off the bones. Return the meat to the soup. Adjust the seasonings, if needed. Discard the bay leaves.

RUSTIC RYE BREAD

This beautiful bread has just a touch of sweetness, a crusty top, and a firm texture. It holds up well to sandwiches and is a hearty accompaniment to pea soup.

MAKES 1 LOAF

1 PACKAGE (¼ OUNCE) OR 1 SCANT TABLESPOON ACTIVE DRY YEAST

1¼ CUPS WARM WATER (105°F TO 115°F)

1 TABLESPOON LIGHT BROWN SUGAR

1 TABLESPOON BUTTER, AT ROOM TEMPERATURE

1 TEASPOON SALT

½ CUP RYE FLOUR (PREFERABLY COARSE)

2¼ CUPS UNBLEACHED BREAD FLOUR

1. In a large bowl, sprinkle the yeast over the warm water, stir, and add the brown sugar. Set aside until the yeast begins to foam, about 5 minutes. Add the butter, salt, and rye flour. Gradually add the bread flour, mixing until a dough forms. Let the dough rest for 15 minutes.

2. Turn the dough out onto a lightly floured surface and knead until the dough is smooth, adding flour if needed to keep from sticking.

3. Place the dough in a lightly greased bowl, turn to coat, cover, and let rise for 1 hour. Punch the dough down and shape into a round loaf. Place on a lightly greased baking sheet. Cover and let rise until almost doubled in bulk, about 45 minutes.

4. Preheat the oven to 375°F.

5. Bake until a wooden skewer inserted into the center of the loaf comes out clean and dry, about 30 minutes. Transfer to a rack to cool.

Swedish Yellow Pea Soup with Pork
(WITH) Swedish Pancakes

SWEDISH YELLOW PEA SOUP WITH PORK

Pea soup is regarded as a national dish in Sweden. It has been served every Thursday in Swedish homes and cafes for hundreds of years, almost always accompanied by very thin pancakes that are buttered and then rolled up. **MAKES 6 TO 8 SERVINGS**

2 CUPS DRIED SWEDISH YELLOW
    PEAS (SEE NOTE), RINSED AND
    PICKED OVER

3 QUARTS WATER

1 POUND MEATY FRESH PORK HOCK OR
    A 2½- TO 3-POUND BONE-IN PORK
    SHOULDER

2 MEDIUM ONIONS, SLICED

½ TEASPOON GROUND GINGER

¼ TEASPOON GROUND ALLSPICE

1 TEASPOON SALT

⅛ TEASPOON GROUND WHITE PEPPER

Note: The classic Swedish yellow peas are whole, not split. If you cannot find whole yellow peas, you can substitute yellow split peas, but expect the soup to be thicker.

1. In a soup pot, combine the peas and water (to cover). Soak overnight. Do not change the water.

2. Cover the pot, place over high heat, and bring to a boil. Remove any pea skins that rise to the surface. Add the pork, onions, ginger, allspice, salt, and white pepper. Cover and simmer until the pork and peas are tender, about 3 hours.

3. Remove the pork and pull the meat off the bones. Cut into small chunks and return to the pot.

SWEDISH PANCAKES

Bake these in a Swedish *plattarpanna* if you have one. A plett (which is what it's called in English) is a pan with little pancake-shaped indentations about 3 inches in diameter. If you don't have one, simply make thin pancakes in a heavy skillet or on a griddle. If you are serving these pancakes for breakfast or for dessert, fill with lingonberry jam and top with whipped cream. **MAKES ABOUT 24 SMALL, THIN PANCAKES**

3 LARGE EGGS

1 CUP HEAVY (WHIPPING) CREAM

1 CUP ALL-PURPOSE FLOUR

2 CUPS WHOLE OR 2% MILK

4 TABLESPOONS (½ STICK) BUTTER, MELTED

¼ TEASPOON SALT

SHORTENING, MELTED, OR OIL BUTTER

1. In a bowl, beat together the eggs and cream until blended. Add the flour, mixing until the batter is smooth. Gradually add the milk and stir in the butter and salt.

2. Heat a pancake pan (or skillet) until a drop of water sizzles when dropped onto the surface. Brush with melted shortening or oil.

3. Make pancakes using about 2 tablespoons of batter for each one. When the surface begins to bubble and get dry, turn over and cook until golden brown.

4. Serve with butter.

Bloody Mary Sippy Soup
⬤Ⱳ⬤ Overnight Mini Croissants

BLOODY MARY SIPPY SOUP

Consider this a way to start out a New Year's brunch party. It's pretty, delicious, and really easy to make. If you don't want to spike the soup, omit the vodka. Offer the mini croissants in a basket. **MAKES 4 REGULAR SERVINGS OR 12 SHOOTER SERVINGS**

2 CUPS BASIC VEGETABLE BROTH OR
    BASIC CHICKEN STOCK (PAGE 12 OR 6)
    OR LOW-SODIUM STORE-BOUGHT
1 CAN (14.5 OUNCES) DICED TOMATOES
1 MEDIUM TOMATO, DICED
1 CUP DICED CELERY
2 TEASPOONS WORCESTERSHIRE SAUCE

2 TEASPOONS TABASCO SAUCE
½ CUP VODKA (OPTIONAL)
SALT
½ CUP SOUR CREAM
1 TABLESPOON GRATED HORSERADISH,
    PREFERABLY FRESH
SMALL CELERY RIBS WITH LEAVES

1. In a large saucepan, combine the broth or stock, canned and fresh tomatoes, celery, Worcestershire sauce, and Tabasco sauce. Bring to a simmer and cook for 2 minutes.

2. Working in batches if necessary, transfer the soup to a blender and puree until smooth. Return the soup to the saucepan and add the vodka (if using). Heat through. Add salt to taste.

3. Combine the sour cream and horseradish.

4. Serve the soup in cups or in 2-ounce shot glasses. Top with a dollop of the horseradish cream and garnish with a small celery rib.

OVERNIGHT MINI CROISSANTS

Don't let the idea of making your own croissants scare you. They are simply yeast-raised pastries, and refrigerating the dough makes it a whole lot easier to handle. This recipe makes a lot of mini croissants—bake them ahead and freeze them until you're ready to serve. If frozen, they can be thawed in a 300°F oven in just a few minutes. **MAKES 64 MINI CROISSANTS**

1 PACKAGE (¼ OUNCE) OR 1 SCANT
    TABLESPOON ACTIVE DRY YEAST
1 CUP WARM WATER (105°F TO 115°F)
½ CUP WHOLE OR 2% MILK,
    AT ROOM TEMPERATURE
3 TABLESPOONS SUGAR
2 LARGE EGGS

1½ TEASPOONS SALT
4 CUPS ALL-PURPOSE FLOUR,
    PLUS ADDITIONAL FOR ROLLING
    THE DOUGH
4 TABLESPOONS (½ STICK) BUTTER,
    MELTED, PLUS 8 OUNCES (2 STICKS)
    COLD BUTTER, CUT UP

1. In a 1-quart bowl, sprinkle the yeast over the warm water. Let stand until the yeast looks foamy, about 5 minutes. Add the milk, sugar, one of the eggs, the salt, and 1 cup of the flour and whisk to make a smooth batter. Blend in the melted butter. Set aside.

2. Measure the remaining 3 cups flour into a large bowl or a food processor. Cut in the cold butter (with a pastry cutter or two knives, or with 15 to 20 on/off pulses in the processor) until the pieces are no larger than peas.

3. Pour the yeast mixture over the flour mixture. Stir with a wooden spoon or rubber spatula just until the flour is moistened. Cover tightly and chill at least 4 hours or overnight.

4. Turn the chilled dough out onto a lightly floured surface and knead about 6 times. Divide the dough into quarters. Divide each quarter in half and shape each half into a disk.

5. Working with 1 disk at a time (refrigerate the remaining disks), on a floured surface, roll out to an 8-inch round. Cut into 8 pie-shaped wedges. Roll up each wedge, starting with the wide end, and place on an ungreased baking sheet. Curve the ends of each roll into a crescent shape. Cover loosely and let rise in a warm place until about doubled in bulk, about 1 hour.

6. Preheat the oven to 325°F. Beat the remaining egg with 1 tablespoon water and brush this mixture over each roll. Bake until golden, 10 to 12 minutes. Transfer to a rack to cool.

Borscht ⬤ Russian Black Bread

BORSCHT
....

Borscht is the Russian word for "soup." History says that borscht was and is one of the most popular dishes in Russia, commonly appearing at the end of the eighteenth century. Red beets as well as cabbage are common ingredients because they grow well in northern climates and are easy to store. Meat, fish, and mushrooms might also be ingredients in a soup called borscht. For those without access to meat, borscht was made only with vegetables. This recipe is the basic version; vary it according to what meats and vegetables you have on hand. **MAKES 6 SERVINGS**

1 POUND BEEF STEW MEAT

3 QUARTS WATER

1 MEDIUM ONION, CHOPPED

2 TABLESPOONS BUTTER OR
    VEGETABLE OIL

2 MEDIUM BEETS, PEELED AND CUT
    INTO THIN STICKS

6 CUPS CHOPPED CABBAGE
    (ABOUT ½ POUND)

4 SMALL BOILING POTATOES

1 MEDIUM CARROT, CUT INTO
    MATCHSTICKS

2 MEDIUM TOMATOES, CHOPPED, OR
    1 CAN (14.5 OUNCES) DICED OR
    STEWED TOMATOES

1 TEASPOON CIDER VINEGAR

SALT AND GROUND BLACK PEPPER

SOUR CREAM

DRIED DILLWEED

1. In a large soup pot, combine the meat and water. Bring to a boil; then reduce to a simmer. Add the onion, cover, and cook over low heat until the meat is fork-tender, about 2 hours.

2. Melt the butter in another pot. Add the beets, cabbage, potatoes, carrot, tomatoes, and vinegar. Cook over medium heat, partially covered, until softened, about 15 minutes. Add to the pot with the meat and continue simmering until the vegetables are cooked, 30 to 45 minutes. (The longer the simmer, the more flavorful the soup becomes.) Season to taste with salt and pepper. Serve bowlfuls with a dollop of sour cream and a sprinkle of dillweed.

RUSSIAN BLACK BREAD

If you have any of this bread left after dinner, make grilled cheese sandwiches for lunch the next day. The molasses, chocolate, and coffee granules turn it a glorious color. **MAKES 1 LARGE LOAF**

2 PACKAGES (¼ OUNCE EACH) OR
    2 SCANT TABLESPOONS ACTIVE
    DRY YEAST

2 CUPS WARM WATER (105°F TO 115°F)

3 TABLESPOONS BUTTER, AT ROOM
    TEMPERATURE

3 TABLESPOONS DISTILLED WHITE
    VINEGAR

3 TABLESPOONS DARK MOLASSES

1 SQUARE (1 OUNCE) UNSWEETENED
    CHOCOLATE, MELTED

2 TEASPOONS SALT

2 TEASPOONS INSTANT COFFEE
    GRANULES

1½ TABLESPOONS GROUND
    FENNEL SEEDS

1 CUP DARK RYE FLOUR

3 TO 4 CUPS BREAD FLOUR

1. In a large bowl, combine the yeast and warm water. Let stand until the yeast begins to foam, about 5 minutes. Stir in the butter, vinegar, molasses, chocolate, salt, coffee granules, fennel seeds, and rye flour. Add 2 cups of the bread flour and beat well. Cover and let rest for 15 minutes until the mixture begins to rise.

2. Stir in enough of the remaining bread flour to make a soft, smooth dough. Turn out onto a floured surface and knead until smooth, 5 to 10 minutes. Place the dough in a lightly greased bowl, cover, and let rise until doubled in bulk, about 1 hour.

3. Punch the dough down and shape into a round loaf. Place loaf on a lightly greased baking sheet. Cover and let rise until almost doubled in bulk, about 45 minutes.

4. Preheat the oven to 350°F.

5. Bake until a wooden skewer inserted into the center of the loaf comes out clean and dry, 30 to 40 minutes. Cool on a rack.

VARIATION

Bread Machine Method

Place all of the ingredients into a bread machine and program the machine to "dough." When the machine stops, proceed with shaping and baking as described in the main recipe.

Cabbage and Apple Soup
⬤ Cheese and Olive Bread

CABBAGE AND APPLE SOUP

This combination not only is classic, but also offers up a healthy mix of vitamins, minerals, and fiber. **MAKES 12 SERVINGS**

12 CUPS SHREDDED CABBAGE,
    RED OR GREEN
3 GRANNY SMITH APPLES, PEELED
    AND THINLY SLICED
1 ONION, THINLY SLICED
2 TABLESPOONS LIGHT BROWN SUGAR
1 TABLESPOON SALT
6 BLACK PEPPERCORNS
½ CUP RED WINE VINEGAR OR
    BALSAMIC VINEGAR
6 CUPS BASIC CHICKEN STOCK, TWO-
    FOR-ONE BEEF STOCK, OR BASIC
    VEGETABLE BROTH (PAGE 6, 9, OR 12)
    OR LOW-SODIUM STORE-BOUGHT

6 SLICES BACON, COOKED TO CRISP
    AND CRUMBLED
1 POUND GROUND BEEF, CRUMBLED
2 BRATWURST OR POLISH
    SAUSAGES, DICED
3 TABLESPOONS WORCESTERSHIRE SAUCE
2 CUPS DICED FRESH TOMATOES
    OR 1 CAN (14.5 OUNCES) DICED
    TOMATOES
SOUR CREAM

In a large soup pot, combine the cabbage, apples, onion, brown sugar, salt, peppercorns, vinegar, stock, bacon, beef, sausages, and Worcestershire sauce and bring to a simmer, stirring, over medium heat. Simmer, covered, for 1 hour. Add the tomatoes and cook until heated through. Serve hot with dollops of sour cream.

VARIATIONS

To turn this into a vegetarian soup, eliminate the bacon, beef, and sausages, and use vegetable broth in place of the chicken or beef stock.

To use this recipe with leftover pot roast, place it along with its cooking juices into a large soup pot. Add all of the ingredients for this soup, except the beef, sausages, and bacon.

CHEESE AND OLIVE BREAD

Speckled with cheese and dotted with olives, this bread is a showstopper when shaped into a twisted loaf. **MAKES 1 FAT LOAF**

1 CUP WARM WATER (105°F TO 115°F)

1 PACKAGE (¼ OUNCE) OR 1 SCANT TABLESPOON ACTIVE DRY YEAST

1 TABLESPOON SUGAR

¾ TEASPOON SALT

1 LARGE EGG

3 CUPS UNBLEACHED BREAD FLOUR

1 CUP SHREDDED SHARP CHEDDAR CHEESE

¾ CUP CHOPPED PITTED KALAMATA OLIVES

1. In a bowl, combine the warm water, yeast, and sugar. Let stand until the yeast begins to foam, about 5 minutes. Stir in the salt, egg, and 1 cup of the flour. Beat with a spoon until smooth. Stir in the remaining 2 cups flour, ½ cup at a time, stirring until a shaggy dough forms.

2. Turn the dough out onto a floured surface and knead by hand until the dough is smooth, about 5 minutes. Knead in the cheese and olives until evenly blended into the dough. Place the dough in a greased bowl, turn to coat, cover, and let rise until doubled in bulk, about 45 minutes.

3. Divide the dough in half. Shape each half into a narrow strand about 16 inches long. Twist the two strands into a ropelike loaf and place on a lightly greased baking sheet. Cover and let rise until almost doubled in bulk, about 45 minutes.

4. Preheat the oven to 400°F.

5. Spray the loaf with water and bake until lightly browned, 20 to 25 minutes. Cool on a rack.

Onion Barley Soup with Mushrooms
WITH Honey Bran Muffins

ONION BARLEY SOUP WITH MUSHROOMS

You won't miss the meat in this hearty, richly flavored soup. I keep a supply of dried mushrooms on hand so when the first blustery winter day arrives, I can make this for lunch. Cremini mushrooms, which are dark button-size mushrooms, are actually young portobellos. **MAKES 6 SERVINGS**

1 CUP BOILING WATER

½ OUNCE DRIED MUSHROOMS, SUCH AS
   SHIITAKE OR CHANTERELLES

3 TEASPOONS TOASTED SESAME OIL

2 MEDIUM ONIONS, COARSELY CHOPPED

2 TEASPOONS CHOPPED FRESH GINGER

4 CLOVES GARLIC, MINCED

3 CUPS SLICED CREMINI MUSHROOMS

1 TEASPOON LIGHT BROWN SUGAR

⅔ CUP PEARL BARLEY

¼ CUP DRY SHERRY

3 TABLESPOONS SOY SAUCE

2 CUPS WATER

1½ CUPS TWO-FOR-ONE BEEF STOCK
   (PAGE 9) OR LOW-SODIUM
   STORE-BOUGHT

1. In a heatproof bowl, combine the boiling water and dried mushrooms. Cover and let stand 30 minutes to reconstitute. Drain the mushrooms into a sieve set over a bowl, reserving the soaking liquid. Slice the reconstituted mushrooms, discarding the stems.

2. Heat 2 teaspoons of the oil in a heavy soup pot over medium-high heat. Add the onions, ginger, and garlic and cook until lightly browned, about 3 to 5 minutes, stirring regularly. Add the remaining 1 teaspoon oil to the pot along with the reconstituted mushrooms, cremini, brown sugar, barley, sherry, soy sauce, reserved mushroom liquid, 2 cups water, and stock and bring to a boil. Reduce to a simmer, cover, and cook until the barley is tender, about 50 minutes. Ladle into soup bowls.

HONEY BRAN MUFFINS

Grainy, full of fiber, and fragrant of honey, these muffins not only are excellent served with soup for supper, but are also perfect for breakfast, brunch, or lunch.

MAKES 12

1½ CUPS 100% BRAN CEREAL

1¼ CUPS WHOLE OR 2% MILK

1 EGG, BEATEN

⅓ CUP BUTTER, MELTED

½ CUP HONEY

1¼ CUPS ALL-PURPOSE FLOUR

1 TABLESPOON BAKING POWDER

½ TEASPOON SALT

1 CUP CHOPPED DATES, RAISINS, OR CHOPPED FRESH APPLE

¼ CUP TOASTED WHEAT GERM

1. Preheat the oven to 400°F. Line 12 muffin cups with paper liners or coat with cooking spray.

2. In a large bowl, mix the bran cereal and milk and let stand 5 minutes. Stir in the egg, butter, and honey.

3. In a medium bowl, combine the flour, baking powder, salt, and dates, raisins, or apple. Add to the bran mixture and mix until the dry ingredients are moistened.

4. Spoon the batter into the muffin cups and sprinkle with the wheat germ. Bake until golden, 18 to 20 minutes. Remove from the tins and cool on a rack.

German Potato Soup
⬤ with Pumpernickel Soup Bowls

GERMAN POTATO SOUP

Soup served in a bread bowl has been a novelty on restaurant menus for as long as I can remember. It can really be done with any bread with a firm crust and with any soup. This combination is inspired by a classic Bavarian pairing. **MAKES 6 SERVINGS**

1 TABLESPOON BUTTER

1 LARGE ONION, CHOPPED

6 CUPS BASIC CHICKEN STOCK OR TWO-FOR-ONE BEEF STOCK (PAGE 6 OR 9) OR LOW-SODIUM STORE-BOUGHT

4 LARGE BOILING POTATOES, PEELED AND DICED

2 TABLESPOONS ALL-PURPOSE FLOUR

½ CUP LIGHT SOUR CREAM

½ CUP WHOLE OR 2% MILK

1 CUP SHREDDED COOKED CORNED BEEF

½ CUP SHREDDED SWISS CHEESE

PUMPERNICKEL SOUP BOWLS (SEE NEXT RECIPE)

1 TABLESPOON CHOPPED FRESH PARSLEY

1. Melt the butter in a heavy-bottomed soup pot over medium heat. Add the onions and cook until they are soft, 5 to 10 minutes. Add the stock and potatoes. Cover and simmer until the potatoes are tender, about 25 minutes.

2. In a medium bowl, stir together the flour, sour cream, and milk. Add a little hot soup to the mixture; then stir the mixture into the pot of soup. Add the corned beef to the soup and simmer 10 minutes. Stir in the cheese.

3. Ladle the soup into the bread bowls and top with the toasted lid of the bread bowl. Garnish with parsley and serve.

PUMPERNICKEL SOUP BOWLS

You'll need to make these bread bowls before you cook the soup. Allow about four hours to prepare them or make them a day ahead. **MAKES 6 SOUP BOWLS**

½ CUP PLUS 1¼ CUPS WARM WATER
   (105°F TO 115°F)
1 PACKAGE (¼ OUNCE) OR 1 SCANT
   TABLESPOON ACTIVE DRY YEAST
1 TABLESPOON DARK MOLASSES
1½ CUPS WHOLE WHEAT FLOUR
½ CUP RYE FLOUR

1 CUP UNBLEACHED BREAD FLOUR
⅓ CUP NONFAT DRY MILK POWDER
1 TABLESPOON CARAWAY SEEDS
1 TEASPOON SALT
1 TABLESPOON BUTTER, PLUS
   MELTED BUTTER FOR BRUSHING
   ON THE LOAVES

1. In a small bowl, combine ½ cup of the warm water, the yeast, and molasses. Set aside until the mixture begins to foam, about 5 minutes.

2. In a food processor or bowl, combine the whole wheat, rye, and bread flours, dry milk, caraway seeds, salt, and butter. Stir in the 1¼ cups warm water along with the yeast mixture to make a stiff dough. Add more water if necessary to make a dough that is soft and pliable. Or, process the dough in the food processor until it comes together in a ball and spins around the bowl about 25 times. Let the dough rest for 15 minutes.

3. Place the dough in a lightly greased bowl, turn to coat, cover, and let rise until doubled in bulk, about 1 hour.

4. Divide the dough into 6 equal parts. Shape each part into a round ball. Place on 2 greased baking sheets and let rise until puffy, 45 minutes to 1 hour.

5. Preheat the oven to 350°F.

6. Brush the loaves with water and bake until a wooden skewer inserted into the center of a loaf comes out clean and dry, 25 to 35 minutes. Brush with melted butter and cool completely on a rack.

7. To serve, slice a shallow cap off the top of each loaf. Remove the soft interior of the loaves and reserve for another use. Brush the cut side of the cap with butter and toast under the broiler until heated through.

Ham and Fingerling Potato Soup
(WITH) Popovers

HAM AND FINGERLING POTATO SOUP

After a holiday meal, we always have leftover ham. I use the ham bone to make ham bone soup and the ham chunks in this soup. Fingerlings, halved lengthwise, are the perfect size. **MAKES 4 TO 6 SERVINGS**

1 POUND FINGERLING POTATOES, SCRUBBED AND HALVED LENGTHWISE

1 RIB CELERY, DICED

1 SMALL ONION, CHOPPED

1 CUP DICED COOKED HAM

4 CUPS BASIC CHICKEN STOCK OR TWO-FOR-ONE BEEF STOCK (PAGE 6 OR 9) OR LOW-SODIUM STORE-BOUGHT

5 TABLESPOONS BUTTER

5 TABLESPOONS ALL-PURPOSE FLOUR

2 CUPS WHOLE OR 2% MILK, HEATED TO SIMMERING

SALT AND GROUND BLACK PEPPER

1. In a 4-quart soup pot, combine the potatoes, celery, onion, ham, and stock and bring to a boil. Reduce the heat to medium and cook until the potatoes are tender, about 20 minutes.

2. Melt the butter in a small saucepan over medium-low heat. Whisk in the flour and cook, stirring constantly, until thickened, about 1 minute. Whisk in the milk slowly, so that lumps will not form. Continue stirring over medium-low heat until thick, 4 to 5 minutes. Stir the milk mixture into the soup and cook until heated through. Add salt and pepper, to taste. Serve hot.

POPOVERS

For the best "pop," mix this batter hours ahead or even the day before. When we have company, I like to prepare the batter ahead and keep it in a covered pitcher so we can bake popovers at the drop of a hat. This batter will make six large popovers or twelve small ones, but the recipe can be easily tripled. What's more, it can be mixed in the blender. **MAKES 6 LARGE OR 12 SMALL POPOVERS**

1 CUP ALL-PURPOSE FLOUR

1 CUP WHOLE OR 2% MILK

1 TABLESPOON SOFTENED BUTTER OR
VEGETABLE OIL

½ TEASPOON SALT

3 LARGE EGGS

1. If you are baking the popovers right away, preheat the oven to 375°F. Grease and flour 12 muffin cups or six 6-ounce custard cups. Place in the oven to preheat along with the oven.

2. In a blender, combine the flour, milk, butter or oil, salt, and eggs and process for 2½ minutes. Scrape down the sides of the container and check for dry flour stuck to the sides or bottom. Pour the batter into a pitcher and let stand, covered, for 30 minutes (or up to 12 hours refrigerated).

3. Pour the batter into the preheated baking cups, filling each about three-quarters full. Bake until dark brown, puffy, and crispy, 40 to 45 minutes for small popovers or 50 minutes for large popovers. Serve immediately.

Lamb Meatball and Root Vegetable Soup WITH Bazlama (Turkish Flatbread)

LAMB MEATBALL AND ROOT VEGETABLE SOUP

When it's a cold and blustery day, a pot of soup simmering on the stove makes even subzero temperatures bearable. Shredded kale adds a nice, colorful touch, not to mention a nourishing boost. **MAKES 4 SERVINGS**

½ POUND GROUND LEAN LAMB

2 TABLESPOONS CHOPPED
    FRESH PARSLEY

¼ CUP SHORT-GRAIN RICE

1 TEASPOON SALT PLUS ADDITIONAL
    FOR SEASONING

¼ TEASPOON GROUND BLACK PEPPER
    PLUS ADDITIONAL FOR SEASONING

ALL-PURPOSE FLOUR

4 CUPS LAMB, BEEF, OR CHICKEN STOCK

1 ONION, FINELY CHOPPED

2 CARROTS, DICED

1 CUP FINELY DICED CELERIAC
    (CELERY ROOT)

1 MEDIUM BOILING POTATO, PEELED
    AND CHOPPED

3 TOMATOES, CHOPPED

2 CUPS SHREDDED KALE LEAVES

2 LEMONS, SLICED

1. In a bowl, combine the lamb, parsley, rice, salt, and pepper. Shape into small meatballs. Roll the meatballs in flour and chill for 20 minutes.

2. In a soup pot, combine the stock, onion, carrots, celeriac, and potato. Bring to a simmer over medium-high heat, uncovered, and cook for 20 minutes. Add the meatballs, return to a simmer, and cook until the meatballs are cooked through, 25 to 30 minutes longer.

3. Add the tomatoes and kale. Heat just until the kale is wilted, about 10 minutes. Season to taste with salt and pepper and serve. Garnish with the sliced lemon.

BAZLAMA (TURKISH FLATBREAD)

We enjoyed this flatbread on a trip to Turkey, where it was cooked on the ceramic sides of outdoor fire pits. Here, we bake them on a pizza stone in the oven. **MAKES 4**

1 PACKAGE (¼ OUNCE) OR 1 SCANT
    TABLESPOON ACTIVE DRY YEAST
2 CUPS WARM WATER (105°F TO 115°F)
1 TABLESPOON SUGAR

2 TEASPOONS SALT
½ CUP YOGURT (WHOLE MILK OR
    FAT-FREE)
4 CUPS ALL-PURPOSE FLOUR

1. In a large bowl, sprinkle the yeast over the warm water and stir in the sugar and salt. Let stand until the yeast begins to foam, about 5 minutes. Add the yogurt and flour, and beat until satiny and stretchy, about 5 minutes. The dough will be soft but not sticky.

2. Turn the dough out onto a lightly floured surface and shape it into a ball. Cover the dough with a damp cloth and let rise at room temperature for 3 hours.

3. Position a pizza stone on the middle rack of the oven and preheat to 500°F.

4. Cut the dough into 4 portions. Shape into rounds and flatten each to make 10-inch rounds as though you were making pizza. Cover the rounds with a cloth and let the dough rest for 15 minutes.

5. Transfer 1 round of dough to the pizza stone. Bake until brown spots appear on the bottom, about 5 minutes. Flip the bread over and bake for an additional minute. Remove the bread and wrap it in a clean kitchen towel to keep warm. Repeat with the remaining dough rounds. To serve, tear into pieces. Leftover flatbreads will keep, wrapped tightly, for two days. To keep them longer, wrap and freeze.

Beet and Red Cabbage Soup
WITH Ground Beef Pasties

BEET AND RED CABBAGE SOUP

The perfect partner for this brilliant and simple-to-make soup is a ground beef pasty. The combination makes a wonderful wintertime lunch. **MAKES 6 SERVINGS**

6 CUPS TWO-FOR-ONE BEEF STOCK (PAGE 9) OR LOW-SODIUM STORE-BOUGHT

1 SMALL HEAD RED CABBAGE (ABOUT 1¼ POUNDS)

1 TABLESPOON LEMON JUICE

3 LARGE BEETS, PEELED AND SHREDDED

½ TEASPOON CARAWAY SEEDS

½ TEASPOON GROUND BLACK PEPPER

SOUR CREAM

Bring the stock to a boil in a large soup pot. Add the cabbage, lemon juice, beets, caraway seeds, and pepper. Cover and simmer over medium-low heat until the cabbage is tender, about 30 minutes. Serve hot, topped with a spoonful of sour cream.

GROUND BEEF PASTIES

Pasties are meat-filled pies that miners in Minnesota and Michigan carried to work in their lunch boxes. The pasties were often baked fresh in the morning and wrapped so well that they were still warm at lunchtime. Today, they round out a vegetable soup menu for dinner. In this version, I use ground beef rather than beef cubes. Pasties can be made ahead and frozen before or after baking. If frozen unbaked, allow an additional ten to fifteen minutes of baking time. **MAKES 6**

3 CUPS ALL-PURPOSE FLOUR

½ TEASPOON SALT

8 OUNCES (2 STICKS) COLD BUTTER, CUT INTO SMALL PIECES

1 LARGE EGG

1 POUND EXTRA-LEAN GROUND BEEF

1 MEDIUM ONION, CHOPPED

8 OUNCES BUTTON MUSHROOMS, CHOPPED

2 CLOVES GARLIC, MINCED

1 TEASPOON SALT

¼ CUP CHOPPED FRESH PARSLEY

1. In a food processor or in a medium bowl, combine the flour and salt. Cut in the butter (by hand with a pastry blender or two knives, or with on/off pulses in the processor) until the butter is the size of small peas. If using a food processor, transfer the mixture to a bowl.

2. Break the egg into a glass measuring cup and add enough water to come to ½ cup. Beat lightly. Add about 2 tablespoons of the egg mixture at a time to the flour mixture and stir until the dough forms a ball, adding more water if necessary, 1 tablespoon at a time. Gather the mixture into a ball. Wrap and chill for 30 minutes.

3. Heat a large nonstick skillet over medium-high heat. Add the ground beef, onion, mushrooms, garlic, and salt and cook, breaking up the beef, until the meat is browned, about 25 minutes. Remove from heat and let cool. Stir in the parsley.

4. Preheat the oven to 425°F. Cut the pastry into 6 equal parts. On a floured board, roll out each to make an 8-inch round. Spread about ½ cup of the cooled filling onto half of each pastry round. Moisten the edges of the round with water. Fold the uncovered half over the filling and lightly press the edges together. Dampen the edges and seal using a fork. Place the filled pasties, or turnovers, on an ungreased baking sheet and bake until lightly browned, 20 to 25 minutes. Serve warm.

Quinoa Vegetable Soup
(WITH) Savory Cheese Mini Loaves

QUINOA VEGETABLE SOUP

Quinoa is not a true cereal grain, but has similar characteristics. Nutritionally, it has a high protein content, making it a wonderful substitute for wheat or rice—and it's gluten free. It is closely related to plants such as beets and spinach, and has a delicious, grainy flavor and texture. **MAKES 4 SERVINGS**

1 CUP QUINOA

1½ CUPS WATER

2 TABLESPOONS OLIVE OIL

1 CUP CHOPPED LEEKS OR GREEN
    ONIONS (SCALLIONS)

1 TEASPOON DRIED TARRAGON

6 CUPS BASIC VEGETABLE BROTH OR
    BASIC CHICKEN STOCK (PAGE 12 OR 6)
    OR LOW-SODIUM STORE-BOUGHT

1 PACKAGE (10 OUNCES) MIXED THAWED
    FROZEN CARROTS, CORN, AND PEAS

SALT AND GROUND BLACK PEPPER

1 TO 1½ CUPS BUTTERMILK

1. Soak the quinoa in water to cover for 5 minutes (soaking helps quinoa to cook evenly). Drain and transfer to a 2-quart pot. Add the 1½ cups water and bring to a boil. Cover tightly, reduce the heat to a simmer, and cook until the quinoa is bite-tender, about 15 minutes.

2. Heat the oil in another pot over medium heat. Add the leeks or green onions and cook until the vegetables are cooked, about 4 minutes. Stir in the tarragon and cook for 1 minute. Add the broth or stock and bring to a boil. Stir in the frozen vegetables and the cooked quinoa. Cover and continue to cook until the vegetables are tender, 3 to 5 minutes. Season to taste with salt and pepper. Drizzle buttermilk in a swirl on top of each portion of the soup.

SAVORY CHEESE MINI LOAVES

These no-knead loaves have a brioche-like texture and an equally rich flavor.

MAKES 4 LOAVES

1 PACKAGE (¼ OUNCE) OR 1 SCANT TABLESPOON ACTIVE DRY YEAST

½ CUP WARM WATER (105°F TO 115°F)

½ CUP NONFAT DRY MILK POWDER

2 LARGE EGGS PLUS 1 EGG BEATEN WITH A PINCH OF SALT (FOR GLAZING THE LOAVES)

1 TEASPOON SALT

¼ TEASPOON CAYENNE PEPPER

2 CUPS UNBLEACHED BREAD FLOUR

4 TABLESPOONS (½ STICK) BUTTER, AT ROOM TEMPERATURE

4 OUNCES SWISS OR GRUYÈRE CHEESE, FINELY DICED

¼ CUP GRATED SWISS, GRUYÈRE, OR CHEDDAR CHEESE

1. In the large bowl of a stand mixer, sprinkle the yeast over the warm water. Stir in the dry milk. Let stand until the yeast begins to foam, about 5 minutes.

2. Mix in the 2 eggs, salt, cayenne pepper, and 1 cup of the bread flour to make a smooth dough. Gradually work in the remaining flour and the butter to make a smooth and elastic dough. Cover the bowl and let rise at room temperature until doubled in bulk, about 1½ hours. Add the 4 ounces of cheese and mix for about 1 minute.

3. Turn the dough out onto a floured surface and divide into 4 parts. Shape each into a round loaf and place on a greased baking sheet or into 4 small greased loaf pans. Let rise until almost doubled in bulk, 45 minutes to 1 hour.

4. Preheat the oven to 400°F.

5. Gently brush the risen loaves with the egg-salt glaze and sprinkle with the grated cheese, about 1 tablespoon per loaf. Bake until golden brown and the loaves sound hollow when tapped, 20 to 25 minutes. Transfer to a rack to cool and remove from the pans (if using).

Mulligan Stew
WITH Irish Brown Soda Bread

MULLIGAN STEW

Mulligan stew, sometimes called hobo stew, is simply an Irish stew that includes meat, potatoes, vegetables, and whatever else can be scared up. This recipe is a little unusual in that the stew meat is not browned before being cooked with the vegetables. **MAKES 8 SERVINGS**

2 POUNDS BEEF STEW MEAT, CUT INTO 1-INCH CUBES

4 MEDIUM THIN-SKINNED YELLOW OR RED POTATOES, UNPEELED, QUARTERED

4 MEDIUM CARROTS, CUT INTO 2-INCH PIECES

4 SMALL ONIONS, QUARTERED

1 SMALL (½ POUND) RUTABAGA OR TURNIP, PEELED AND CUT INTO 1-INCH CUBES

3 SPRIGS PARSLEY

1 TABLESPOON SUGAR

2 TEASPOONS SALT

¼ TEASPOON GROUND BLACK PEPPER

2 TABLESPOONS ALL-PURPOSE FLOUR

½ CUP RED WINE OR WATER

1. In a 4-quart soup pot, combine the meat and cold water to cover, about 4 cups, and bring to a boil. Add the potatoes, carrots, onions, rutabaga or turnip, parsley, sugar, salt, and pepper. Simmer, tightly covered, over low heat until the meat is tender, about 2 hours 30 minutes.

2. In a cup, mix the flour and wine or water until smooth. Stir into the stew and cook for 15 minutes, stirring frequently, to thicken the stew.

IRISH BROWN SODA BREAD

A quick bread, this loaf slices best on the day after it's made, although it makes for excellent eating while hot or toasted. **MAKES 1 LOAF**

4 CUPS WHOLE WHEAT FLOUR

2 CUPS UNBLEACHED
   ALL-PURPOSE FLOUR

2 TABLESPOONS BUTTER, AT ROOM
   TEMPERATURE, PLUS MELTED BUTTER
   FOR THE TOP OF THE LOAF

1½ TEASPOONS SALT

1½ TEASPOONS BAKING SODA

2¼ CUPS BUTTERMILK

1. Preheat the oven to 400°F. Lightly grease a baking sheet.

2. In a medium bowl, combine the whole wheat and all-purpose flours. Blend the butter into the flours using a mixer or pastry blender. Add the salt and baking soda. Gradually add the buttermilk, stirring until a stiff dough forms.

3. Shape the dough into a ball and place on the baking sheet. Flatten into a round about 2 inches thick. Using a razor blade, French *lame*, or sharp knife, score a cross on the top from edge to edge.

4. Bake until browned and a wooden skewer inserted into the center of the loaf comes out dry, 35 to 40 minutes. Brush with melted butter and transfer to a rack to cool.

Roasted Potato Cheddar Soup
(WITH) Alfalfa Sprout Flatbread

ROASTED POTATO CHEDDAR SOUP

The rich flavor of this simple soup comes from the roasted potatoes.

MAKES 6 SERVINGS

12 SLICES BACON

4 LARGE BAKING POTATOES, PEELED
AND CUT INTO ½-INCH CUBES

4 GREEN ONIONS (SCALLIONS), CHOPPED

8 TABLESPOONS (1 STICK) BUTTER

½ CUP ALL-PURPOSE FLOUR

6 CUPS WHOLE OR 2% MILK, HEATED

1¼ CUPS (ABOUT 4 OUNCES) SHREDDED
CHEDDAR CHEESE, MILD OR SHARP

1 CUP SOUR CREAM

1 TEASPOON SALT

1 TEASPOON GROUND BLACK PEPPER

1. Preheat the oven to 450°F. Arrange the bacon slices in a shallow roasting pan and bake until crisp. Remove from the oven and pour off all but 1 tablespoon of the drippings. Crumble the bacon and set aside.

2. Add the potato cubes to the pan and roll them around until coated with the bacon fat. Spread in a single layer. Return to the oven and roast until the potatoes are tender, about 20 minutes. Add the green onions and roast 3 minutes longer.

3. Melt the butter in a large saucepan over medium heat. Stir in the flour. Whisk in the milk and heat to boiling, whisking all the time. Cook until thickened. Add the roasted potatoes and green onions and stir in the cheese, sour cream, salt, and pepper. Serve garnished with crumbled bacon.

ALFALFA SPROUT FLATBREAD

Wonderfully chewy and grainy, alfalfa sprouts add not only moistness but nutrition and flavor to this bread. This can be a sticky dough to handle, so oil your fingers before patting the dough out flat. **MAKES 16 PIECES**

1 CUP RYE FLOUR

1 CUP WHOLE WHEAT FLOUR

¾ CUP NONFAT DRY MILK POWDER

½ CUP SESAME SEEDS

½ CUP UNSALTED ROASTED
    SUNFLOWER SEEDS

1 TEASPOON SALT

½ CUP PACKED ALFALFA SPROUTS,
    CHOPPED

3 TABLESPOONS CANOLA, OLIVE,
    OR COCONUT OIL

1 CUP WATER

1 EGG, BEATEN

1. Preheat the oven to 450°F. Grease and flour a 10 × 15-inch baking sheet.

2. In a large bowl, combine the rye flour, whole wheat flour, dry milk, sesame seeds, sunflower seeds, and salt. Add the sprouts, oil, and water and blend well. Mix in the egg.

3. Spread the mixture on the baking sheet and use your fingers to pat the dough out to about ¼-inch thickness. Pierce all over with a fork. Bake until the top feels dry, 10 to 12 minutes; then turn the broiler on and broil about 6 inches from the heat until browned. When cooled, the bread becomes crisp. Break or cut into 16 pieces. To store, wrap tightly and freeze in an airtight container.

Sunchoke and Golden Potato Soup
WITH Wild Rice Pecan Bread

SUNCHOKE AND GOLDEN POTATO SOUP

Growing up on a farm in northern Minnesota, I remember digging up the roots of the tall yellow-flowering plants that grew next to all the outbuildings. I loved the sweet, mellow flavor of sunchokes then and still do today. They are also known as Jerusalem artichokes or sunroots, though they have no relation to Jerusalem or to artichokes! You can simply scrub and eat sunchokes peel and all, since most of the nutritional value is in the peel. **MAKES 4 SERVINGS**

2 TABLESPOONS BUTTER

1 SWEET ONION, FINELY CHOPPED

2 RIBS CELERY, CHOPPED

2 CLOVES GARLIC, MINCED

1 POUND SUNCHOKES, SCRUBBED
    AND CUBED

2 MEDIUM YELLOW POTATOES, SCRUBBED
    AND CUBED

4 CUPS BASIC CHICKEN STOCK (PAGE 6)
    OR LOW-SODIUM STORE-BOUGHT

1 CUP HEAVY (WHIPPING) CREAM

SALT AND GROUND BLACK PEPPER

SALTED ROASTED SUNFLOWER SEEDS

1. Heat the butter in a soup pot over medium-high heat. Add the onion, celery, and garlic and cook until the onion is soft but not brown, about 5 minutes.

2. Add the sunchokes, potatoes, and stock and bring to a simmer. Reduce the heat to low and cook until the sunchokes and potatoes begin to break down, 45 minutes to 1 hour.

3. Puree the soup in a blender. Add the cream and season to taste with salt and pepper. Serve garnished with the sunflower seeds.

WILD RICE PECAN BREAD

Wild rice and pecans add not only a nutty flavor to this bread but great texture too. When shaping the dough, pour a small amount of oil onto a paper towel and rub it gently onto the work surface, or coat the work surface and your hands with cooking spray to prevent the dough from sticking. **MAKES 2 LOAVES**

2 PACKAGES (¼ OUNCE EACH) OR 2 SCANT TABLESPOONS ACTIVE DRY YEAST

2 CUPS WARM WATER (105°F TO 115°F)

2 TEASPOONS SUGAR

2 TEASPOONS SALT

4 TO 4½ CUPS UNBLEACHED BREAD FLOUR OR ALL-PURPOSE FLOUR, PLUS ADDITIONAL FLOUR IF NEEDED FOR SHAPING

½ CUP CHOPPED TOASTED PECANS

½ CUP COOKED, COOLED WILD RICE

1. In a large bowl, preferably of a stand mixer, dissolve the yeast in the warm water. Add the sugar. Let stand until the yeast begins to foam, about 5 minutes.

2. Stir in the salt and 2 cups of the flour, mixing until the batter is smooth. Let rest 15 minutes. Add the pecans and wild rice. Stir in the remaining flour, ½ cup at a time, to make a stiff dough. Sprinkle additional flour onto a work surface and turn the dough out onto it. Knead gently until the flour is worked into the dough, about 5 minutes. Place the dough in an oiled bowl and turn to coat. Let rise in a warm place, covered, until doubled in bulk, about 1 hour.

3. Divide the dough into two equal parts. Shape each into a round or oblong loaf. Place on a lightly greased baking sheet, cover, and let rise until almost doubled in bulk, about 45 minutes.

4. Preheat the oven to 450°F.

5. With a sharp knife, make 3 or 4 slashes about ⅛-inch deep on each loaf. Spray the loaves with water. Bake until the loaves are crusty and a wooden skewer inserted into the center of a loaf comes out clean and dry, about 20 minutes. Transfer to a rack to cool.

Feijoada ●WITH● French Twist Bread

FEIJOADA

Spicy and stick-to-the-ribs, this hearty winter soup is a Brazilian classic. It gets better when it is made ahead and reheated the next day. To toast the farina, sprinkle it into a nonstick skillet, place over medium heat, and stir until golden and toasted, about 10 minutes. In Brazil this classic soup is served with toasted manioc, which is cassava root. Manioc is not easily found here; farina is a good substitute.

MAKES 8 SERVINGS

2 CUPS DRIED BLACK BEANS, RINSED AND PICKED OVER

½ TEASPOON SALT

1 BAY LEAF

1 TABLESPOON OLIVE OIL

4 CUPS CHOPPED ONION

3 CLOVES GARLIC, MINCED

¾ POUND SMOKED TURKEY SAUSAGE, CUT INTO ½-INCH CUBES

1¾ CUPS CHOPPED TOMATOES

¼ TEASPOON GROUND CUMIN

⅛ TEASPOON RED-PEPPER FLAKES

2⅔ CUPS HOT COOKED RICE (COOKED WITHOUT SALT)

1 CUP CHOPPED ORANGES

¼ CUP CHOPPED FRESH PARSLEY

1 TEASPOON GRATED ORANGE ZEST

⅓ CUP FARINA, TOASTED

1. In a 4- to 5-quart Dutch oven or heavy soup pot, combine the beans with water to cover by 2 inches and bring to a boil. Boil over high heat for 2 minutes. Remove from the heat, cover, and let stand 1 hour.

2. Drain the beans and return to the pot. Add 5 cups fresh water, the salt, and bay leaf. Cover, bring to a simmer, and cook until the beans are tender, about 3 hours. Set aside.

3. Heat the oil in a large nonstick skillet over medium-high heat. Add the onion and garlic and cook until tender, about 5 minutes. Add the sausage, tomatoes, cumin, and pepper flakes. Cook until heated through, about 10 minutes.

4. Serve the sausage mixture over the rice and beans. Top with the oranges, parsley, and orange zest. Sprinkle with toasted farina.

FRENCH TWIST BREAD

This classic crusty white bread bakes up into a lovely, golden twisted loaf.

MAKES 1 LOAF

1 PACKAGE (¼ OUNCE) OR 1 SCANT
    TABLESPOON ACTIVE DRY YEAST
1 CUP WARM WATER (105°F TO 115°F)

2 TEASPOONS SUGAR
3 CUPS ALL-PURPOSE FLOUR
1 TEASPOON SALT

1. In a large bowl, sprinkle the yeast over the warm water, stir, and add the sugar. Let stand until the yeast foams, about 5 minutes. Add 1½ cups of the flour and the salt. Stir until the batter is smooth. Stir in enough of the remaining flour to make a soft dough.

2. Turn the dough out onto a floured surface. Knead until smooth and elastic, about 10 minutes, adding enough flour to keep the dough from sticking to your hands. Cover and let rise for 15 minutes.

3. Divide the dough in half, shaping each portion into a ball. Cover with plastic wrap and let rest 30 minutes. Roll each ball into a 15-inch-long rope.

4. Twist the ropes together, stretching into an 18-inch-long twisted loaf. Pinch the ends to seal. Place diagonally on a baking sheet coated with cooking spray. Let rise, uncovered, in a warm place until doubled in bulk, about 45 minutes.

5. Preheat the oven to 400°F.

6. Spray the dough lightly with water. Bake the bread for 10 minutes and spray again with water. Continue baking until lightly browned, about 10 minutes longer. Transfer to a rack to cool.

Scandinavian Fruit Soup
⬤WITH Orange Toasts

SCANDINAVIAN FRUIT SOUP

Compotes of dried fruit are classic holiday desserts in Scandinavian and other European countries. This might be served over creamy cooked rice, or with a topping of whipped cream, sour cream, or heavy pouring cream. Not too sweet, the soup is sometimes served for brunch or a light lunch or as the main course on Christmas Eve. **MAKES 8 TO 10 SERVINGS**

1 BAG (12 OUNCES) MIXED DRIED FRUIT (APRICOTS, PEARS, APPLES, PRUNES, AND LIGHT OR DARK RAISINS)

4 CUPS WATER

1 CINNAMON STICK

3 LEMON SLICES, CUT ⅓-INCH THICK

½ TO 1 CUP SUGAR, TO TASTE

4 CUPS APPLE JUICE

2 TABLESPOONS POTATO STARCH OR CORNSTARCH

¼ CUP WATER

1. In a 4-quart saucepan, combine the dried fruit, water, cinnamon stick, lemon slices, and ½ cup of the sugar. Bring to a simmer over medium-high heat and cook, uncovered, until the fruits are reconstituted and tender but still hold their shapes, 45 minutes to 1 hour. With a slotted spoon, transfer the fruit to a serving bowl.

2. Bring the apple juice to a boil in a small saucepan. Meanwhile, mix the starch with ¼ cup water. Add to the boiling juice and stir until thickened and clear. Taste and add more sugar, if desired.

3. Pour the thickened juice over the fruit in the bowl. Serve warm or chilled.

ORANGE TOASTS

These cookie-like toasts can be made ahead and stored, tightly covered, in the freezer for up to two months. **MAKES 2 TO 3 DOZEN**

8 TABLESPOONS (1 STICK) BUTTER,
    AT ROOM TEMPERATURE
½ CUP SUGAR

1 TABLESPOON GRATED ORANGE ZEST
1 LOAF ITALIAN OR FRENCH BREAD, CUT
    INTO ¼-INCH SLICES

1. Preheat the oven to 350°F. Line a baking sheet with parchment paper.

2. In a small bowl, mix together the butter, sugar, and orange zest. Spread the butter mixture on both sides of each bread slice and place them on the prepared baking sheet.

3. Bake until lightly browned and crisp, 10 to 15 minutes. Serve warm or let cool and store in an airtight container.

INDEX